# THE ESSENTIAL HUAINANZI

TRANSLATIONS FROM THE ASIAN CLASSICS

TRANSLATIONS FROM THE ASIAN CLASSICS

*Editorial Board*

Wm. Theodore de Bary, Chair
Paul Anderer
Donald Keene
George A. Saliba
Wei Shang
Haruo Shirane
Burton Watson

# THE ESSENTIAL
# Huainanzi

## Liu An, King of Huainan

TRANSLATED, EDITED, AND SELECTED BY

John S. Major • Sarah A. Queen • Andrew Seth Meyer • Harold D. Roth

COLUMBIA UNIVERSITY PRESS • NEW YORK

COLUMBIA UNIVERSITY PRESS
*Publishers Since 1893*
New York   Chichester, West Sussex
cup.columbia.edu

Copyright © 2012 Columbia University Press
All rights reserved

Library of Congress Cataloging-in-Publication Data
Huainan zi. English. Selections.
   The essential Huainanzi / Liu An, King of Huainan ; translated, edited, and selected by John S. Major . . . [et al.].
       p. cm.   (Translations from the Asian classics)
   Includes bibliographical references (p.   ) and index.
   ISBN 978-0-231-15980-7 (cloth : alk. paper)
   ISBN 978-0-231-15981-4 (pbk. : alk. paper)
   ISBN 978-0-231-50145-3 (e-book)
   I. Liu, An, 179–122 B.C.   II. Major, John S.   III. Title.
   BL1900.H824E5 2012
   320.01—dc23
                                                    2011033920

Columbia University Press books are printed on permanent and durable acid-free paper.

This book is printed on paper with recycled content.

CONTENTS

Sketch of Early Chinese History,
with Special Reference to the *Huainanzi*   vii

*Introduction*   1

1. *Originating in the Way*   13
2. *Activating the Genuine*   27
3. *Celestial Patterns*   39
4. *Terrestrial Forms*   49
5. *Seasonal Rules*   57
6. *Surveying Obscurities*   67
7. *Quintessential Spirit*   73
8. *The Basic Warp*   83
9. *The Ruler's Techniques*   95
10. *Profound Precepts*   111
11. *Integrating Customs*   123
12. *Responses of the Way*   135

13. Boundless Discourses   145

14. Sayings Explained   153

15. An Overview of the Military   165

16. and 17.
    A Mountain of Persuasions and A Forest of Persuasions   177

18. Among Others   189

19. Cultivating Effort   197

20. The Exalted Lineage   211

21. An Overview of the Essentials   225

   Glossary of Personal Names   233

   Brief Bibliography   243

   Index   245

## SKETCH OF EARLY CHINESE HISTORY, WITH SPECIAL REFERENCE TO THE *HUAINANZI*

ca. 3500–2000 B.C.E.: Era of legendary sage-rulers
  Appearance of advanced Neolithic jade-working cultures in several parts of China; complex chieftainships develop into protostates. The supposed era of the Divine Farmer, the Yellow Emperor, and other mythical sage-rulers and culture heroes.
ca. 1950–1550 B.C.E.: Xia dynasty
  Dynasty supposedly founded by the flood-tamer Yu the Great. Beginning of the Bronze Age, beginning of hereditary monarchy. Last ruler is Tyrant Jie.
ca. 1550–1046 B.C.E.: Shang dynasty
  Founded by Tang the Victorious. High Bronze Age culture: elaborate tombs and worship of royal ancestors, divination by means of oracle bones, earliest Chinese writing. Last ruler is Tyrant Djou.
1046–771 B.C.E.: Western Zhou dynasty
  Founded by Kings Wen and Wu, consolidated by the Duke of Zhou. China is divided into numerous states ruled by aristocrats owing ritual and military support to the Zhou kings.
722–481 B.C.E.: Spring and Autumn period
  Named for a chronicle kept by the dukes of Lu. Decline of Zhou royal power, emergence of large, powerful states and the *ba* "hegemon" system. Lifetime of Confucius (551–479 B.C.E.).
481–221 B.C.E.: Warring States period
  Constant interstate warfare. Emergence of *shi* "knights" as a key social class.

Numerous political thinkers debate ways to create an orderly, safe, and well-governed society.

221–206 B.C.E.: Qin dynasty

Last Zhou king dies in 256 B.C.E. State of Qin begins campaign to conquer remaining warring states and consolidate their territory into a single empire. Campaign succeeds in 221; ruler takes the title First Emperor of Qin. Ambitious but overreaching centralization of power. First Emperor dies in 210; Qin state collapses in 206.

206 B.C.E.–7 C.E.: Western (or Former) Han dynasty

206 B.C.E.: Liu Bang proclaims himself king of Han; takes title of emperor in 202. Liu Chang becomes first king of Huainan in 196.

195–188 B.C.E.: Emperor Hui.

188–180 B.C.E.: Interregnum of Empress Dowager Lü.

180–157 B.C.E.: Emperor Wen. Liu Chang dies in 174; kingdom of Huainan temporarily abolished. Liu An becomes second king of Huainan in 164.

157–141 B.C.E.: Emperor Jing. Kingdom of Huainan becomes a center of learning.

141–87 B.C.E.: Emperor Wu. *Huainanzi* presented to emperor in 139 B.C.E. Liu An dies and kingdom of Huainan ends in 122 B.C.E.

# THE ESSENTIAL HUAINANZI

INTRODUCTION

The *Huainanzi* (*The Master of Huainan*) is a compendium of knowledge dating from early in China's Han dynasty (206 B.C.E.–220 C.E.). It was compiled under the auspices of, and probably with the active participation of, Liu An (179?–122 B.C.E.), the king of Huainan. Liu An was an influential member of the imperial family who ruled a sizable kingdom within the Han Empire. He also was known as an essayist, critic, poet, and patron of learning.

The *Huainanzi* was completed and presented to the imperial throne in 139 B.C.E. Its twenty-one chapters contain a comprehensive survey of contemporary knowledge, from self-cultivation techniques to the arts of rulership and from cosmology and geography to public speaking, military affairs, and the importance of education. The book's final chapter summarizes the entire work and claims that it synthesizes the best features of all other schools of thought, thereby creating a compact yet comprehensive distillation of all knowledge necessary for ruling the empire. For readers today, it opens a fascinating window into the intellectual and political life of China in the second century B.C.E.

## Historical Background

For much of the first millennium B.C.E., China was divided into a large number of states ruled by members of a hereditary aristocracy. Those rulers were nominally subject to the authority of the kings of the Zhou dynasty (1046–256), but after the eighth century B.C.E. the power of the Zhou kings waned, and they had little control over state affairs. For a time, during the Spring and Autumn period (722–481), the state rulers themselves tried to keep order, recognizing a succession of first-among-equals strongmen called *ba* (hegemons) who exercised authority on behalf of the Zhou kings. But that system eventually broke down, and during the Warring States period (481–221), the states grew larger and more powerful but fewer in number as the larger states conquered and absorbed their smaller neighbors. Warfare and treachery were commonplace, and philosophers and political theorists had only moderate success devising systems of rulership that would restore order once again.

In the mid-third century B.C.E., just as the enfeebled Zhou dynasty was coming to an end, the king of the state of Qin embarked on a conscious program of conquest, intended to defeat the other states and bring all of China under his own dominion. Abolishing hereditary offices, the king instituted a merit-based bureaucracy in the state of Qin and mobilized the whole population for the twin purposes of agriculture and war. His campaign was successful, and the last of the Zhou-era states submitted to Qin in 221 B.C.E. Taking the newly coined title Qin Shihuangdi (First Emperor of Qin), he extended his strict laws and bureaucratic government throughout the country. He then embarked on an ambitious—and, as it proved to be, overly ambitious—program of public works: building roads, canals, a section of the Great Wall, and his own huge, magnificent tomb. When the First Emperor died in 210, the country erupted in rebellion and civil war, and the Qin dynasty collapsed. The causes of that collapse were complex, but the explanation widely accepted at the time emphasized the populace's resentment of the burden of taxes and labor service placed on them, as well as the regime's policy of inflicting severe punishments for even petty crimes.

The principle of a united China endured, however, after some initial backtracking. In 206 B.C.E., the rebel chieftain Liu Bang proclaimed himself king of Han, and four years later, having defeated the last of his rivals, he assumed the title of emperor. Having come to power, he had to decide what his new government would look like and to what extent it would reflect the centralizing tendencies of Qin. Initially the new emperor instituted a hybrid system, keeping most of western China under direct imperial control and dividing the lands in the rich eastern parts of the country into kingdoms, semiautonomous realms that were handed over to the emperor's important allies and relatives. At the time, this would have been seen as a perfectly normal policy, sanctified by centuries of use. Soon, however, the Han dynasty found itself involved in a generations-long struggle to define the proper relationship between the imperial government and the neofeudal kingdoms. Rebellions and plots against the imperial throne by various regional kings were brutally suppressed in 196, 174, and 154 B.C.E. Some scholars suggest that at least some of these "rebellions" were provoked, and perhaps fabricated, by imperial authorities as a way of eliminating the regional kings and bringing their territory under imperial control.

Liu An, the patron and editor of the *Huainanzi*, was a grandson of the Han dynasty's founder, Liu Bang. Liu An's father, Liu Chang, had been established as king of Huainan in 196 B.C.E., when he was still an infant. (The name of the kingdom means "south of the Huai River." At its largest extent, it encompassed the present-day Anhui and Jiangxi provinces and some adjacent territories.) In 174, the youthful Liu Chang was accused of rebellion and died on the road to exile. Although the kingdom of Huainan was temporarily abolished, it was reestablished (with much less territory) in 164, when Liu An, still in his teens, was named the second king of Huainan. He grew up to be a talented and ambitious monarch whose royal palace became a magnet for writers and intellectuals. At some point, Liu An began working with some of his guest-scholars to produce a book that would synthesize the best points of all schools of thought and provide infallible guidance on how a government should be run. That book is what we now know as the *Huainanzi*.

The fourth Han sovereign, Emperor Jing (r. 157–141 B.C.E.), also was a grandson of the founder and thus was Liu An's cousin. Much of the *Huainanzi* was compiled during Emperor Jing's reign, and it is quite possible that the writing of this manifesto for imperial government reflected Liu An's hope that he might succeed his cousin as emperor. (Unlike later European monarchies, Chinese dynasties did not always pass down the throne to the eldest son of the late ruler; succession could also run from brother to brother, cousin to cousin, and so on.) That did not happen, however. Instead, a teenage son of Emperor Jing, Liu Che, mounted the throne. Known to posterity as Emperor Wu (the Martial Emperor), he reigned from 141 to 87 B.C.E., winning a reputation as the Han dynasty's longest-ruling and most successful emperor.

Having been passed over in the imperial succession, Liu An tried to find another outlet for his ambitions. In 139 B.C.E., he traveled to the Han capital at Chang'an and presented his treatise on good government, the *Huainanzi*, to the imperial throne. He evidently intended to establish himself as a trusted elder cousin (in effect, an honorary uncle) and personal adviser to the young emperor. Records tell us that Emperor Wu was "delighted" with the book, but Liu An himself failed to gain much influence at court. He returned to Huainan and in 122 was accused of harboring imperial ambitions. He committed suicide rather than face prosecution, the kingdom of Huainan was abolished, and Liu An's extensive library and other personal possessions were confiscated by the throne. Even though Liu An died in disgrace, the *Huainanzi* lived on. It never achieved canonical status (it was not, for example, part of the curriculum of studying for the imperial civil service examinations), but the *Huainanzi* endured through the centuries, attracting the attention of numerous commentators and intellectuals for the inherent interest of its ideas, the beauty of its prose, and its comprehensive approach to understanding the cosmos and the place of humans in it.

## The *Huainanzi*

The *Huainanzi* consists of twenty-one chapters. The final chapter, "An Overview of the Essentials," summarizes and characterizes the entire work. Written in an elaborate style of prose-poetry, that chapter probably was recited orally at the imperial court when Liu An presented the book to Emperor Wu. The "Overview" claims that the book's twenty substantive chapters encompass the best features of all earlier thinkers and thus supersede them. Moreover, the chapters leave out nothing of importance and so constitute a complete, unique, and infallible guide to the policies that should be followed by the imperial clan in governing the empire. The book envisions an emperor who has undergone rigorous training in the techniques of self-cultivation, leading to a state of sagehood (that is, being perfectly aligned with the basic forces of the cosmos); who has been comprehensively educated in history, statesmanship, rhetoric, and other necessary qualities; and who rules through loyal ministers and reliable bureaucrats, supported by the Lords of the Land—hereditary aristocrats like Liu An himself. It envisions an imperial establishment that is adaptable to changing times but preserves the best features of the past. Liu An's vision of empire reflected his own position and his own self-interest. In the end, though, that vision was overtaken by the imperial regime's centralizing tendencies and by an imperial ideology that differed significantly from Liu An's intellectual program. Yet some of its basic ideas remained influential, including the notion that the emperor should have the qualities of a sage and that his rule should be so attuned to cosmic forces and cycles as to seem effortless.

### Sources and Claims

In the early Han period, Liu An's *Huainanzi* became part of a lively, energetic, sometimes acrimonious multipart conversation among scholars and administrators about the nature of the cosmos, the role of humans in it, the structure and function of government, and other fundamental issues. Some intellectuals of the time took the position that a single text—for example, the *Spring and Autumn Annals* (*Chunqiu*) or one of its principal commentaries or the *Changes* (*Yijing* or *Zhouyi*)—constituted a complete and infallible (if properly interpreted) source of all knowledge and wisdom. Others advocated a doctrine (imperfectly understood today and still debated by scholars) known as Huang-Lao that supposedly combined the teachings of Laozi (that is, the *Daodejing*) and the Yellow Emperor. Others, like Liu An, advocated drawing on a diverse menu of texts to formulate a syncretic doctrine. Earlier works of this type, such as the *Mr. Lü's Spring and Autumn Annals* (*Lüshi chunqiu*), directly influenced the *Huainanzi*. In turn, the *Huainanzi* makes the extraordinary claim that it distills and encompasses all essential knowledge, thus rendering all earlier books superfluous and making it unnecessary to compose any more new ones. Not surprisingly, that claim was not widely endorsed by contemporaries. Still, the *Huainanzi* offers a very wide-ranging and informative look at the intellectual currents in the early Han.

## Root and Branch

The central organizing metaphor of the *Huainanzi* is the concept of roots and branches—in other words, that certain ideas, concepts, institutions, and texts are fundamental, while others are derivative or peripheral. Put another way, the roots are associated with principles and the Way, and the branches are associated with "affairs," or actualizations of the principles of the Way. The first eight chapters of the work are "root" chapters; the next twelve deal with "branch" issues; and the last summarizes and makes claims for the work as a whole. The root chapters build on one another to create a framework for the branch chapters that follow.

Chapter 1 deals with the Way (*dao*), the indivisible monad that is both the universal source of all things and the all-encompassing totality of everything.

Chapter 2 describes how individual humans can align themselves with the Way to achieve extraordinary states of accomplishment such as the Genuine or the Perfected.

Chapters 3, 4, and 5 form a cosmological trilogy of chapters that examine, respectively, astronomy and astrology, geography (both real and mythical) and the interactions of topography and living beings, and the calendar and the appropriate rituals and emblems for every month and season. These three chapters correspond structurally to the familiar triad in early Chinese thought—Heaven, Earth, and Man—in the order in which they emerge from the cosmic root.

Chapter 6 introduces the concept of resonance, the idea that every stimulus evokes a response conveyed through the medium of *qi*. In principle, these stimuli and responses should be comprehensible through an understanding of cosmic regularities, but the chapter admits that in practice many of them remain mysterious.

Chapter 7 covers the theory and techniques of personal self-cultivation, fundamental to success as a ruler (political and administrative techniques of rulership are considered "branch" phenomena).

Chapter 8 articulates a theory of history that sees humans progressing from a "root" state of primitive communitarianism, associated with the Way and its Potency, through successively elaborate forms of culture associated with "branch" virtues such as Humaneness and Rightness, down to the present day when laws and punishments have become necessary for government. The self-cultivated ruler is urged to adhere to the root while making properly expedient use of branch techniques.

Chapters 9 through 20 describe various branch phenomena, including rulership and administration (9), the relationship between government and moral values (10), customs and ritual (11), qualities of the ideal ruler (12), the concept of change in historical context (13), proverbial wisdom (14), the military (15), rhetoric (16 and 17), the vagaries of human affairs (18), the necessity of education and personal effort (19), and Moral Potency as the foundation of government (20). Obviously the classification of these matters as branch phenomena does not imply that they are unimportant, only that they are derived from fundamental principles, rather than being fundamental in their own right.

## Key Concepts in the *Huainanzi*

The *Way* (*dao*) is the source of everything in the universe and embraces all things in their totality. Nothing can exist apart from or in contrast to the Way; the Way cannot be negated. Even the term itself is provisional. In fact, the Way is not namable because to name it would be to differentiate it from something else. (As the opening line of the *Laozi* famously puts it, "The Way that can be called 'The Way' is not the everlasting Way.") According to the *Huainanzi*, the key to success in all human activities is that they be attuned to the Way. The term also can be used to denote a specific doctrine, teaching, or technique (for example, "the Way of charioteering").

*Potency* (*de*) is the activation of the Way in the phenomenal world. The word *de* is etymologically related to another word (also pronounced *de*) that means "to obtain," so potency has the connotation of "to accumulate." For example, during the spring and summer, the potency of yang accumulates while the potency of yin reciprocally diminishes. But in autumn and winter, yin's potency accumulates while yang's potency diminishes. The sage-ruler accumulates potency, allowing him to bestow rewards on the deserving. Therefore, *de* also has the sense of "reward" or "benefit." When the term occurs in the *Huainanzi* in contexts that are clearly Confucian in orientation (for example, in regard to such virtues as Humaneness and Rightness), we translate it as "Moral Potency." (Older, and in our view less apt, translations of this difficult word include "power" and "virtue.")

*Qi* means both "matter" and "energy." Everything that exists is made of *qi*, and every action is a manifestation of *qi* energy. *Qi* comes in various textures, from the most ethereal and refined to the coarse and lumpish. Ethereal *qi* is heavenly, and coarse *qi* is earthly. Spirits are made of highly refined *qi*, but ordinary physical matter is made of coarse *qi*. Highly refined states of consciousness such as tranquillity and clarity are manifestations of ethereal *qi*. *Qi* consequently serves as a vibrating, resonant medium that conveys responses to stimuli. In medical and self-cultivation contexts, *qi* means "vital energy" or "vital breath," the animating principle of a living body. The principal aims of various techniques of self-cultivation are to refine the body's *qi*, to attain deep states of insight, and to control and direct the flow of energy within the body.

*Wu* and *you* are paired antonyms that mean "to be without" and "to have," "nonexistence" and "existence," "nothing" and "something." We live in the world of "something," but "nothing" is both temporally and conceptually prior to "something." *Wu* contains myriad potentialities, but *you* is reduced to a single instantiation. For that reason, the *Huainanzi* (like the Daoist classics the *Laozi* and the *Zhuangzi*) exhibits a strong preference for *wu* over *you*.

In the *Huainanzi*'s cosmology, the primal unity of the undifferentiated Way divides into *yin* and *yang*, two reciprocal forces that are in a constant state of motion and transformation. Yin and yang are complementary rather than antagonistic. They are paired opposites, each containing the germ of, and ultimately evolving to become, the other. Yin is dark, female, moist, low-lying, cool, oviparous, and winter; and yang correspondingly is bright, male, dry, high, warm, viviparous, and summer. Unlike some other Han texts, the *Huainanzi* does not conspicuously privilege yang over yin but regards both as cosmic forces necessary for the universe to function.

The *Five Phases* (*wuxing*) represent the five paradigmatic manifestations of *qi*: Wood, Fire, Earth, Metal, and Water. (The term *wuxing* is sometimes translated as "five elements," but this is misleading because the five are paradigms, not constituents, of physical phenomena.) The five are "phases" of *qi* in the same sense that steam, liquid water, and ice are "phases" of $H_2O$. All phenomena can be classified as belonging to one or another of the Five Phases, as well as being yin or yang.

*Resonance* (*ganying*) refers to the ability of a stimulus to evoke a response through the vibrating medium of *qi*, even in the absence of a perceptible physical connection between the two. The classic example is that if the "C" string of one musical instrument is plucked, the "C" string of a nearby instrument will vibrate. Chapter 6 of the *Huainanzi* describes resonance as being both crucial to the workings of the cosmos and deeply mysterious and hard to fathom.

*Nature* (*xing*) is the quality that makes a thing itself, the attributes that are present from birth in a living creature. "Nature" is often contrasted with deliberate human undertakings, so it is said that to run and kick is the nature of a horse, while to control a horse with bit and reins is to impose human will on the animal.

*Self-cultivation* (*yang shen*) refers to a variety of meditative techniques and disciplines aimed at refining and controlling one's store of vital energy to attain a state of authenticity that is a manifestation of "quintessential spirit" (*jingshen*). These are collectively referred to as "the techniques of the mind." The results of successful self-cultivation are described with a variety of terms denoting superior attainments: both the Superior Man (*junzi*) and the Sage (*sheng*) are regarded as active participants in the human realm of affairs, while the Genuine (*zhenren*) and the Perfected (*zhiren*) are mysterious, self-sufficient beings beyond the reach of ordinary concerns. One consequence of self-cultivation can be the achievement of "spirit-illumination" (or "spiritlike illumination"), an ability to see deeply into matters hidden from the perception of ordinary humans.

*Wu wei* literally means "without acting." In the *Huainanzi*, it generally does not refer to a state of utter inaction but to the ability of a person (especially a ruler) to be so attuned to the Way and therefore so filled with Potency that his desires are translated into reality without any visible effort on his part. Things that occur through *wu wei* appear to come about "naturally" or "spontaneously" (*ziran* [thus of itself]).

*Transformation* (*hua*) is the most profound of several terms for change ("change," "alteration," "shift," and so on) in the *Huainanzi*. A sage-ruler is able to "transform the people" by projecting his Potency in such a way as to evoke a spontaneous positive response in the natures of the people in his realm.

*Humaneness* (*ren*), *Rightness* (*yi*), *Ritual* (*li*), and *Music* (*yue*) are virtues and social phenomena associated especially with the teachings of Confucius and his followers. In the *Huainanzi*, these are taken to be valuable, indeed essential, qualities of a well-governed society in the conditions that obtain in the present day. But they are derived, rather than fundamental, qualities ("branches" rather than "roots"). Thus government conducted by means of these virtues is inferior in principle to the primitive harmony brought about by the sages of antiquity, who, being perfectly attuned to the Way, transformed the people by means of non-action.

## Sources of the *Huainanzi*

True to its stated claim to draw on the best ideas of all previous thinkers and texts, the *Huainanzi* quotes, paraphrases, alludes to, and echoes a very wide range of earlier materials. It treats four texts as canonical; that is, it usually quotes them by name and regards them as authoritative in affirming or ratifying a position. These four are the *Laozi*, the *Odes*, the *Changes*, and the *Documents*. The *Huainanzi* also draws heavily on many other texts but seldom or never refers to them by title.

Chapter 1 of the *Huainanzi* is heavily based on the *Laozi*, which therefore can be said to form the root of the work's root chapters. Interestingly, the *Laozi* is not referred to by name in *Huainanzi* 1. Instead, it appears that the authors of the opening chapter of the *Huainanzi* assumed that its readers were thoroughly familiar with its source text. But the *Laozi* is quoted extensively by name in *Huainanzi* 12 and in many other chapters of the text.

The *Odes* (a collection of some three hundred poems comprising liturgical hymns, dynastic legends, folk songs, and other genres), the *Changes* (a divination text consulted for aid in making decisions), and the *Documents* (a collection of supposedly ancient historical documents of varying degrees of reliability) became closely associated with the Confucian tradition during the Han dynasty. The *Huainanzi* quotes these texts, usually by name, most often in the "branch" chapters of the text and only seldom in the "root" chapters. This is consistent with the *Huainanzi*'s position that the Confucian virtues, like Humaneness, Rightness, Propriety, and Music, are derived properties of the Way.

The *Huainanzi* also draws extensively on the *Zhuangzi* (the second great work, along with the *Laozi*, of pre-Han Daoism), which forms the philosophical basis for *Huainanzi* 2 and 7 and is often alluded to (but not usually cited by name) in other chapters, both "root" and "branch." Several *Huainanzi* chapters allude to the *Hanfeizi* (which argues for hard-nosed political centralism and performance-based rewards and punishments to achieve political goals), the *Xunzi* (a work in the Confucian tradition that advocates a pragmatic approach to political and administrative issues and places great emphasis on the need for education and moral cultivation), and the *Guanzi* (itself a highly eclectic work dealing with government administration, cosmology, self-cultivation, and other matters). The *Huainanzi* also draws on, or at least shares material with, earlier syncretic texts such as the *Shizi* (*Master Shi*) and the *Lüshi chunqiu*.

Individual chapters of the *Huainanzi* can often be associated with particular source texts. *Huainanzi* 3 borrows from astronomical and cosmological texts like the "Tian wen" (Questions About Heaven) section of the poetic anthology *Chuci* (*Elegies of Chu*). *Huainanzi* 4 has much in common with the *Shanhaijing* (*Classic of Mountains and Seas*), an account of real and mythical geography within and beyond the borders of China. Much of *Huainanzi* 5 quotes from (or shares a source text with) the *Lüshi chunqiu*, while *Huainanzi* 15 draws on a rich tradition of pre-Han military texts such as the *Sunzi bingfa* (*Master Sun's Arts of War*). In addition, portions of the *Huainanzi* apparently quote from or are based on earlier texts that have been lost and are now unknown or known only by title. For example, several sections of *Huainanzi* 3 quote verbatim from a short work known as the "Wuxing zhan" (Stations of the Five Planets), a previously unknown text archaeologically recovered at Mawangdui, Changsha, in Hunan Province, in 1973. Probably many other passages in the *Huainanzi* are quoted from lost and now untraceable sources.

The fact that much of the *Huainanzi* is taken from earlier sources does not mean, however, that the text is simply a grab bag of recycled materials. The genius of Liu An and his court scholars was precisely that, drawing on early China's rich textual tradition and creating new material as needed, they formulated a comprehensive and persuasive view of the world and how it should be ruled by a sagelike, cultivated, and morally potent sovereign.

## About This Book

*The Essential Huainanzi* is an abridgment of *The Huainanzi: A Guide to the Theory and Practice of Government in Early Han China*, the first complete English translation of Liu An's great work. Although about 20 to 30 percent of each chapter is included in this abridged volume, most of the ancillary features of the unabridged volume, such as the appendices explaining technical terms and an extensive bibliographical essay, have been omitted. Our aim in this book is to create a highly readable condensation of the *Huainanzi* while making it easy to refer to the unabridged work for readers who wish to do so. A few, very inconspicuous corrections to the translation have been made in this abridged volume; otherwise, the corresponding material in the unabridged and abridged texts is identical.

The introduction to each of the chapters of the abridged translation (except that to chapter 21 itself) begins by quoting the chapter summary from *Huainanzi* 21, "An Overview of the Essentials." After this self-introductory passage, we briefly describe the content of the chapter, its sources, the significance of the chapter title, and the place of the chapter in the work as a whole. Considerably longer and more detailed chapter introductions may be found in the unabridged edition.

Section numbers (not present in the original Chinese text of the *Huainanzi*) were added to the unabridged translation, both to reveal underlying structural features of the text and to facilitate references to the translation itself. The numbers of sections quoted in full or in part in this volume match the section numbers in the unabridged translation.

We were careful to preserve in the formatting of our translations, in both the unabridged edition and this book, such formal characteristics as block prose, parallel prose (set line for line and indented), and verse (set line for line and indented even more). These features are important to appreciating the literary qualities of the text as well as the rhetorical force of its arguments.

We omitted most of the footnotes in the abridged edition, except for the explanatory footnotes necessary for understanding special terms, historical anecdotes, and the like. Those readers who require such information can find footnotes explaining textual issues, cross-references, and other scholarly questions in the corresponding passages in the unabridged translation.

The proper names of persons, identified in footnotes in the unabridged translation, are collected in a glossary at the end of this volume, to reduce further the distraction of numerous footnotes to the text.

For readers who might wish to consult the Chinese text on which our translation is based, the unabridged translation is keyed by chapter, page, and line to D. C. Lau, *A Concordance to the Huainanzi* (*Huainanzi zhuzi suoyin*) (Hong Kong: Commercial Press, 1992).

We already have defined some of the key terms in the *Huainanzi*, but a fuller explanation of these and other terms may be found in two appendices in the unabridged translation volume: appendix A, "Key Chinese Terms and Their Translations," and appendix B, "Categorical Terms."

In this book's short bibliography, we mention two Chinese editions of the *Huainanzi* and a few key Western-language translations and studies. A more extensive bibliography of translations and studies, along with a brief account of the transmission and textual history of the *Huainanzi*, may be found in the unabridged translation volume, in appendix C, "A Concise Textual History of the *Huainanzi* and a Bibliography of *Huainanzi* Studies."

Further information about the historical background, the intellectual and political life of the early Han dynasty, the sources of the *Huainanzi*, the state of modern *Huainanzi* studies, and other related matters can found in the general introduction to the unabridged translation. Likewise, more detailed information on individual chapters can be found in the chapter introductions of that work.

We gratefully acknowledge the contribution to the complete translation, and to this abridged volume, of two colleagues: Michael Puett, who participated in the translation of chapter 13, and Judson Murray, who participated in the translation of chapter 21.

We hope that this abridged edition of the *Huainanzi* will be read with interest and pleasure and that it will stimulate some readers to explore further in the field of *Huainanzi* studies.

# One

## ORIGINATING IN THE WAY

"Originating in the Way"
>[begins with] the six coordinates contracted and compressed
>and the myriad things chaotic and confused.
>[It then] diagrams the features of the Grand One
>and fathoms the depths of the Dark Unseen,
>thereby soaring beyond the frame of Empty Nothingness.
>By relying on the small, it embraces the great;
>by guarding the contracted, it orders the expansive.

It enables you to understand
>the bad or good fortune of taking the lead or following behind
>and the benefit or harm of taking action or remaining still.

If you sincerely comprehend its import, floodlike, you can achieve a grand vision.
>If you desire a single expression to awaken to it:
>"Revere the heavenly and preserve your genuineness."
>If you desire a second expression to comprehend it:
>"Devalue things and honor your person."
>If you desire a third expression to fathom it:
>"Externalize desires and return to your genuine dispositions."
>If you grasp its main tenets,
>inwardly you will harmonize the Five Orbs
>and enrich the flesh and skin.

> If you adhere to its models and standards
> and partake of them to the end of your days,
they will provide the means
> to respond and attend to the myriad aspects of the world
> and observe and accompany its manifold alterations,
> as if rolling a ball in the palm of your hand.
> Surely it will suffice to make you joyous!
>
> —"An Overview of the Essentials" (21.2)

"Originating in the Way" (Yuan dao), the first of the eight foundational or "root" chapters of the text, is significant because it provides the cosmological basis for the entire *Huainanzi* collection. It opens with a beautiful poetic rhapsody on the cosmology of the Way (*dao*) and its Potency (*de*) in the tradition of the *Laozi*, certainly one of the canonical sources for this essay and for the book as a whole. In it we see a detailed examination of how these cosmic foundations are manifested in the world and an in-depth description of how sages are able to use their unique penetrating vision of these foundations, attained through self-cultivation, to bring peace and harmony to the realm. Coming at the beginning of the entire twenty-one-chapter book and presented to the court at a time when its compiler, Liu An, was trying to dissuade his nephew, Emperor Wu, from accepting the arguments of his Confucian (*ru*) advisers, this chapter serves a number of purposes.

First, even though the chapter never directly affirms a particular intellectual affiliation, its cosmological, psychological, and political philosophy shows its indebtedness to the *Laozi* and some other important early Daoist sources on the relationship of cosmology and self-cultivation to rulership. Only such an ideal of rulership comprehends the inner workings of the cosmos and applies that wisdom to governing in harmony with them. Second, as the opening chapter of the collection, "Originating in the Way" sets out general themes that will be pursued in more detail in much of the remainder of the work, such as cosmology, human psychology and self-cultivation, and political philosophy. Its importance to understanding the entire book and seeing it in a clearer light cannot be overemphasized.

Perhaps the most important focus of this chapter is on how the Way generates and infuses the innate natures of all things and guides their spontaneous interaction through a series of regular patterns such as the movements of the stars and planets and the structured flow of vital energies in the human being. Taken together, these natures and patterns form a "normative natural order." Sages accord with this order through a self-cultivation process that is described in this chapter. Its authors recommend practices that empty out consciousness to attain psychological states of tranquillity and freedom from self that, when they are applied to daily affairs, produce clear cognition, unbiased attitudes, and effortless action that yield a spontaneous harmony with the normative natural order. This cognitive mode is the essence of skilled rulership.

# One

## 1.1

As for the Way:
It covers Heaven and upholds Earth.
>It extends the four directions
>and divides the eight end points.
>So high, it cannot be reached.
>So deep, it cannot be fathomed.
>It embraces and enfolds Heaven and Earth
>It endows and bestows the Formless.
>Flowing along like a wellspring, bubbling up like a font,
>it is empty but gradually becomes full.
>Roiling and boiling,
>it is murky but gradually becomes clear.

Therefore,
>pile it up vertically: it fills all within Heaven and Earth.
>Stretch it out horizontally: it encompasses all within the Four Seas.
>Unwind it limitlessly: it is without distinction between dawn and dusk.
>Roll it out: it expands to the six coordinates.[1]
>Roll it up: it does not make a handful.

---

1. That is, the three dimensions: up-down, front-back, and left-right.

It is constrained but able to extend.
It is dark but able to brighten.
It is supple but able to strengthen.
It is pliant but able to become firm.
It stretches out the four binding cords and restrains yin and yang.
It suspends the cosmic rafters and displays the Three Luminaries.
Intensely saturating and soaking,
Intensely subtle and minute,
Mountains are high because of it.
Abysses are deep because of it.
Beasts can run because of it.
Birds can fly because of it.
The sun and moon are bright because of it.
The stars and timekeepers move because of it.
*Qilins* wander freely because of it.
Phoenixes soar because of it.[2]

## 1.3

The most exalted Way
     generates the myriad things but does not possess them,
     completes the transforming images but does not dominate them.
Creatures that walk on hooves and breathe through beaks, that fly through the air and wriggle on the ground,
     depend on it for life, yet none understands its Potency;
     depend on it for death, yet none is able to resent it.
     Those who attain it and profit are unable to praise it;
     those who use it and lose are unable to blame it.
          It gathers and collects yet is not any richer for it.
          It bestows and confers yet it not diminished by it.
          It cycles endlessly yet cannot be fathomed.
          It is delicate and minute yet cannot be exhausted.
          Pile it up, but it will not get higher;
          Collapse it, but it will not get lower.
          Add to it, but it will not increase.

---

2. The *qilin* was a mythical animal with the head of a lion or dragon, horns, the body of a horse, and hooves like those of a goat or deer. The phoenix (*fenghuang*) was a mythical bird somewhat resembling a peacock or a pheasant. Both were said to appear only during times of good government.

Take away from it, but it will not decrease.
Split it, but it will not get thinner.
Kill it, but it will not be destroyed.
Bore into it, but it will not deepen.
Fill it in, but it will not get shallower.
Hazy! Nebulous! You cannot imagine it.
Nebulous! Hazy! Your use will not exhaust it.
Dark! Obscure! It responds formlessly.
Deep! Penetrating! It does not act in vain.
It rolls and unrolls with the firm and the pliant.
It bends and straightens with the yin and the yang.

## 1.5

Therefore,
the affairs of the world cannot be deliberately controlled.
You must draw them out by following their natural direction.
The alterations of the myriad things cannot be fathomed.
You must grasp their essential tendencies and guide them to their homes.

When a water mirror comes in contact with shapes, it is not because of wisdom and precedent that it is able to flawlessly reflect the square, round, crooked, and straight. Therefore, the echo does not respond at random, and the shadow does not independently arise. They mimic sounds and forms and tacitly grasp them.

That which is tranquil from our birth is our heavenly nature. Stirring only after being stimulated, our nature is harmed. When things arise and the spirit responds, this is the activity of perception. When perception comes into contact with things, preferences arise. When preferences take shape and perception is enticed by external things, our nature cannot return to the self, and the heavenly patterns are destroyed.

Thus those who break through to the Way do not use the human to change the heavenly. Externally they transform together with things, but internally they do not lose their genuine responses.

They attain Nothing, but their needs are provided for.
They are always on the move but find a place to lodge for the night.

Small and great, tall or short, each has its proper role. The myriads spring forth and leap and prance in profusion, yet they do not lose track of their norms.

So when they rest above, the people do not find them heavy.
When they are located in front, the multitudes do not injure them.
All the world returns to them
The wicked and perverse fear them.

It is because they do not compete with the myriad things that none is able to compete with them.

## 1.8 (in part)

Therefore,
> those who break through to the Way return to clarity and tranquillity.
> Those who look deeply into things end up not acting on them.
> If you use calmness to nourish your nature,
> and use quietude to transfix your spirit,
> then you will enter the heavenly gateway.

What we call "Heaven"
>> is pure and untainted.
>> Unadorned and plain,

it has never begun to be tainted with impurities.
> What we call "human"
>> is biased because of wisdom and precedent.
>> Devious and deceptive,

it is what looks back to past generations and interacts with the vulgar.
> Thus,
>> that the ox treads on cloven hooves and grows horns
>> and that the horse has a mane and square hooves,

This is heavenly [i.e., natural].
> Yet to put a bit in a horse's mouth
> and to put a ring through an ox's nose,

This is human.
> Those who comply with Heaven roam with the Way.
> Those who follow the human interact with the mundane.

Now,
> you cannot talk to a fish in a well about great things because it is confined by its narrow space.
> You cannot talk to a summer bug about the cold because it is restricted to its season.
> You cannot talk to petty scholars about the Utmost Way because they are confined by the mundane and bound up by their teaching.

Thus sages
> do not allow the human to obscure the heavenly
> and do not let desire corrupt their genuine responses.
> They hit the mark without scheming;
> they are sincere without speaking;

>    they attain without planning;
>    they complete without striving.
>
> Their vital essence circulates into the Magical Storehouse, and they become human along with what fashions and transforms them.

## 1.9 (in part)

Therefore,
>    sages internally cultivate the root [of the Way within them]
>    and do not externally adorn themselves with its branches.
>    They protect their Quintessential Spirit
>    and dispense with wisdom and precedent.
>    In stillness they take no deliberate action, yet there is nothing left undone.
>    In tranquillity they do not try to govern, but nothing is left ungoverned.
>    What we call "no deliberate action" is to not anticipate the activity of things.
>    What we call "nothing left undone" means to adapt to what things have [already] done.
>    What we call "to not govern" means to not change how things are naturally so.
>    What we call "nothing left ungoverned" means to adapt to how things are mutually so.
>    The myriad things all have a source from which they arise;
>    [the sages] alone understand how to guard this root.
>    The hundred endeavors all have a source from which they are produced;
>    [the sages] alone understand how to guard this gateway.
>    Thus exhausting the inexhaustible,
>    reaching the limit of the infinite,
>    illuminating things without bedazzling them,
>    and inexhaustibly responding to things like an echo [responds to sound]:
> This is what we call "being released by Heaven."

## 1.10

Thus those who attain the Way:
>        Their wills are supple, but their deeds are strong.
>        Their minds are empty, but their responses are dead on.
> What we mean by a supple will is
>    being pliant and soft, calm, and tranquil;

hiding when others do not dare to;
acting when others are unable to;
being calm and without worry;
acting without missing the right moment;
and cycling and revolving with the myriad things.
Never anticipating or initiating
but just responding to things when stimulated.

Therefore,
the honored invariably take their titles from the base,
and those of high station invariably take what is below as their foundation.
They rely on the small to embrace the great;
they rest in the inner to regulate the outer;
they act pliantly to become firm;
they utilize weakness to become strong;
they cycle through transformations and push where things are shifting;
they attain the Way of the One and use the few to correct the many.

What we mean by strength of deeds is
responding with alacrity when encountering alterations;
pushing away disasters and warding off difficulties;
being so strong that there is nothing unvanquished;
facing enemies, there are none that are not humiliated;
responding to transformations by gauging the proper moment
and being harmed by nothing.

Therefore,
if you wish to be firm, you must guard it by being pliant.
If you wish to be strong, you must protect it by being supple.
When you accumulate pliability, you become firm.
When you accumulate suppleness, you become strong.
Keep a close watch on what you are accumulating
in order to know the tendencies toward fortune or misfortune.

Strength defeats what is not its equal. When it encounters its equal, it is neutralized.

Pliability defeats what exceeds itself. Its power cannot be measured.
Thus when an army is strong, it will be destroyed.
When a tree is strong, it will be broken.
When leather armor is hard, it will split open.
Because teeth are harder than the tongue, they wear out first.
Therefore, the pliant and weak are the supports of life,
and the hard and strong are the disciples of death.

## 1.12

Of all things under Heaven, none is more pliant and supple than water. Nonetheless, it is
> so great that its limits cannot be reached;
> so deep that it cannot be fathomed;
> so high that it reaches the infinite;
> so distant it merges into the boundless.
> Increasing and decreasing, draining away and filling up,
> it circulates without restraints into the immeasurable.
> When it ascends into the heavens, it becomes the rain and the dew.
> When it descends to the earth, it becomes moisture and dampness.
> If the myriad things do not gain it, they will not be born.
> If the various endeavors do not gain it, they will not succeed.
> It completely embraces the various things without partiality or favoritism.
> It seeps through to the tiniest of creatures without seeking their gratitude.
> Its richness sustains the entire world without being depleted.
> Its Potency extends to the hundred clans without being expended.
> It circulates [everywhere], yet we cannot exhaust it.
> It is so subtle that we cannot seize it in our hands.
> Strike it, and it is not wounded.
> Pierce it, and it is not injured.
> Chop it, and it is not cut apart.
> Try to set it alight, and it will not burn.
> Seeping, draining, flowing, disappearing,
> Mixing and blending, intertwining with [things], it cannot be differentiated.
> It is so sharp it can pierce a hole in metal and stone.
> It is so strong it can give sustenance to the entire world.
> It dissolves into the realm of the Formless,
> And soars beyond the region of the Nebulous.
> It meanders its way through the rivers and valleys,
> and surges out into the vast wildernesses.
> Depending on whether it is abundant or deficient,
> it takes from or gives to Heaven and Earth.
> It gives to the myriad things equally without preferences.

Therefore,
> without being partial or impartial, gushing and undulating, it totally merges with Heaven and Earth.

Without favoring the left or the right, coiling and swirling, it ends and begins with the myriad things.

This is what we call "Perfect Potency."

The reason that water is able to achieve its Perfect Potency within the entire world is that it is gentle and soaking, moist and slippery. Thus, in the words of Lao Dan:

> The most pliant things in the world
> ride roughshod over the most rigid.
> [This is because] they emerge from the Nonexistent
> and enter into the Seamless.

I thereby understand the benefits of taking no action.

> Now the Formless is the Great Ancestor of things,
> and the Toneless is the Great Ancestor of sound.
> Their son is light;
> their grandson is water;

And both are generated by the Formless.

> Light can be seen but cannot be held;
> water can be held but cannot be destroyed.

Thus of all things that have shapes, none is more honored than water.

## 1.14

> Joy and anger are aberrations from the Way;
> worry and grief are losses of Potency.
> Likes and dislikes are excesses of the mind;
> lusts and desires are hindrances to nature.
>> Violent anger ruins the yin;
>> extreme joy collapses the yang.
>> The suppression of vital energy brings on dumbness;
>> fear and terror bring on madness.
>> When you are worried, aggrieved, or enraged,
>> sickness will increasingly develop.
>> When likes and dislikes abundantly pile up,
>> misfortunes will successively follow.

Thus,
> when the mind is not worried or happy, it achieves the perfection of Potency.
> When the mind is inalterably expansive, it achieves the perfection of tranquillity.

> When lusts and desires do not burden the mind, it achieves the perfection of emptiness.
> When the mind is without likes and dislikes, it achieves the perfection of equanimity.
> When the mind is not tangled up in things, it achieves the perfection of purity.

If the mind is able to achieve these five qualities, then it will break through to spiritlike illumination. To break through to spiritlike illumination is to realize what is intrinsic.

Therefore,

> if you use the internal to govern the external,
> then your various endeavors will not fail.
> If you are able to realize internally,
> then the external can be attended to.
> If you realize it internally
> then your Five Orbs[3] will be in repose;
> worries and anxieties will be at peace.
> Your sinews will be powerful, and your muscles will be strong;
> your ears and eyes will be acute and clear.
> Though you are placid and calm, you do not waver.
> Though you are hard and strong, you do not break.
> There is nothing you overshoot
> and nothing you fall short of.
> When you dwell in the small, you will not be cramped;
> when you dwell in the great, you will be unrestrained.
> Your soul will not be agitated;
> your spirit will not be troubled.
> Clear and limpid, still and calm,
> you will become a hero to the entire world.

## 1.17

The mind is the master of the Five Orbs. It regulates and directs the Four Limbs and circulates the blood and vital energy, gallops through the realms of accept-

---

3. The Five Orbs correspond to the five organs of the human physiology. They were thought to be important generative and coordinating junctures for the dynamic matrix of *qi* that composed the mind–body system: the lungs, liver, spleen, gall bladder, and kidneys. The term refers to organic systems, not just to the physical viscera; hence we speak of the pulmonary, hepatic, choleric, splenic, and renal orbs.

ing and rejecting, and enters and exits through the gateways and doorways of the hundreds of endeavors. Therefore if you do not realize it [your intrinsic nature] in your own mind and still want to control the entire world, this is like having no ears yet wanting to tune bells and drums and like having no eyes and wanting to enjoy patterns and ornaments. You will, most certainly, not be up to the task.

Thus the world is a spiritlike vessel: you cannot act deliberately on it; you cannot control it. Those who attempt to deliberately act on it will be defeated by it; those who try to control it will lose it. Now the reason that Xu You devalued the world and would not trade places with Yao was because he had the intention of leaving the world behind. Why was this so? Because he thought that you should act on the world by adapting to it [and not trying to force your own will on it].

The essentials of the world:
    do not lie in the Other
    but instead lie in the self;
    do not lie in other people
    but instead lie in your own person.
When you fully realize it [the Way] in your own person, then all the myriad things will be arrayed before you. When you thoroughly penetrate the teachings of the techniques of the mind, then you will be able to put lusts and desires, likes and dislikes, outside yourself.

Therefore [if you realize the Way],
    there is nothing to rejoice in and nothing to be angry about,
    nothing to be happy about and nothing to feel bitter about.
    You will be mysteriously unified with the myriad things,
    and there is nothing you reject and nothing you affirm.
    You transform and nourish a mysterious resplendence
    and, while alive, seem to be dead.

# Two

## ACTIVATING THE GENUINE

"Activating the Genuine" exhaustively traces the transformation [of things] from their ends to their beginnings;
>infuses and fills the essence of Something and Nothing;
>distinguishes and differentiates the alterations of the myriad things;
>unifies and equates the forms of death and life.

It enables you to
>know to disregard things and return to the self;
>investigate the distinctions between Humaneness and Rightness;
>comprehend the patterns of identity and difference;
>observe the guiding thread of Utmost Potency;
>and know the binding cords of alterations and transformations.
>Its explanations tally with the core of the Profound Mystery
>and comprehend the mother of creation and transformation.

"An Overview of the Essentials" (21.2)

"Activating the Genuine" is the second of the eight "root" or foundational chapters of the text and serves as a companion to chapter 1, "Originating in the Way," in its overarching cosmology and self-cultivation themes. Whereas "Originating in the Way" is very much indebted to the

*Laozi*, "Activating the Genuine" is thoroughly steeped in the *Zhuangzi*, three of whose authorial voices are powerfully represented in its pages.[1]

All the principal themes of chapter 2 are found in the *Zhuangzi*. These include cosmogony, the precariousness of life, the existence of archaic utopias governed by spiritually perfected sage-rulers, the devolution of history and the degradation of spiritual realization that have occurred over time, the nature of perfected human beings, the Way as the source of the entire universe, the spiritual perfection of sages who through meditative "inner cultivation" return to the wellsprings of the spirit that lie deep within human nature, and the importance of the right balance of nature and destiny in the human ability to attain sage-rulership and spiritual fulfillment.

The authors of chapter 2 hark back to the Utopian past of "great perfection," in which the people lived in simplicity and harmony with one another and with all creatures. They were led by Genuine human beings, now rare but still present, who, expert in the "techniques of the Way," embraced Potency and lived in accord with the foundations of the cosmos. Deeply grounded in an internal experience of all aspects of the transcendent Way, these Perfected persons bring a dispassionate clarity to ruling the people and influence them toward tranquillity and harmony simply by their presence. Yet these Genuine human beings are not fundamentally different from other people: they share a natural tendency for the senses to perceive clearly and to be naturally tranquil but easily disturbed by lusts and desires. These sages differ from others, however, in how they use the meditational "techniques of the mind" in order to keep their spirits clear, their minds empty of desires and preferences, and their consciousness illumined and impartial. They thus allow their own natures to engender spontaneous and genuine responses to things and so to cultivate the internal and use it to rule the external. The authors of chapter 2 criticize the current-day disciples of Confucius and Mozi for failing to do this, observing that their Way is external and derived from the branches rather than from these internal psycho-spiritual roots. As the authors say, when what is external does not disturb what is internal, then nature can function spontaneously and harmoniously and will achieve Potency. Thus the genuine responses of our innate natures to the many life situations that constitute our destiny are completely facilitated and the Way is fully embodied. This is the foundation of enlightened rulership.

---

1. These three voices are the authentic writings of Zhuang Zhou, the "Primitivist," and the "Syncretist." The *Zhuangzi* is a layered text, written by several hands over a period of time, and some of its latest portions might be roughly contemporaneous with the *Huainanzi*.

# Two

## 2.2 (in part)

The Great Clod[1]
   loads me with a body,
   burdens me with a life,
   eases me with old age,
   rests me with death.
That I found it good to live is the very reason why I find it good to die.
   [You can] hide a boat in a ravine,
   hide a fishing net in a marsh:
people call this "secure."
However, in the middle of the night, a strong man can put [the boat] on his back and run off with it, and the sleeper does not know about it. It is appropriate to hide small things within the large. But if you do so, your thing just might vanish from you. But if you hide the world in the world, then there is nothing that can conceal its form.

   How can it be said that things are not grandly indiscriminate? You once happen on the shape of a human being and are especially pleased. But humanity has a thousand alterations and ten thousand transformations, never reaching its limit, wearing out and then renewing; should not your joy be incalculable? Compare it to a dream:

---

1. "The Great Clod" is a slightly ironic Daoist term for the physical world.

> In a dream we become a bird and fly into the sky.
>
> In a dream we become a fish and disappear into the deep.

When we are dreaming, we do not know it is a dream; only after we awaken do we realize it is a dream. Only when we have a great awakening do we realize that this present moment is the ultimate dream. In the beginning before I was born, how could I have known the joy of being alive? Now in this moment when I have not yet died, how can I know that death is not also joyful?

In ancient times, Gongniu Ai suffered from a cyclical illness: every seven days he would transform into a tiger. His older brother opened his door and entered to spy on him, and when he did, the tiger snatched and killed him. Thus,

> his [outer] patterns and markings became those of a beast;
>
> his fingernails and teeth shifted and changed;
>
> his consciousness and mind altered;
>
> his spirit and form transformed.

When he was a tiger, he did not know that he had ever been a human being. When he was a human being, he knew nothing about being a tiger. These two alternated in opposition, yet each found joy in the form it took. Cleverness and confusion displace [each other] endlessly, and who knows from what they spring?

> When water approaches winter, it congeals and becomes ice.
>
> When ice welcomes spring, it melts and becomes water.

Ice and water shift and change in the former and latter positions as if they were running around in an eternal circle; which has the time to know bitterness or joy?

## 2.3

Among the people of antiquity were some who situated themselves in the chaotic and obscure. Their spirit and vital energy did not leak out to their exteriors. The myriad things were peaceful and dispassionate and so became contented and tranquil. The *qi* of [baleful comets such as] "magnolias," "lances," "colliders," and "handles" was in every case blocked and dissipated so that they were unable to cause harm. At that time, the myriad peoples were wild and untamed, not knowing East from West;

> they roamed with their mouths full,
>
> drummed on their bellies in contentment.
>
> In copulation they followed the harmony of Heaven;
>
> in eating they accorded with the Potency of Earth.

They did not use minute precedent or "right and wrong" to surpass one another. Vast and boundless, this is what we call "Grand Order." And so those in high station

directed [ministers] on their left and right and did not pervert their natures;
possessed and pacified [the people] and did not compromise their Potency.
Thus,
> Humaneness and Rightness were not proclaimed, and the myriad things flourished.
> Rewards and punishments were not deployed, and all in the world were respected.

Their Way could give rise to great perfection, but it is difficult to find a quantitative measure for it. Thus,
> calculating by days there is not enough;
> calculating by years there is surplus.
> Fish forget themselves in rivers and lakes.
> Humans forget themselves in the techniques of the Way.

The Genuine of antiquity stood in the foundation of Heaven and Earth, were centered in uninterrupted roaming, embraced Potency, and rested in harmony. The myriad things were to them like smoke piling higher. Which of them would willingly create discord in human affairs or use things to trouble their nature and destiny?

## 2.4

The Way has both a warp and a weft linked together. [The Perfected] attain the unity of the Way and join with its thousand branches and ten thousand leaves. Thus
> because they have it in high position, they can promulgate their decrees;
> because they have it in low position, they can forget their baseness;
> because they have it in poverty, they can take pleasure in their work;
> because they have it in distress, they can be settled amid danger.

When the great cold arrives, frost and snow descend: only then do we understand the vigor of pine and cypress;

Withstanding difficulties, walking into danger, with profit and harm arrayed before them: only then do we understand how sages do not lose the Way.

Thus those who are able to
> wear on their heads the Great Circle [of Heaven] will traverse the Great Square [of Earth];
> mirror Vast Purity will contemplate Great Luminosity;
> stand amid Vast Peace will be situated in the great hall;
> roam amid Dark Obscurity will have the same brilliance as the sun and moon.

Thus,
> they take the Way as their pole;
> Potency as their line;
> Rites and Music as their hook;
> Humaneness and Rightness as their bait;
> they throw them into the rivers;
> they float them into the seas.

Though the myriad things are boundless in numbers, which of them will they not possess?

## 2.6

> To grasp the intensely bright and not blacken it,
> act with the perfectly pure and not sully it,
> rest in profound obscurity and not darken it,
> sit at the pivot of Heaven and not destroy it,
> to be unobstructed by the Mengmen or Zhonglong mountains,
> unhindered by swift currents, deep chasms, or the depths of Luliang,
> unimpeded by the obstructions of Taihang, Shijian, Feihu, or Gouwang.
> Only those who embody the Way are able to not be defeated [by these things].

For these reasons, their persons reside on rivers and seas, and their spirits roam under the palace gateway. Had they not attained the One Source, how could they have reached this point?

For these reasons, residing with the Perfected
> makes families forget their poverty,
> makes kings and dukes scorn honors and riches

and delight in poverty and baseness,
> makes the brave deflate their anger
> and makes the greedy diminish their desires.
> They sit and do not teach;
> they stand and do not dispute.
> When they are empty, they go;
> when they are full, they return.

Thus they do not speak and can quench others with harmony.
For these reasons, [those who embody] the Utmost Way take no action.
> Now a dragon, then a snake,
> they expand and contract,
> coil and uncoil,
> and alter and transform with the seasons.

Outside, they follow prevailing customs;
inside, they guard their nature.
Their ears and eyes are not dazzled.
Their thoughts and reflections are not entangled.

Those who in this way lodge their spirit maintain the simple in order to roam in vast purity, draw into compliance the myriad things, and cause the many excellences to germinate.

For these reasons,
the spirit will depart from those who belabor their spirit;
the spirit will lodge with those who rest their spirit.

The Way emerges from the One Source, penetrates the Nine Gateways, is scattered through the Six Crossroads, and is displayed in the domain of the boundless. It is still and silent and thereby empty and nonexistent. It is not that it acts on things; it is that things act on themselves. For these reasons, when affairs comply with the Way, it is not that the Way has accomplished them but that the Way has impelled them.

## 2.11

The nature of water is clear, yet soil sullies it.
The nature of humans is tranquil, yet desires disorder it.

What human beings receive from Heaven are [the tendencies]
for ears and eyes [to perceive] colors and sounds,
for mouth and nose [to perceive] fragrances and tastes,
for flesh and skin [to perceive] cold and heat.

The instinctive responses are the same in everyone, but some penetrate to spiritlike illumination, and some cannot avoid derangement and madness. Why is this? That by which they [these tendencies] are controlled is different.

Thus,
the spirit is the source of consciousness. If the spirit is clear, then consciousness is illumined.
Consciousness is the storehouse of the mind. If consciousness is impartial, then the mind is balanced.
No one can mirror himself in flowing water, but [he can] observe his reflection in standing water because it is still.
No one can view his form in raw iron, but [he can] view his form in a clear mirror because it is even.

Only what is even and still can thus give form to the nature and basic tendencies of things. Viewed from this perspective, usefulness depends on what is not used. Thus when the empty room is pristine and clear, good fortune will abide there.

 If the mirror is bright, dust and dirt cannot obscure it.

 If the spirit is clear, lusts and desires cannot disorder it.

To work at reclaiming the Quintessential Spirit once it has already overflowed externally is to lose the root and seek it in the branches. If external and internal do not tally and you desire to interact with things; if you cover your mysterious light and seek to know [things] with the ears and eyes; this is to discard your brilliance and follow your blindness. This is called "losing the Way." When the mind goes somewhere, the spirit swiftly lodges there. By returning the spirit to emptiness, this lodging dissolves and is extinguished. This is the wandering of the sage.

 Thus those in antiquity who ordered the world invariably penetrated the basic tendencies of nature and destiny. Their taking and giving were not necessarily the same, [but] they were as one in uniting with the Way.

> You do not refrain from wearing fur in summer because you cherish it but because it is too hot for your person.
>
> You do not refrain from using a fan in winter to conserve it but because it is too cold for comfort.

The sages

> assess their bellies and eat;
>
> measure their frames and dress.

They compose themselves, that is all; from whence can the mind of greed and dissipation arise?

 Thus,

> a person who can have the world is invariably someone who will not strive for it.
>
> A person who can possess fame and praise is invariably someone who will not scurry in search of them.

The sage has broken through to it. Having broken through to it, the mind of lust and desire is external [to him].

## 2.12

The disciples of Confucius and Mozi all teach the techniques of Humaneness and Rightness to the age, yet they do not avoid destruction. If they personally cannot practice [their teachings], how much less may those they teach? Why is this? Because their Way is external. To ask the branches to return to the roots: if even Xu You could not do it, how much less the common people? If you genuinely break through to the basic tendencies of nature and destiny, so that Humaneness and Rightness adhere [to your actions], how then can choosing and discarding suffice to confuse your mind?

If
>   the spirit has no obstruction and the mind has no burden,
>   if they are pervasively comprehending and minutely penetrating,
>   calm and quiescent and free of tasks,
>   without any congealing or stagnancy,
>   attentive in empty stillness,

then
>   power and profit cannot lure them;
>   logicians cannot delight them;
>   sounds and colors cannot corrupt them;
>   beauty cannot debauch them;
>   wisdom cannot move them;
>   courage cannot frighten them;

This is the Way of the Genuine. Those who are like this shape and forge the myriad things and in their being human are conjoined with what creates and transforms.
>   Amid Heaven and Earth,
>   in space and time,

nothing can destroy or impede them.
>   What generates life is not life;
>   what transforms things is not transformation.

Their spirits:
>   cross Mount Li or the Taihang [Mountains] and have no difficulty;
>   enter the Four Seas or the Nine Rivers and cannot be trapped;
>   lodge in narrow defiles and cannot be obstructed;
>   spread across the realm of Heaven and Earth and are not stretched.

If you do not penetrate to this [point],
>   though your eyes enumerate a group of one thousand sheep,
>   though your ears distinguish the tones of the eight winds,
>   your feet perform the "Northern Bank" dance;
>   your hands execute the "Green Waters" rhythm;
>   your intelligence encompasses Heaven and Earth;
>   your brilliance illuminates the sun and moon;
>   your disputations unknot linked jewels;
>   your words add luster to jade and stone;

These will still be of no aid to governing the world.

## 2.13

> Tranquillity and calmness are that by which the nature is nourished.
> Harmony and vacuity are that by which Potency is nurtured.
> When what is external does not disturb what is internal, then our nature attains what is suitable to it.
> When the harmony of nature is not disturbed, then Potency will rest securely in its position.
> Nurturing life so as to order the age,
> embracing Potency so as to complete our years,

This may be called being able to embody the Way.

> Those who are like this:
>> Their blood and pulse have no sluggishness or stagnation;
>> their five orbs have no diseased *qi*;
>> calamity and good fortune cannot perturb them;
>> blame and praise cannot settle on them like dust;

thus can they reach the ultimate. [However,] if you do not have the age, how can you succeed? If you have the right character but do not meet your time, you will not even be able to safeguard your person. How much less so one who is without the Way!

> Moreover, the instinctive responses of human beings are for
>> the ears and eyes to respond to stimulus and movement,
>> the mind and awareness to recognize worry and happiness.
>> The hands and feet to rub at pains and itches and to avoid cold and heat.

This is how we interact with things.

>> If a wasp or a scorpion stings your finger, your spirit cannot remain placid.
>> If a mosquito or a gadfly bites your flesh, your nature cannot remain settled.

The worries and calamities that come to disturb your mind are not limited to the poisonous bites of wasps or scorpions or the annoyance of mosquitoes and gadflies, yet you want to remain tranquil and vacuous. How can it be done?

>> The ears of one whose eyes are examining the tip of an autumn hair will not hear the sound of thunder and lightning.
>> The eyes of one whose ears are harmonizing the tones of jade and stone will not see the form of Mount Tai.

Why is this? They are attending to what is small and forgetting what is big. Now the arrival of the myriad things, pulling and plucking at my nature, grabbing and grasping at my feelings, is like a spring or fountain, even if one wanted to not be ruled [by them], could this be achieved?

Now a person who plants a tree irrigates it with springwater and beds it in fertile soil. If one person nurtures it and ten people harvest it, there will certainly be no spare splinters; how much less if the entire kingdom hacks at it together? Though one wanted it to live for a long time, how could this be accomplished?

If you leave a basin of water in the courtyard to settle for one full day, you will still not be able to see your eyebrows and lashes. If you muddy it with no more than one stir, you will not be able to distinguish square from circular. The human spirit is easy to muddy and difficult to clarify, much like the basin of water. How much more so when an entire age stirs and disturbs it; how can it attain a moment of equanimity?

# Three

## CELESTIAL PATTERNS

"Celestial Patterns" provides the means by which to
>  harmonize the *qi* of yin and yang,
>  order the radiances of the sun and moon,
>  regulate the seasons of opening [spring/summer] and closing [fall/
>     winter],
>  tabulate the movements of the stars and planets,
>  know the permutations of [their] retrograde and proper motion,
>  avoid the misfortunes associated with prohibitions and taboos,
>  follow the responses of the seasonal cycles,
>  and imitate the constancy of the Five Gods.

It enables you to
>  possess the means to gaze upward to Heaven and uphold what to
>     follow
>  and thereby avoid disordering Heaven's regularities.
>
>  "An Overview of the Essentials" (21.2)

The term *tian wen* (celestial patterns) means "astronomy" in modern Chinese, but the classical term has a much broader reach, encompassing also astrology, cosmology, calendrics, mathematical harmonics, and meteorology. Although some passages in *Huainanzi* 3 may strike modern readers as both obscure and highly technical, from the point of view of Han intellectual history, this chapter treats its topics in rather general terms, omitting the sorts of technical detail that would be the province of specialists. Although the chapter is not a manual for practicing astrologers, attentive readers would learn enough to be able to participate in a discussion in which these topics arose (such as a court debate about astrologically based policy).

This chapter draws on, and is generally consistent with, a substantial body of pre-Han and Han astronomical and astrological lore. Some of its source texts still exist, notably a poetical catechism called "Questions about Heaven," which is included in an ancient anthology of poetry, the *Chuci* (*Elegies of Chu*). In fact, portions of 3.1, 3.4, 3.13–3.16, and 3.25 give direct answers to that text's questions. Other sections of the chapter appear to be "set pieces" quoted from writings that are no longer extant, so whose existence can only be inferred. Lending strength to that inference is section 3.6, quoted from a text that was unknown until a manuscript copy was recovered archaeologically from a tomb at Mawangdui (near Changsha, Hunan Province) in 1973.

The principal message of this chapter is that all things in the cosmos are interconnected and that human plans and intentions are subject to the influence of various cosmic cycles and correlations. Section 3.2, for example, discusses the influence of yin and yang on the behavior and transformations of various creatures. Section 3.6 gives correlates for each of the five naked-eye planets. Section 3.28 (as well as sections 3.29–3.31, which are not included here) demonstrates the numerological links between weights and measures and the musical notes of the five-tone and twelve-tone scales. Other passages, not included in this abridged version, give correlates for the eight winds (3.12), the interactions of yin and yang with the twelve lunar months (3.16), the twenty-four fifteen-day periods of the solar year (3.18), and the twelve-year orbital cycle of the planet Jupiter (3.33), among many other topics. The reader will learn from these passages that such cycles and correlations must be understood and taken into account in the formulation of policy.

# Three

## 3.1

When Heaven and Earth were yet unformed, all was
  ascending and flying,
  diving and delving.
Thus it was called the Grand Inception.
  The Grand Inception produced the Nebulous Void.
  The Nebulous Void produced space-time;
  space-time produced the original *qi*.
A boundary [divided] the original *qi*.
  That which was pure and bright spread out to form Heaven;
  that which was heavy and turbid congealed to form Earth.
  It is easy for that which is pure and subtle to converge
  but difficult for the heavy and turbid to congeal.
Therefore
  Heaven was completed first;
  Earth was fixed afterward.
  The conjoined essences of Heaven and Earth produced yin and yang.
  The supersessive essences of yin and yang caused the four seasons.
  The scattered essences of the four seasons created the myriad things.
  The hot *qi* of accumulated yang produced fire; the essence of fiery *qi* became the sun.

> The cold *qi* of accumulated yin produced water; the essence of watery *qi* became the moon.
>
> The overflowing *qi* of the essences of the sun and the moon made the stars and planets.
>
> > To Heaven belong the sun, moon, stars, and planets;
> > to Earth belong waters and floods, dust and soil.
>
> In ancient times Gong Gong and Zhuan Xu fought, each seeking to become the thearch.[1] Enraged, they crashed against Mount Buzhou;[2]
>
> > Heaven's pillars broke;
> > the cords of Earth snapped.
> > Heaven tilted in the northwest, and thus the sun and moon, stars and planets shifted in that direction.
> > Earth became unfull in the southeast, and thus the watery floods and mounding soils subsided in that direction.

## 3.2

> > The Way of Heaven is called the Round;
> > the Way of Earth is called the Square.
> > The square governs the obscure;
> > the circular governs the bright.
> > The bright emits *qi*, and for this reason fire is the external brilliance of the sun.
> > The obscure sucks in *qi*, and for this reason water is the internal luminosity of the moon.
> > Emitted *qi* endows;
> > retained *qi* transforms.
>
> Thus yang endows and yin transforms.
>
> > The unbalanced *qi* of Heaven and Earth, becoming perturbed, causes wind;
> > the harmonious *qi* of Heaven and Earth, becoming calm, causes rain.
>
> When yin and yang rub against each other, their interaction produces thunder.
>
> > Aroused, they produce thunderclaps;
> > disordered, they produce mist.
> > When the yang *qi* prevails, it scatters to make rain and dew;

---

1. "Thearch" is our translation of the Chinese word *di*. Its connotations of divine rulership emphasize the transcendent qualities of a sage-emperor (whether mythical or real) empowered by the Way.
2. Mount Buzhou was a mythical mountain northwest of China, considered to be the pivot point of the cosmos.

when the yin *qi* prevails, it freezes to make frost and snow.
Hairy and feathered creatures make up the class of flying and walking things and are subject to yang.
Creatures with scales and shells make up the class of creeping and hiding things and are subject to yin.
The sun is the ruler of yang. Therefore, in spring and summer animals shed their fur; at the summer solstice, stags' antlers drop off.
The moon is the fundament of yin. Therefore when the moon wanes, the brains of fish shrink; when the moon dies, wasps and crabs shrivel up.
Fire flies upward;
water flows downward.

Thus,
the flight of birds is aloft;
the movement of fishes is downward.
Things within the same class mutually move one another;
root and twig mutually respond to each other.

Therefore,
when the burning mirror sees the sun, it ignites tinder and produces fire.
When the square receptacle sees the moon, it moistens and produces water.
When the tiger roars, the valley winds rush;
when the dragon arises, the bright clouds accumulate.
When *qilins* wrangle, the sun or moon is eclipsed;
when the leviathan dies, comets appear.
When silkworms secrete fragmented silk, the *shang* string [of a stringed instrument] snaps.
When meteors fall, the Bohai[3] surges upward.

## 3.3

The feelings of the rulers of men penetrate to Heaven on high.

Thus,
if there are punishments and cruelty, there will be whirlwinds.
If there are wrongful ordinances, there will be plagues of devouring insects.
If there are unjust executions, the land will redden with drought.
If there are unseasonable ordinances, there will be great excess of rain.
The four seasons are the officers of Heaven.

---

3. The Bohai is a shallow body of water forming China's northeastern coast, bounded by the Liaodong and Shandong peninsulas.

The sun and moon are the agents of Heaven.
The stars and planets mark the appointed times of Heaven.
Rainbows and comets are the portents of Heaven.

## 3.6

What are the five planets?

The East is Wood. Its god is Tai Hao. His assistant is Gou Mang. He grasps the compass and governs spring. His spirit is Year Star [Jupiter]. His animal is the Bluegreen Dragon. His musical note is *jue*; his days are *jia* and *yi*.

The South is Fire. Its god is Yan Di. His assistant is Zhu Ming. He grasps the balance beam and governs summer. His spirit is Sparkling Deluder [Mars]. His animal is the Vermilion Bird. His musical note is *zhi*; his days are *bing* and *ding*.

The Center is Earth. Its god is the Yellow Emperor. His assistant is Hou Tu ["Sovereign of the Soil"]. He grasps the marking cord and governs the four quarters. His spirit is Quelling Star [Saturn]. His animal is the Yellow Dragon. His musical note is *gong*; his days are *wu* and *ji*.

The West is Metal. Its god is Shao Hao. His assistant is Ru Shou. He grasps the T-square and governs autumn. His spirit is Great White [Venus]. His animal is the White Tiger. His musical note is *shang*; his days are *geng* and *xin*.

The North is Water. Its god is Zhuan Xu. His assistant is Xuan Ming. He grasps the weight and governs winter. His spirit is Chronograph Star [Mercury]. His animal is the Dark Warrior. His musical note is *yu*; his days are *ren* and *gui*.

## 3.24

In the third [and final] month of spring, abundant thunder sounds forth, bringing in the rains.

In the third [and final] month of autumn, the *qi* of Earth has not yet become [completely] quiescent, and one gathers in the killed things. All crawling things become torpid and hide away, and country dwellers shut their gates. Gray Woman comes out and brings down frost and snow.

Thus the *qi* of the twelve times of the year progress until they reach an end [again] in the second month of spring, when what has been stored away is received forth [again] and the cold is shut away. Then Tranquil Woman drums and sings to regulate the harmony of Heaven and to make grow the hundred kinds of cereals, the beasts and birds, and the herbs and trees.

In the first month of summer the crops ripen; the cries of pheasants and pigeons become prolonged, causing the emperor to look forward to the annual harvest.
Thus,
> if Heaven does not give forth yin, the myriad things cannot be born;
> if Earth does not give forth yang, the myriad things cannot grow to maturity.
> Heaven is round;
> Earth is square;

the Way is exactly in the middle.
> The sun [produces] accretion;
> the moon [produces] paring away.
> When the moon reverts [in its course], the myriad creatures die.
> When the sun attains its apogee, the myriad creatures are born.
> Separated from mountains, the *qi* of mountains is hidden away.
> Separated from water, aquatic insects become dormant.
> Separated from trees, leaves wither.

When the sun is not seen for five days, [the ruler] will lose his throne. Even a [ruler who is a] sage cannot withstand this.

## 3.25

The sun rises up from the Bright Valley, bathes in the Pool of Xian, and rests in the Fusang Tree.[4] This is called Dawn Light.

Ascending the Fusang Tree, it thereupon commences its journey. This is called Emergent Brightness.
> [When the sun] reaches the Bent Slope, this is called Dawn Brilliance.
> [When the sun] reaches the Steaming Spring, this is called the Morning Meal.
> [When the sun] reaches the Mulberry Field, this is called the Late-Morning Meal.
> [When the sun] reaches the Balance Beam of Yang, this is called Within the Angle.
> [When the sun] reaches Kun Wu, this is called the Exact Center.
> [When the sun] reaches the Bird Roost, this is called the Lesser Return.

---

4. All the places mentioned in this passage are mythical or astral, not actual geographical locations. The Fusang Tree was a magical mulberry tree on which the sun-crow perched before beginning its daily trip across the sky.

[When the sun] reaches the Valley of Grief, this is called the Dinner Hour.
[When the sun] reaches Woman's Sequence, this is called the Great Return.
[When the sun] reaches the Angle of the Abyss, this is called the Raised Pestle.
[When the sun] reaches Carriage Stone, this is called the Descending Pestle.

[When the sun] reaches the Fountain of Grief, it halts; its female attendant rests her horses. This is called the Suspended Chariot.

[When the sun] reaches the Abyss of Anxiety, this is called Yellow Dusk.

[When the sun] reaches the Vale of Obscurity, this is called Definite Dusk.

The sun enters the floodwaters of the Abyss of Anxiety; sunrise emerges from the drainage stream of the Vale of Obscurity. [The sun] travels over the nine continents, [passing through] seven resting places, [covering a distance of] 507,309 *li*. The divisions [of its journey] make dawn, daylight, dusk, and night.

## 3.28

Thus it is said, "The Way begins with one." One [alone], however, does not give birth. Therefore it divided into yin and yang. From the harmonious union of yin and yang, the myriad things were produced. Thus it is said,

"One produced two,
two produced three,
three produced the myriad things."

[With regard to] Heaven and Earth, three months make one season. Thus a sacrifice of three [types or portions of] cooked grains are used in mourning rites. The year continues for three shifts [of seasons] to make the seasonal nodes [complete their cycle]. Armies emphasize three signal flags in order to maintain control.

Using three to examine matters: $3 \times 3 = 9$. Thus the Yellow Bell pitch pipe is nine inches long and harmonizes with the note *gong*. Furthermore, $9 \times 9 = 81$. Thus the number of the Yellow Bell is established therein. Yellow is the color of the Potency of Earth; the bell is that by which the [seeds of] *qi* are sown. At the winter solstice the *qi* of accretion produces Earth; the color of Earth is yellow. Thus the [note of the winter solstice] is called Yellow Bell.

The number of pitch pipes is six, classified as female and male [for a total of twelve]. Thus it is said there are twelve bells to act as adjuncts to the twelve months. Each of the twelve is based on three. Thus if one sets up [the number] one and triples it eleven times [i.e., $3^{11}$], the total is 177,147. The Great Number of the Yellow Bell is thereby revealed.

## 3.41

Of those prized by the heavenly spirits, none is more prized than the Bluegreen Dragon. The Bluegreen Dragon is otherwise called the Heavenly Unity, or otherwise *taiyin*. [The country corresponding to] the place where *taiyin* dwells cannot retreat but can advance. [The country corresponding to] the place beaten against by the Northern Dipper cannot withstand attack.

When Heaven and Earth were founded, they divided to make yin and yang.

> Yang is born from yin;
> yin is born from yang;

they are in a state of mutual alternation. The four binding cords [of Heaven] communicate with them.

> Sometimes there is death;
> sometimes there is birth.

Thus are the myriad things brought to completion.

[Of all creatures that] move and breathe, none is more prized than humans. [The bodily] orifices, limbs, and trunk all communicate with Heaven.

> Heaven has nine layers; man also has nine orifices.
> Heaven has four seasons, to regulate the twelve months;
> Man also has four limbs, to control the twelve joints.
> Heaven has twelve months, to regulate the 360 days;
> Man also has twelve joints, to regulate the 360 nodes.

A person who undertakes affairs while not obeying Heaven is someone who deviates from what gave birth to him.

# Four

## TERRESTRIAL FORMS

"Terrestrial Forms" provides the means by which to
>    encompass the length from north to south,
>    reach the breadth from east to west,
>    survey the topography of the mountains and hillocks,
>    demarcate the locations of the rivers and valleys,
>    illuminate the master of the myriad things,
>    know the multitude of categories of living things,
>    tabulate the enumerations of mountains and chasms,
>    and chart the roadways far and near.

It enables you to
>    circulate comprehensively and prepare exhaustively,
>    so that you cannot be roused by things
>    or startled by oddities.

"An Overview of the Essentials" (21.2)

"Terrestrial Forms" is an account of world geography from the point of view of the Western Han dynasty. It ignores political geography (such as the states of the Warring States period or the kingdoms, provinces, and counties of the Han Empire) and gives only a cursory account of the physical geography of China itself. It names the provinces, mountains, and marshes associated with the eight directions and the center, as well as the eight winds, and gives an extensive list of rivers and their sources. But the authors of "Terrestrial Forms" appear to be more interested in the wider world beyond China's borders, with an emphasis on the mythical, the magical, the distant, and the strange. Special attention is given to Mount Kunlun, the mountain at the center of the world, associated with the goddess known as the Queen Mother of the West and her elixir of immortality. Sections 4.15 and 4.16 list various strange and grotesque peoples living beyond the boundaries of the known world, along with various mythical places such as the land of the Torch Dragon and the grave-mound of Lord Millet.

This chapter emphasizes that physical features of terrain interact in important ways with plants, animals, and people. Section 4.8, for example, contends that various topographical features have specific physical effects on the people who live near them; section 4.9 (not included here) makes a similar case for types of soil. The chapter also has a section (4.11) that proposes a kind of zoological taxonomy based on physical features of various animals. Section 4.18 describes an evolutionary process that gives rise to various kinds of living creatures, and section 4.19 (not included here) describes an analogous process for the growth of minerals in the soil.

In general, the chapter's analytical viewpoint involves understanding the influences and cyclical transformation of yin and yang and the Five Phases. The chapter's sources include the "Questions About Heaven" poetical catechism of the *Chuci* anthology, the compendium of real and mythical geography known as the *Shanhaijing* (*Classic of Mountains and Seas*), and most likely other texts that are no longer extant. The chapter's understanding of world geography is based on the work of the cosmographer Zou Yan (fl. ca. 300 B.C.E.). He proposed that China (which was divided into nine provinces by the mythical hero Yu the Great after he had drained away the waters of the Great Flood) was situated in the southeastern corner of a great square continent divided into nine subcontinents. The great continent was itself one of nine such continents, all surrounded by a boundless ocean. This schematic view of world geography accounted for the location of Mount Kunlun to China's northwest and for the observable fact that China is bordered on the east and the southeast by water.

This chapter reminds the reader that while China is the "Middle Kingdom," it also is part of a much larger terrestrial world. And like chapter 3 (with which it forms a pair), it stresses that everything in the world is interconnected and in a constant state of flux.

# Four

### 4.1 (in part)

Everything that exists on earth lies
    within the six coordinates [and]
    within the outer limits of the four directions.
    To illuminate it, [it has] the sun and moon;
    for its warp threads, [it has] the stars and planets;
    to regulate it, [it has] the four seasons;
    to control it, [it has] the great Year Star.
Between Heaven and Earth are nine continents and eight pillars. The dry land has nine mountains; the mountains have nine passes. There are nine marshes, eight winds, and six rivers. . . .

### 4.2 (in part)

The expanse within the four seas measures 28,000 *li* from east to west and 26,000 *li* from south to north. There are 8,000 *li* of watercourses passing through six valleys; there are six hundred named streams. There are 3,000 *li* of roads and paths.

    Yu employed Tai Zhang to measure the earth from its eastern extremity to its western extremity. It measured 233,500 *li* and 75 double paces. He also employed Shu Hai to measure from its northern extremity to its southern extremity. It measured 233,500 *li* and 75 double paces.

## 4.4

The waters of the Yellow River issue from the northeast corner of the Kunlun Mountains and enter the ocean, flowing [eastward] along the route of Yu through the Piled-Stone Mountains.[1]

The Vermilion River issues from the southeast corner and flows southwest to the Southern Sea, passing to the east of Cinnabar Marsh. The Weakwater [River] issues from the southwest corner; when it reaches Heli, its overflowing waves pass through the Flowing Sands and flow south to enter the Southern Sea. The Yang River issues from the northwest corner and enters the Southern Sea south of [the country of] the Winged People.

The four streams [originate in] the divine springs of the [Yellow] Emperor, from which can be concocted all kinds of medicinal substances to bring physical well-being to the myriad creatures.

## 4.5

If you climb to a height double that of the Kunlun Mountains, [that peak] is called Cool Wind Mountain. If you climb it, you will not die. If you climb to a height that is doubled again, [that peak] is called Hanging Gardens. If you ascend it, you will gain supernatural power and be able to control the wind and the rain. If you climb to a height that is doubled yet again, it reaches up to Heaven itself. If you mount to there, you will become a spirit. It is called the abode of the Supreme Thearch.

The Fu [= Fusang] Tree in Yang Province is baked by the sun's heat. The Jian Tree on Mount Duguang, by which the gods ascend and descend [to and from Heaven], casts no shadow at midday. If one calls [from that place], there is no echo. It forms a canopy over the center of the world. The Ruo Tree is to the west of the Jian Tree. On its branches are ten suns; its blossoms cast light upon the earth.

## 4.8

In the [fabric of] the earth's shape,
>   east and west are the weft;
>   north and south are the warp.

---

1. Kunlun is the name of a mythical mountain or mountain range northwest of China, home of the goddess Queen Mother of the West and associated with the elixir of immortality. It is not necessarily identical with the actual mountain range north of Tibet that bears the same name. The Piled-Stone Mountains are a mythical mountain range for which various early texts give different and inconsistent locations.

Mountains are the cumulative [result of] accretion;
valleys are the cumulative [result of] cutting away.
High places govern birth;
low places govern death.
Hills govern maleness;
valleys govern femaleness.
Water [congealed] in a round shape forms pearls;
water [congealed] in a square shape forms jade.

Clear water yields gold; the dragon's lair in the depths yields the quintessential beauty of jade.

Various sorts of earth give birth [to living creatures], each according to its own kind.

For this reason,

> The *qi* of mountains gives birth to a preponderance of men.
> The *qi* of low wetlands gives birth to a preponderance of women.
> The *qi* of dikes produces many cases of muteness.
> The *qi* of wind produces many cases of deafness.
> The *qi* of forests produces many cases of paralysis of the legs.
> The *qi* of wood produces many cases of spinal deformity.
> The *qi* of seashores produces many cases of ulcerations of the lower extremities.
> The *qi* of stone produces much strength.
> The *qi* of steep passes produces many cases of goiter.
> The *qi* of heat produces many cases of early death.
> The *qi* of cold produces much longevity.
> The *qi* of valleys produces many cases of rheumatism.
> The *qi* of hills produces many cases of rickets.
> The *qi* of low-lying places produces much human fellow-feeling.
> The *qi* of mounds produces much covetousness.
> The *qi* of light soil produces much hastening after profit.
> The *qi* of heavy soil produces much sluggishness.
> The sound of clear water is small;
> the sound of muddy water is great.
> People [who live near] rushing water are light;
> people [who live near] placid water are heavy.

The central region produces many sages.

All things are the same as their *qi*; all things respond to their own class. Thus,

> In the south are herbs that do not die;
> In the north is ice that does not melt.

In the east are countries of superior people.
In the west is the corpse of Xing Can.

## 4.11

All birds and fish are born of yin but are of the class of yang creatures. Thus birds and fish are oviparous. Fish swim through water; birds fly in the clouds. Thus at the beginning of winter, swallows and sparrows enter the sea and transform into clams.[2]

   The myriad [living] creatures all are born as different kinds.
      Silkworms eat but do not drink.
      Cicadas drink but do not eat.
Mayflies neither eat nor drink. Armored and scaly creatures eat during the summer but hibernate in the winter.
      Animals that eat without mastication have eight bodily openings and are oviparous.
      Animals that chew have nine bodily openings and are viviparous.
Quadrupeds do not have feathers or wings. Animals that have horns do not have upper [incisor] teeth.
   [Some] animals do not have horns and are fat but do not have front teeth.
   [Other animals] have horns and are fat but do not have back teeth.
   Creatures born during the day resemble their fathers;
   creatures born at night resemble their mothers.
   Extreme yin produces females;
   extreme yang produces males.
Bears hibernate, and birds migrate seasonally.

## 4.14 (in part)

Wood overcomes Earth, Earth overcomes Water, Water overcomes Fire, Fire overcomes Metal, Metal overcomes Wood. Thus,
   grain is born in the spring and dies in the fall.
   Legumes are born in the summer and die in the winter.
   Wheat is born in the autumn and dies in the summer.
   Green vegetables are born in the winter and die in midsummer.

---

2. In early China, it was widely believed that species of animals could transform into other animals in the same yin-yang/Five Phase category. For another example see 5.3, in which field mice are said to change into quail.

When Wood is in its prime, Water is old, Fire is about to be born, Metal is paralyzed [imprisoned], and Earth is dead.

When Fire is in its prime, Wood is old, Earth is about to be born, Water is paralyzed, and Metal is dead.

When Earth is in its prime, Fire is old, Metal is about to be born, Wood is paralyzed, and Water is dead.

When Metal is in its prime, Earth is old, Water is about to be born, Fire is paralyzed, and Wood is dead.

When Water is in its prime, Metal is old, Wood is about to be born, Earth is paralyzed, and Fire is dead.

## 4.18 (in part)

Downyhair gave birth to Oceanman.[3] Oceanman gave birth to Ruojun. Ruojun gave birth to sages; sages gave birth to ordinary people. Thus creatures with scanty hair are born from ordinary people.

Winged Excellence gave birth to Flying Dragon. Flying Dragon gave birth to the phoenix. The phoenix gave birth to the symurgh. The symurgh gave birth to ordinary birds. Feathered creatures in general are born from ordinary birds.

Hairy Heifer gave birth to Responsive Dragon. Responsive Dragon gave birth to Establish Horse. Establish Horse gave birth to the *qilin*. The *qilin* gave birth to ordinary beasts. Hairy animals in general are born from ordinary beasts.

Scaly One gave birth to Wriggling Dragon. Wriggling Dragon gave birth to Leviathan. Leviathan gave birth to Establish Emanation. Establish Emanation gave birth to ordinary fishes. Scaly creatures in general are born from ordinary fishes.

Armored Abyss gave birth to First Dragon. First Dragon gave birth to Dark Sea-Turtle. Dark Sea-Turtle gave birth to Divine Tortoise. Divine Tortoise gave birth to ordinary turtles. Armored creatures in general are born from ordinary turtles.

---

3. All the names given in this section are fanciful or allegorical and, as such, are not included in the "Glossary of Personal Names."

# Five

## SEASONAL RULES

"Seasonal Rules" provides the means by which to
>   follow Heaven's seasons above,
>   use Earth's resources below,
>   determine standards and implement correspondences,
>   aligning them with human norms.

It is formed into twelve sections to serve as models and guides.
>   Ending and beginning anew,
>   they repeat limitlessly,
>   adapting, complying, imitating, and according
>   in predicting bad and good fortune.
>   Taking and giving, opening and closing,
>   each has its prohibited days,
>   issuing commands and administering orders,
>   instructing and warning according to the season.

[It] enables the ruler of humankind to know the means by which to manage affairs.

"An Overview of the Essentials" (21.2)

"Seasonal rules" is the third part of a trilogy with chapters 3 and 4. Having established, in those chapters, the patterns of Heaven (and their astrological significance) and the shape of Earth (and how creatures interact with topography), the *Huainanzi*'s authors turn here to the role of monthly and seasonal ritual time in the proper governing of the empire. Reflecting the annual waxing and waning of the powers of yin and yang and the successive seasonal potency of each of the Five Phases (Wood, Fire, Earth, Metal, and Water), the chapter prescribes ritual behavior, colors of vestments, and actions of government for each of the year's twelve months; proscribes certain other behaviors and actions; and warns of the bad consequences of applying the rules appropriate to any one season inappropriately to any of the others.

The first twelve sections of the chapter are substantially identical to a text, generally known as the *Yue ling* (*Monthly Ordinances*), that is preserved in the first twelve chapters of the syncretic text *Lüshi chunqiu* (*Mr. Lü's Spring and Autumn Annals*, ca. 240 B.C.E.) and also in the Han ritual compendium the *Liji* (*Record of Rites*). Perhaps the *Huainanzi* version was borrowed (with small but systematic differences) from the *Lüshi chunqiu* version, but it also is possible that both drew on a now unknown source text. Unlike the *Lüshi chunqiu* and *Liji* versions of the text, the *Huainanzi* divides the year not into the four natural seasons of the solar year but into five seasons (with the third month of summer being treated as an artificial fifth season, "midsummer") so as to make all the ritual prescriptions of the seasons conform to the correlative cosmology of the Five Phases. The chapter thus integrates yin-yang and Five Phase theory in a detailed and holistic fashion for the guidance of government policy throughout the year. *Huainanzi* 5 also contains three otherwise unknown additional sections that complement the material in the twelve month-by-month sections.

The excerpts included here are 5.3, the ordinances for the third and last month of spring (representing all of the first twelve sections of the text); 5.13, which relates the monthly ordinances particularly to the seasons and the directions; and 5.15, which describes the annual round of yang and yin (and the government's corresponding social policies) through the use of tool metaphors, a trope highly characteristic of the *Huainanzi*.

# Five

### 5.3

In the final month of spring, Zhaoyao[1] points to *chen* [east-southeast]. [The lunar lodge] Seven Stars culminates at dusk; Ox Leader culminates at dawn. [Spring] occupies the east. Its days are *jia* and *yi*. Its beasts are [those of the] scaly [class]. Its [pentatonic] note is *jue*. The pitch pipe [of the third month] is Maiden Purity. The number [of spring] is eight. Its flavor is sour. Its smell is rank. Its sacrifices are made to the door god. From the body of the sacrificial victim, the spleen is offered first.

The *tong* tree begins to bloom. Field mice transform into quail. Rainbows first appear. Duckweed begins to sprout. The Son of Heaven wears bluegreen clothing. He mounts [a carriage drawn by] azure dragon [horses]. He wears azure jade [pendants] and flies a bluegreen banner. He eats wheat with mutton. He drinks water gathered from the eight winds and cooks with fire [kindled from] fern stalks. The imperial ladies of the Eastern Palace wear bluegreen clothing with bluegreen trim. They play the *qin* and the *se*. The weapon [of spring] is the spear. The domestic animal [of spring] is the sheep. [The Son of

---

1. Zhaoyao is a star at the end of the "handle" of the Northern Dipper, which acts as a celestial dial making a complete circuit of the horizon in a year. Here it is described as pointing in succession to the months and their associated directions.

Heaven] holds the dawn session of court in the corner [chamber of the Mingtang] to the right of the Bluegreen Yang Chamber.²

[He orders] the Master of Boats to turn over the boats [to inspect them] five times over and five times back and then to deliver a report [on their condition] to the Son of Heaven. The Son of Heaven thereupon boards his boats for the first time [in the new year]. A sturgeon is offered in the inner chamber of the [ancestral] temple, and prayers are made that the wheat should bear grain.

In this month, the production of *qi* reaches its fullest, [and] yang *qi* is released. Young plants grow no more, and the sprouting plants attain their maximum growth, but they cannot [yet] be gathered in. The Son of Heaven orders those in authority to open the granaries and storehouses to assist the impoverished and the bereft, to relieve the exhausted and [those who are] cut off [from their families], and to open the strong rooms and treasuries to distribute rolls of silk. He sends embassies to the nobles, inquires after eminent scholars, and performs courtesies to the worthy. He orders the Minister of Works, when the seasonal rains are about to descend, to mount his carriage as the water descends and, following all of the roads from the capital city, make an inspection of the plains and uncultivated fields, repairing the dikes and embankments, channeling the ditches and watercourses, following to its end every road and comprehending every byway,

> beginning at the metropolis,
> stopping [only] upon reaching the border.

Those who hunt, [whether with] nets or with arrows, with rabbit snares or bird nets, or by putting out poisoned bait, are prohibited from going out from the nine gates [of the city]. [The Son of Heaven] also [issues] a prohibition to the foresters in the wilderness, [saying that there must be] no cutting down of mulberry trees or cudrania trees. The turtledove spreads its wings, [and] the crested hoepoe lands in the mulberry tree. Preparing plain cocoon frames, round baskets and rectangular baskets, the royal consort and the royal concubines fast and perform austerities. Then they go to the mulberry [groves] in the eastern suburbs where

> the lady overseers initiate
> and supervise [the work of] sericulture.

[He] commands [those in charge of] the five storehouses to order the workmen to inspect the gold and iron, the pelts and hides, the sinew and horn, the ar-

---

2. The Mingtang (Bright Hall) was a temple in which the ruler worshipped Heaven. Different descriptions of this hallowed structure are found in a number of early texts. The *Huainanzi* depicts it as a structure containing nine rooms, in which the ruler performs rituals corresponding to the months and the seasons.

rowshaft bamboo and the bow-wood, the grease and glue, the cinnabar and lac, [seeing to it that] there is none that is not excellent. Selecting an auspicious day in the last ten day period of the month, [he holds] a great musical performance, which brings jubilation. Moreover [he orders] bulls to be mated with cows and stallions with mares; afterward the female animals are driven out to their herdsmen. He orders on behalf of the kingdom an exorcism at the nine gates [of the capital city], [and] sacrificial [animal victims] are torn apart in order to bring an end to the *qi* of springtime.

If the ordinances for this month are observed, sweet rain will fall during the three ten-day periods of the month. If, during the last month of spring, the ordinances of winter were carried out, then cold *qi* would from time to time issue forth; all the plants and trees would wither; and the state would [suffer] great fear. If the ordinances of summer were carried out, the people would [suffer] epidemics; the seasonal rains would not fall; and nothing would grow on the mountains and tumuli. If the ordinances of autumn were carried out, Heaven would produce a flood of yin. Rains would fall [unseasonably] early, [and] military rebellions would break out.

The third month governs villages. Its tree is the pear.

## 5.13

There are five positions.

The extreme limit of the eastern region begins from Stele-Stone Mountain, passing through the Land of Chaoxian[3] and the Land of Giants. In the east it reaches the place from whence the sun rises, the land of the Fu [-Sang] tree, the wild fields of the Green-Land trees. The places ruled by Tai Hao and Gou Mang [encompass] 12,000 *li*.[4]

The ordinances [of the East] say: Hold fast to all prohibitions. Open what is closed or covered. Penetrate to the utmost all blocked-up passes. Extend to the frontiers and passes. Wander afar. Reject resentment and hatred. Free slaves and those condemned to hard labor [for crimes]. Avoid mourning and grief. Refrain from imposing corporal punishments. Open gates and dams. Proclaim a [general] distribution of wealth [from the public treasury]. Harmoniously resolve [any] resentment [that may be] abroad. Pacify the four directions. Act with pliancy and kindness. Put a stop to hardness and [overbearing] strength.

---

3. Chaoxian is an ancient Chinese name for Korea.
4. Section 5.13 deals with geography on a grand scale, describing not only China ("the central region") but also fantastic regions beyond China's frontiers, ruled by mythical beings.

The extreme limit of the southern region begins from outside [= beyond] [the country of] the people of North-Facing Doors and passes through the country of Zhuan Xu. It extends to the wild lands of Stored Fire and Blazing Winds. The regions governed by the Vermilion Thearch and Zhu Rong encompass 12,000 *li*.

The ordinances [of the south] say: Ennoble the virtuous [and] reward the meritorious. Show kindness to the beneficent and excellent. Come to the aid of the hungry and thirsty. Raise up those who display prowess in agriculture. Relieve the poor and destitute. Show kindness to orphans and widows. Grieve with the infirm and ill. Dispense great emoluments [and] carry out great bestowals of rewards. Raise up ruined lineages. Support those who have no posterity. Enfeoff nobles. Establish [in office] worthy assistants.

The extreme limits of the central region extend from Kunlun east through the region of [the two peaks? of] Constancy Mountain. This is where the sun and the moon have their paths. It is the source of the Han and Jiang [= Yangzi] rivers. [Here are] the open fields of the multitudes of people, [the lands] suitable for the five [kinds of] grain. At Dragon Gate the He [= Yellow] and the Qi rivers merge. [Here, Yu the Great] took swelling earth to dam the floodwaters and traced out the [nine] provinces. [These territories] extend eastward to Stele-Stone Mountain. The territories governed by the Yellow Emperor and the Sovereign of the Soil encompass 12,000 *li*.

The ordinances [of the center] say: Be evenhanded without inconsistency. Be enlightened without petty fault finding. Embrace, enfold, cover over, [and] enrich as with dew, so that there is none who is not tenderly enwrapped in [the royal] bosom. Be vast and overflowing, without private considerations. Let government be tranquil, to bring about harmony. Succor, nurture, and feed the old and the weak. Send condolences to [the families of] the dead, inquire after the sick, [all] to escort the myriad creatures on their return.

The extreme limits of the regions of the west extend from Kunlun through the Flowing Sands and the Sinking Feathers, westward to the country of Three Dangers. [They extend to] the Walled City of Stone and the Metal Palace [and] the open fields of the people who drink *qi* and do not die. The territories governed by Shao Hao and Ru Shou encompass 12,000 *li*.

The ordinances [of the west] say: Scrupulously use the laws. Punishment of the guilty must be carried out. Take precautions against thieves and robbers. Prohibit sexual license and debauchery. Issue instructions regarding the general collection [of harvest taxes]. Make a careful record of all collections [of revenue]. Repair city walls and outer fortifications. Repair and clear out drainage pipes. Close off footpaths and lanes; block up sluices and ditches. Shut off flowing water, swamps, gorges, and valleys. Guard doors and gates. Set out [in readiness] weapons and armor. Select officials. Punish the lawless.

The extreme limits of the regions of the north extend from the nine marshes and the farthest reaches of Exhaust-the-Summer Gloom, north to the Valley Where Ordinances Cease. Here are the open fields of freezing cold, piled-up ice, snow, hail, frost, sleet, and of pooling, soaking, massed-up water. The regions governed by Zhuan Xu and Xuan Ming encompass 12,000 *li*.

The ordinances [of the north] say: Extend all prohibitions. Firmly shut and store away. Repair [the fortifications of] the frontiers and passes. Fix gates and water barriers. Prohibit walking around [outside the city walls]. Speedily carry out corporal punishments. Kill those who are under sentence of death. Close up the city gates and the gates of the outer fortifications. On a large scale, conduct investigations of strangers. Put a stop to communications and travel. Prohibit the pleasures of the night. Close up [chambers] early and open them late, in order to restrain lewd folk. If lewd persons are already to be found, they must be seized and held under severe restraint. Heaven has already almost completed its cycle: Punishments and executions must [be carried out] without any being pardoned; even in the case of [royal] relatives of surpassing venerableness, the law must be carried out to the full degree.

>There must be no travel by water.
>There must be no opening up of that which is stored away.
>There must be no relaxation of punishments.

## 5.15

Regulating the standards:
For the great regulation of yin and yang, there are six standards.
>Heaven is the marking cord.
>Earth is the level.
>Spring is the compass.
>Summer is the balance beam.
>Autumn is the square.
>Winter is the weight.
>The marking cord is that by which the myriad things are marked out.
>The level is that by which the myriad things are leveled.
>The compass is that by which the myriad things are made round.
>The balance beam is that by which the myriad things are equalized.
>The square is that by which the myriad things are made square.
>The weight is that by which the myriad things are weighed.

The marking cord as a standard:
>It is straight without swerving.
>It is long and inexhaustible.

>It is long enduring and does not wear out.
>It reaches to far distances without deviation.
>It matches Heaven in Potency.
>It matches the spirits in illumination.
>[By its means,] what one desires may be obtained,
>and what one loathes may be caused to perish.

From ancient times to the present, there can be no deviation from its trueness. Its innate Potency is vast and subtle; it is broad and capacious. For this reason, the Supreme Thearch takes it as the ancestor of things.

The level as a standard:
>It is flat and not bumpy,
>balanced and not inconsistent,
>broad and capacious,
>spacious and abundant,
>so as to be harmonious.
>It is pliant and not hard,
>acute but not injurious,
>flowing and not stopped up,
>simple [to use] and unsullied,
>expansively penetrating and [proceeding in] an orderly course.
>It is comprehensive and subtle but not sluggish.
>The level makes things perfectly flat without error,
>thereby the myriad things are leveled.

The people are without malice or scheming; resentment and hatred do not arise. Therefore the Supreme Thearch uses it to make all things level.

The compass as a standard:
>It revolves without repeating itself.
>It is round without turning [from its course].
>Great but without excess,
>broad and spacious,
>feelings and actions are ordered [thereby].
>It is expansively penetrating and [proceeds] on an orderly course.
>Abundant! Simple!
>The hundred forms of resentment do not arise.
>The standard of the compass does not err;
>it gives birth to both *qi* and pattern.

The balance beam as a standard:
>It is deliberate but does not lag behind.
>It is impartial and not resented.
>It bestows but is not benevolent.

It condoles but does not rebuke.
It adjusts to an appropriate level the people's emoluments.
It continues but does not heap up.
Majestic! Brilliant!
Only those [possessing] Potency act thus.
Nurturing, bringing to full growth, transforming, rearing;
the myriad creatures abundantly flourish.
It makes the five [kinds of] grain bear seed,
and the bounded fields be fruitful.

Government [by this standard] does not err; Heaven and Earth are illuminated thereby.

The square as a standard:
It is majestic and not contrary.
It is hard and unbroken.
It seizes but does not provoke resentment,
[Penetrates] within but does no injury.
It is stern and severe but not coercive.
Its ordinances are carried out but without wasteful destruction.
In killing and smiting, its ends are attained;
the enemy is brought to submission.

The square's trueness is without error; all punishments are [thereby] suitably fulfilled.

The weight as a standard:
It is hasty but not excessive.
It kills but does not slaughter.
It is filled to completion.
It is comprehensive and subtle but without sluggishness.
It inflicts destruction on things but does not single things out.
It punishes and kills without pardon.
Sincerity and trustworthiness are essential to it,
Strength and sincerity make it firm.
Cleanse away filth! Chastise the evil!
Wickedness may not be tolerated.

Therefore, if correct [policies] for winter are to be carried out, [the ruler] must appear
weak in order to be strong,
pliant in order to be firm.

The weight's trueness is without error; through it the myriad things are shut away.

In the regulation of the Mingtang,

be tranquil, taking the level as a pattern.
Be active, taking the marking cord as a pattern.
For the government of spring, adopt the compass.
For the government of autumn, adopt the square.
For the government of winter, adopt the weight.
For the government of summer, adopt the balance beam.
Thus dryness and dampness, cold and heat, will arrive in their proper seasonal nodes.
Sweet rain and fertile dew will descend in their proper times.

# Six

## SURVEYING OBSCURITIES

"Surveying Obscurities" provides the means by which to discuss
>   Utmost Essence penetrating the Nine Heavens,
>   Utmost Subtlety sinking into the Formless,
>   Unblemished Purity entering Utmost Clarity,
>   and Luminous Brightness penetrating Dark Obscurity.

It begins by
>   grasping things and deducing their categories,
>   observing them, taking hold of them,
>   lifting them up, and arranging them,
>   and pervasively positing them as categories of similarity,

by which things can be understood as ideas and visualized as forms.
It then
>   penetrates various obstructions,
>   bursts open various blockages,
>   to guide your awareness,
>   to connect it to the Limitless.

[It] then thereby illuminates
>   the stimuli of the various categories of things,
>   the responses of identical *qi*,
>   the unions of yin and yang,
>   and the intricacies of forms and shapes.

It is what leads you to observe and discern in a far-reaching and expansive way.

"An Overview of the Essentials" (21.2)

The first five chapters of the *Huainanzi* establish the characteristics of the Way and its primacy in cosmogony, in the attainment of sagehood, and in the cosmological realms of Heaven, Earth, and Time. In chapter 6, "Surveying Obscurities," the Huainan masters turn to a phenomenon they cannot fully explain, although they are certain that it exists. This is "resonance," which is thought of as a kind of sympathetic vibration in the force field of *qi* that pervades the cosmos. Because resonance acts not only on physical objects but also on emotions and intentions, the actions of humans have clear and predictable effects in the natural world. Impiety, injustice, and bad government lead to human catastrophes and natural disasters, whereas following the Way and instituting good government lead to human happiness and celestial harmony. Accordingly, it is imperative, the chapter maintains, for the ruler to look into the roots of bad and good government, identify himself with the One, and make his actions conform to the Way, so as to lay the foundation for the whole world to be harmonious and tranquil. In the end, however, the means by which resonance operates remain cloaked in obscurity. As the chapter's title implies, the phenomenon can be perceived in its general outlines but not with complete clarity.

Some passages in "Surveying Obscurities" resemble lines in the *Zhuangzi*, the *Lüshi chunqiu*, the *Guanzi*, and other early texts, but the chapter as a whole is not heavily dependent on such texts as sources. Instead, it draws its illustrative material from a body of anecdotal lore in wide circulation in the Warring States and early imperial eras, material that also is used extensively in the later chapters of the *Huainanzi*.

Although "Surveying Obscurities" is one of the shortest chapters in the entire *Huainanzi*, it is arguably also one of the most important because it explains the constant interaction and transformation of all phenomena central to the *Huainanzi*'s worldview.

# Six

### 6.1 (in part)

In ancient times Music Master Kuang played the tune "White Snow" and because of that, spiritlike creatures descended [from heaven]; wind and rain arrived violently; Duke Ping became impotent and ill; and the lands of the state of Jin reddened [with drought].[1]

The Commoner Woman cried out to Heaven. Thunder and lightning beat down; Duke Jing's lookout tower collapsed; his limbs and body were broken and slashed; and floodwaters gushed from the sea.[2]

Now the blind music master and the Commoner Woman
>were of a [social] rank as lowly as swaying weeds;
>their [political] weight was as light as windblown feathers;

yet
>by concentrating their essences and disciplining their intentions,
>abandoning their [mundane] responsibilities and storing up spirit [energy],

upward, they penetrated to ninefold Heaven, rousing and putting into action the utmost essence.

---

1. "White Snow" was a work of sacred music. When Duke Ping (of Jin, r. 557–532 B.C.E.) ordered it played in a secular setting, calamities ensued.
2. The nameless "Commoner Woman" was falsely accused by her sister-in-law of murdering her mother-in-law. Duke Jing of Qi reigned from 547 to 490 B.C.E.

Looking at things from this perspective in regard to the punishments [sent by] Heaven on high: Though one dwells
> in a broad wasteland or a dark valley,
> at a remote distance or a secluded hideaway,
> in a multilayered stone refuge,
> or at a frontier barrier or narrow defile,

there is no place where one may escape them. This is clear.

## 6.2

That things in their [various] categories are mutually responsive is [something] dark, mysterious, deep, and subtle.
> Knowledge is not capable of assessing it;
> argument is not capable of explaining it.

Thus,
> when the east wind arrives, wine turns clear and overflows [its vessels];
> when silkworms secrete fragmented silk, the *shang* string [of a stringed instrument] snaps.

Something has stimulated them.
> When a picture is traced out with the ashes of reeds, the moon's halo has a [corresponding] gap.
> When the leviathan dies, comets appear.

Something has moved them.

Thus, when a sage occupies the throne, he embraces the Way and does not speak, and his nurturance reaches to the myriad people. But when ruler and ministers [harbor] distrust in their hearts, back-to-back arcs appear in the sky. The mutual responses of spirit *qi* are subtle indeed!

Thus,
> mountain clouds are like grassy hummocks;
> river clouds are like fish scales;
> dryland clouds are like smoky fire;
> cataract clouds are like billowing water.

All resemble their forms and evoke responses according to their class.
> The burning mirror takes fire from the sun;
> the square receptacle takes dew from the moon.

Of [all the things] between Heaven and Earth, even a skilled astrologer cannot master all their techniques. [Even] a hand [that can hold] minutely tiny and indistinct things cannot grasp a beam of light. However, from what is within the palm of one's hand, one can trace [correlative] categories to beyond the extreme end point [of the cosmos]. [Thus] that one can set up [these implements] and produce water and fire is [a function of] the mutually [responsive] movement of yin and yang of the same *qi*. That is how Fu Yue bestrode [the lunar lodges] Winnowing Basket and Tail.

Thus,
>maximum yin is freezing cold;
>maximum yang is blazing hot.

The two of them come together and interconnect to bring about harmony, and the myriad things thereby are born. If there were lots of males and no females, how indeed would transformation be able to create [anything]? This is what is known as
>the argument that is not spoken
>and the Way that is not [called] "the Way."

Thus
>to attract those who are far-off [i.e., emissaries], one employs non-action;
>to cherish those who are close by, one employs non-interference.

But only one who "walks by night" is able to have this [technique]. Thus [he] retires [his] fast horses so they [only] make dung, and [his] chariot tracks do not need to extend beyond far-off lands. This is what is called
>>racing while sitting, bathing on dry land,
>>darkness at noon, bright light at night,
>>melting pitch in winter,
>>making ice in summer.

## 6.6

In ancient times, when Wang Liang and Zaofu went driving, [as soon as] they mounted their chariots and took hold of the reins, the horses set themselves in order and wanted to work together.
>They obediently paced in step with one another;
>[whether] pulling hard or easing off, they were as one.
>Their hearts were in tune and their *qi* harmonious;
>their bodies [became] more and more light and coordinated.
>They were content to work hard and happy to go forward;
>they galloped away as if they would vanish.
>They went right and left like [the waving of] a whip;
>they circled around like a jade bracelet.

All people of that era considered [Wang Liang and Zaofu] to be superlative [charioteers], but that was because they had not yet seen any [truly] worthy ones. Now consider the charioteering of Qian Qie and Da Bing. They
>considered reins and bits superfluous,

got rid of whips and cast aside goads.
Before the chariot began to move, it was starting on its own.
Before the horses were given the signal, they were walking on their own.
They paced [like the] sun and moved [like the] moon.
They flashed [like the] stars and advanced [like the] dark.
They raced [like] lightning and leaped [like] ghosts.
> Advancing or withdrawing, gathering strength or stretching out,
> they did not see the slightest barrier.

Thus,
> with no gesturing or pointing,
> with no cursing or scolding,
> they overtook the wild geese flying to Piled-Stone Mountain,
> passed the jungle fowl [flying to] Guyu Mountain.
> Their galloping was like flying;
> their bursts of speed like thread snapping.
> [It was] like riding an arrow or mounting the wind,
> like following a cyclone and returning in an instant.
>> At dawn they started from Fusang
>> and set with the sun at Luotang.

This was taking something unused and obtaining its usefulness: it was not done by examining things through reason or thought or through the exercise of manual skill. Whenever urgent desires took form in the breasts [of Qian Qie and Da Bing], their quintessential spirits were [already] communicated to the six horses. This was a case of using non-driving to go driving.

# Seven

## QUINTESSENTIAL SPIRIT

"Quintessential Spirit" provides the means by which to
>   trace to the source the root from which human life arises
>   and understand what animates humans' form, frame, and nine
>     orifices.

Taking its images from Heaven,
>   it coordinates and identifies humans' blood and $qi$
>   with thunder and lightning, wind and rain;
>   correlates and categorizes humans' happiness and anger
>   with dawn and dusk, cold and heat.
>   Judging the distinctions between life and death,
>   distinguishing the traces of identity and difference,
>   regulating the workings of movement and stillness,

it thereby returns to the Ancestor of nature and destiny.
It is what enables you to
>   cherish and nourish the essence and spirit,
>   pacify and still the ethereal and earthly souls,
>   not change the self on account of things,

and fortify and preserve the abode of Emptiness and Nothingness.

"An Overview of the Essentials" (21.2)

"Quintessential Spirit" is the first chapter of the *Huainanzi* to introduce human beings systematically into the grand scheme of things. The text continues its methodical explication of the underlying powers, patterns, and forces of the cosmos and its creatures before turning, in the later chapters of the work, to illustrations and amplifications of the workings of the Way in the world of affairs.

Chapters 1 and 2 introduced cosmology and ontology; chapters 3 through 5 explored the various dimensions of Heaven, Earth, and Time; and chapter 6 explained the mysterious operations of resonance by which things in the world interact through stimuli and responses. In chapter 7, the authors turn to human beings, the third leg of the early Chinese conceptual tripod of Heaven, Earth, and Man. They identify the Quintessential Spirit as the primordial vital energy of consciousness, what gives humans their distinctive abilities to function cognitively in the outer world and contemplatively in the inner world.

The authors begin by identifying the origins of the Quintessential Spirit in the genesis of the cosmos. It is associated with Heaven and yang energies, in contrast to the physical body, which is associated with Earth and yin energies. Perfected human beings are able to preserve this Quintessential Spirit through a meditative practice ("techniques of the mind") that involves emptying the mind and cultivating tranquillity, a practice described throughout this chapter: human beings tend to lose Quintessential Spirit through an externalizing process that occurs through excessive stimulation of the senses. But adepts at inner-cultivation practice—sages, the "Perfected," and the "Genuine"—prevent this loss by maintaining an inner focus through careful circulation of the vital breath, eventually reaching complete union with the Way and so developing many of its characteristics. Using an enhanced cognitive function referred to as "spiritlike illumination," they maintain this connection throughout their interactions in the phenomenal realm, thus establishing that inner cultivation is the foundation of success in the outer world.

The authors of this chapter express their contempt for two groups of rivals: practitioners of the moving meditation called "Guiding and Pulling" (of the *qi*), portrayed as health fanatics who nurture their bodies at the expense of the minds and spirits; and Confucian literati, who stifle and suppress their true natures in a vain effort to cultivate themselves. This chapter shares a number of phrases and terms with the "inner chapters" of the *Zhuangzi* but also is greatly indebted to the "Inward Training" chapters of the *Guanzi* and probably other works of the inner-cultivation tradition that are now lost.

# Seven

7.1

Of old, in the time before there was Heaven and Earth:
>   There were only images and no forms.
>   All was obscure and dark,
>   vague and unclear,
>   shapeless and formless,
>   and no one knows its gateway.

There were two spirits, born in murkiness, one that established Heaven and the other that constructed Earth.
>   So vast! No one knows where they ultimately end.
>   So broad! No one knows where they finally stop.

Thereupon
>   they differentiated into the yin and the yang
>   and separated into the eight cardinal directions.
>   The firm and the yielding formed each other;
>   the myriad things thereupon took shape.
>   The turbid vital energy became creatures;
>   the refined vital energy became humans.

Therefore,
>   the Quintessential Spirit is of Heaven;
>   the skeletal system is of Earth.
>   When the Quintessential Spirit enters its gateway

and the skeletal system returns to its root,
how can I still survive?
For this reason, the sages
>    model themselves on Heaven,
>    accord with their genuine responses,
>    are not confined by custom,
>    or seduced by other men.
>  They take
>    Heaven as father,
>    Earth as mother,
>    yin and yang as warp,
>    the four seasons as weft.
>    Through the tranquillity of Heaven, they become pure.
>    Through the stability of Earth, they become calm.
Among the myriad things,
>    those who lose this perish;
>    those who follow this live.
>    Tranquillity and stillness are the dwellings of spiritlike illumination;
>    emptiness and nothingness are where the Way resides.
For this reason,
>    those who seek for it externally lose it internally;
>    those who preserve it internally attain it externally as well.
It is like the roots and branches of trees: none of the thousands of limbs and tens of thousands of leaves does not derive from the roots.

## 7.4

> The apertures of perception [eyes and ears] are the portals of the Quintessential Spirit.
> 
> The vital energy and attention are the emissaries and servants of the Five Orbs.
> 
> When the eyes and ears are enticed by the joys of sound and color, then the Five Orbs oscillate and are not stable.
> 
> When the Five Orbs oscillate and are not stable, then the blood and vital energy are agitated and not at rest.
> 
> When the blood and vital energy are agitated and not at rest, then the Quintessential Spirit courses out [through the eyes and ears] and is not preserved.
> 
> When the Quintessential Spirit courses out and is not preserved,

then when either good fortune or misfortune arrives, although it be the size of hills and mountains, one has no way to recognize it.
But
> if you make your ears and eyes totally clear and profoundly penetrating and not enticed by external things;
> if your vital energy and attention are empty, tranquil, still, and serene and you eliminate lusts and desires;
> if the Five Orbs are stable, reposed, replete, and full and not leaking [the vital energies];
> if your Quintessential Spirit is preserved within your physical frame and does not flow out;

then even gazing back beyond bygone ages and looking further than things that are to come; even these things would not be worth doing, much less discriminating between bad and good fortune.

Therefore it is said, "The farther you go, the less you know." This says that the Quintessential Spirit cannot be allowed to be enticed by external things.

Therefore,
> the five colors disrupt the eyes and cause them to be unclear;
> the five sounds confuse the ears and cause them to not be acute;
> the five tastes disrupt the mouth and cause it to lose the ability to taste;
> preferences confuse the nature and cause it to fly about [from one thing to the next].

These four things are how the people of this world commonly nourish their natures.

However, they all are human attachments.

> Therefore it is said:
> "Lusts and desires cause humans' vital energy to dissipate;
> likes and dislikes cause human' minds to tire."

If you do not quickly eliminate them, your attention and vital energy will diminish daily.

## 7.7 (in part)

Those whom we call the Perfected are people whose inborn nature is merged with the Way.
Therefore,
> they possess it but appear to have nothing.
> They are full but appear to be empty.

They are settled in this unity and do not know of any duality
They cultivate what is inside and pay no attention to what is outside.
They illuminate and clarify Grand Simplicity;
taking no action, they revert to the Unhewn.[1]

They embody the foundation and embrace the spirit in order to roam freely within the confines of Heaven and Earth. Untrammeled, they ramble outside this dusty world and wander aimlessly in their taskless calling. Unfettered and unhindered, they harbor no clever devices or cunning knowledge in their minds.

Thus death and life are great indeed, but they do not alter them. Although Heaven and Earth support and nourish, they are not protected by them. They discern the flawless and do not get mixed up with things. While seeing the chaos of affairs, they are able to preserve their origin.

Beings like these
negate obsession and fear
and cast aside sensory perceptions.
Their mental activity is concentrated internally
and penetrates through to comport with the One.
At rest, they have no objectives;
in motion, they set no goals.
Artlessly they go forth;
peacefully they come back.
Their bodies are like withered wood;
their minds are like dead ashes.
They forget the Five Orbs;
lose their physical frames;
know without studying;
see without looking;
complete without acting;
and differentiate without judging.
When stimulated, they respond;
when pressed, they move;
when it is unavoidable, they go forth,
like the brilliant glow of a flame,
like the mimicry of a shadow.

---

1. The "Unhewn" (sometimes also translated as the "Uncarved Block") refers to the original, undifferentiated state of matter: a block of wood or stone that has not yet been carved and therefore retains the possibility of being carved into anything. It is a common Daoist metaphor for the unitary mind of the sage.

Taking the Way as their guiding thread, they are necessarily so. Embracing the foundation of Grand Purity, they contain nothing, and things cannot disturb them. Vast and empty, they are tranquil and without worry.

> Great marshes may catch fire, but it cannot burn them.
> Great rivers may freeze over, but it cannot chill them.
> Great thunder may shake the mountains, but it cannot startle them.
> Great storms may darken the sun, but it cannot harm them.

For this reason,
> they view precious pearls and jade as being the same as gravel.
> They view the supremely exalted and maximally favored [at court] as being the same as wandering guest [scholars].
> They view [the beauties] Mao Qiang and Xi Shi as being the same as funerary figurines.
> They take life and death to be a single transformation
> and the myriad things to be a single whole.
> They merge their vital essence with the Root of Great Purity
> and roam freely beyond the boundless.

They have a vital essence but do not [recklessly] expend it;
and have a spirit but do not [thoughtlessly] use it.
They identify with the artlessness of the Great Unhewn
and take their stand amid the supremely pure.

. . .

This is how their Quintessential Spirit is able to verge upon the Way; this is the roaming of the Perfected.

## 7.8

> If you huff and puff, exhale and inhale,
> blow out the old and pull in the new,
> practice the Bear Hang, the Bird Stretch,
> the Duck Splash, the Ape Leap,
> the Owl Gaze, and the Tiger Stare:

This is what is practiced by those who nurture the body. They are not the practices of those who polish the mind [e.g., the Perfected]. They make their spirit overflow, without losing its fullness. When, day and night, without injury, they bring the spring to external things, they unite with, and give birth to, the seasons in their own minds.

> Moreover, there are those who mortify their bodies without harming their minds,

and those who cede their dwelling [i.e., the mind] without diminishing their Quintessence.

The thinking of the leper is not altered;

the body of the madman not impaired.

But when their spirits eventually make their far-off journey, who will have time to think about what they did [in their lives]? Thus even though the body disappears, the spirit is never transformed. If you use what does not transform in response to transformations, [even through] a thousand alterations and ten thousand evolutions, you will not have begun to reach a limit.

What transforms returns to the Formless;

what does not transform is born together with Heaven and Earth.

A tree dies because its greenness has departed. But can that which gives life to a tree be a tree itself? Analogously, what fills the body is not the body. Thus,

What gives birth to the living never dies, yet that to which it gives birth does die.

What transforms things never transforms, yet that which it transforms does transform.

If you take the world lightly, then your spirit will have no attachments.

If you minimize the myriad things, then your mind will not be led astray.

If you equalize death and life, then your mentality will not be fearful.

If you take all alterations and transformations as [being] the same, then your clarity will not be darkened.

The masses take these as empty words, but I take them as my ideal and prove them true.

## 7.14

Shallow scholars in this declining age do not understand how to get to the origins of their minds and return to their root. They merely sculpt and polish their natures and adorn and stifle their genuine responses in order to interact with their age. Thus,

when their eyes desire something, they forbid it with measures;

when their minds delight in something, they restrict it with rites.

They hasten forth in circles and formally scrape and bow

while the meat goes bad and becomes inedible

and the wine goes sour and becomes undrinkable.

Externally they restrict their bodies;

internally they belabor their minds.

They damage the harmony of yin and yang

and constrain the genuine responses of their nature to fate.

Thus throughout their lives, they are sorrowful people.
> Those who penetrate through to the Way are not like this.
>> They regulate the genuine responses of their natures,
>> cultivate the techniques of the mind,
>> nourish these with harmony,
>> take hold of these through suitability.
>> They delight in the Way and forget what is lowly;
>> They find repose in Potency and forget what is base.
>> Since their natures desire nothing, they attain whatever they desire.
>> Since their minds delight in nothing, there are no delights in which they do not partake.
>> Those who do not exceed their genuine responses do not allow them to tie down their Potency.
>> Those who find ease in their natures do not allow them to injure their inner harmony.

Thus with
> their relaxed bodies and untrammeled awareness,
> their standards and regulations,

they can become models for the empire.

# Eight

## THE BASIC WARP

"The Basic Warp" provides the means by which to
> illuminate the Potency of the great sages
> and penetrate the Way of the Unique Inception.
> Delineating and summarizing the devolution of decadent eras from past to present,
> it thereby praises the flourishing prosperity of earlier ages
> and criticizes the corrupt governments of later ages.

It is what enables you to
> dispense with the acuity and keenness of hearing and sight,
> still the responses and movements of the essence and spirit,
> restrain effusive and ephemeral viewpoints,
> temper the harmony of nourishing your nature,
> distinguish the conduct of [the Five] Thearchs and [Three] Kings,
> and set out the differences between small and great.
>
> "An Overview of the Essentials" (21.2)

"The Basic Warp," the last of the *Huainanzi*'s "root" chapters, uses several different but generally complementary descriptions of an imagined historical past to raise questions about the nature of sage-rulership and to criticize government in the present era. In all these scenarios, an archaic era of agrarian primitivism is idealized as a time when sages, embodying the Way and its Potency, could govern almost invisibly by means of non-action. Both the human and the natural worlds responded resonantly to the sages' superior qualities. Qualities like Humaneness and Music were intrinsic to the sage and were not (as they later became) mere expedients to control the populace in times that departed ever more profoundly from the Way. But inevitably the world began to devolve from the archaic ideal. People perceived deficiencies in their lives and increasingly took steps to satisfy their desires. The more they did so, the more the situation degenerated from primordial simplicity and unity. Thus we find ourselves in an era of discord and turmoil. What is to be done?

The answer is perhaps surprising. Although latter-day calamities have led to suffering and turmoil, they also have created an opportunity for a contemporary ruler—one wise enough to avoid the pitfalls of extravagance, excess, cruelty, and greed—to establish a new era of sagely rule. In tranquil times, there is no need for remarkable men or extraordinary measures. But in times of danger and trouble, a ruler who knows how to embody the unmediated unity of the Grand One, to align himself with the Way and its Potency, to match his actions to the rhythms of the cosmos, and to become imbued with spirit illumination has a golden opportunity to govern as a sage.

The chapter's title, "The Basic Warp," proposes an analogy: the Way, Potency, Humaneness, Rightness, and other qualities of the sage are like the warp threads strung on a loom in preparation for weaving a piece of cloth. Into this warp, the ruler weaves the weft threads of administration to produce the fabric of good government.

The divinities and sage-rulers that appear in this chapter are the common property of a wide range of early Chinese texts. Although "The Basic Warp" is not heavily dependent on any particular source text for its material, its analytical point of view seems clearly grounded in the *Laozi*.

# Eight

## 8.3

The people of antiquity made their *qi* the same as that of Heaven and Earth; they wandered in an era of unity. At that time,
> there was no garnering advantage by praise and rewards,
> no intimidation by mutilations and punishments.
> Ritual and Rightness, purity and modesty, had not yet been established;
> slander and flattery, Humaneness and contempt, had not yet been set up;

and the myriad peoples had not yet [begun to] treat one another with fraud and oppression, cruelty and exploitation—it was as if they were still immersed in turbid obscurity.

Coming down to the era of decline, [it transpired that]
> people were abundant, but wealth was scarce;
> people labored to the utmost, but their nourishment was insufficient.

Thus competition and strife were born, and Humaneness was valued. The Humane and the petty minded were[, however,] not treated equitably.
> Neighbors formed groups,
> and friends formed cabals.
> They promoted falsehood and deceit,
> cherished a spirit of contrivance and artifice,
> and lost [their] natural tendencies.

Thus Rightness was valued.

None of [the people's] feelings associated with yin and yang [i.e., sexual feelings] were free from the stimulation of blood and *qi*. Men and women [therefore] gathered in places and promiscuously dwelt together without distinction. Thus Ritual was valued.

Instinctive feelings overflowed and were mutually conflicting. They could not stop themselves and therefore were discordant. Thus Music was valued.

Thus, Humaneness, Rightness, Ritual, and Music, though able to save [the world] from ruin, are still not the perfection of comprehensive governance.

> Humaneness is able to save people from strife;
> Rightness is able to save people from errors;
> Ritual is able to save people from lewdness;
> Music is able to save people from melancholy.
> When spirit illumination is established in the world, then minds revert to their original state.
> When minds revert to their original state, then people's natures become good.
> When people's natures become good, they are followed by Heaven and Earth and by yin and yang.

Wealth then becomes sufficient. When wealth becomes sufficient, the people are respectful; covetousness, petty mindedness, anger, and competition have no occasion to arise. From this, one can see that [under these circumstances,] there is no need for Humaneness and Rightness.

When the Way and its Potency are established in the world, then the people become pure and simple. Thus

> their eyes are not fixed on beauty;
> their ears are not drawn to sounds.

If there were [entertainers] sitting in rows and singing songs or prancing about with their hair hanging loose—

> even if they were as alluring as Mao Qiang or Xi Shi, [the audience] would take no pleasure in them;
> even if the tunes were "Falling Wings" or "Martial," they would not find any joy in them.

Even if the lewdness had no limit, it would come to nothing.

From this one can see that [under these circumstances,] there is no need for Ritual and Music. Thus,

> when Potency declines, Humaneness is born;
> when conduct fails, Rightness is established.
> When harmony is lost, there are sounds and ditties;
> when rituals are decayed, comportment is gaudy.

Thus,
> if one understands spirit illumination, then one can understand the inadequacy of the Way and its Potency for effecting things;
>
> if one understands the Way and its Potency, then one can understand the inadequacy of Humaneness and Rightness in putting things into practice;
>
> if one understands Humaneness and Rightness, then one can understand the inadequacy of Ritual and Music in regulating conduct.

## 8.7

> The thearch embodies the Grand One;
> the king emulates yin and yang;
> the hegemon[1] follows the four seasons;
> the prince uses the six pitch pipes.

Now the Grand One
> encloses and contains Heaven and Earth,
> weighs on and crushes the mountains and streams,
> retains or emits yin and yang,
> stretches out and drags along the four seasons,
> knots the net of the eight directional end points,
> and weaves the web of the six coordinates.

It renews the dew and universally overflows without partiality; it [causes the] waterflies to fly and wriggling things to move; there is nothing that does not rely on it and its Potency in order to live.

> Yin and yang
> > uphold the harmony of Heaven and Earth and shape the physical forms of the myriad diversities.
> >
> > [They] retain *qi* and transform things in order to bring to completion the kinds of the myriad categories.
>
> They stretch out and draw back,
> roll up and uncoil.
> They sink into the unfathomable,

---

1. The office of "hegemon" was, according to later historical accounts, held in succession by several rulers of large states during the Spring and Autumn period (722–481 B.C.E.). The hegemon was recognized by his fellow rulers as a "first among equals" who wielded authority on behalf of the reigning Zhou king (the Zhou monarchy having, by then, become nearly powerless) to maintain peace and order among the states.

end and begin [again] in emptiness and fullness,
revolving in the without-origin.
The four seasons:
spring birth,
summer growth,
autumn harvest,
winter storage.
For obtaining and bestowing, there are times;
for going out and entering, there are measures.
Opening and closing, expanding and contracting, they do not deviate from their [proper] order;
happiness and anger, hardness and pliancy, do not depart from their principles.
The six pitch pipes are
life and death,
reward and punishment,
granting and taking away.
Anything that is otherwise lacks the Way. Therefore
pay heed to the balance beam and weight, the level and the marking cord;
examine into the light and the heavy.
This is sufficient to govern within the boundaries [of a state].
Therefore one who embodies the Grand One
discerns the true responses of Heaven and Earth
and penetrates the regularities of the Way and its Potency.
His comprehensive brilliance bedazzles like the sun and moon;
his essence and spirit penetrate the myriad things.
His motion and rest are in tune with yin and yang;
his happiness and anger harmonize with the four seasons;
his Moral Potency and magnanimity extend to beyond the borderlands;
and his fame and reputation pass down to later generations.
One who emulates yin and yang
has Potency comparable to Heaven and Earth
and brilliance like that of the sun and moon;
his essence is as comprehensive as that of ghosts and spirits.
He wears roundness as a hat
and squareness as shoes;
he embraces the gnomon
and holds fast to the marking cord.
Within, he is able to govern his person;
without, he is able to win people's minds.

When he promulgates edicts and issues commands, there is no one in the world who does not comply with them.
> One who follows the four seasons
>> is pliant but not fragile,
>> hard but not brittle,
>> lenient but not reckless,
>> demanding but not overbearing.

He is liberal, pliant, responsible, and indulgent in his nourishing the multitudes of creatures; in his Moral Potency he is magnanimous to the simpleminded and forgiving of the deviant; he is devoid of partiality.
> One who uses the six pitch pipes
>> quells disorder and prohibits violence;
>> advances the meritorious and demotes the unworthy.
>> He supports the reliable so as to create order;
>> he drives away the treacherous in order to create peace;
>> he straightens out the bent in order to create uprightness.

He discerns the Way of prohibitions and pardons, openings and closings. He relies on timeliness and utilizes the power of circumstance in order to win over the hearts of the people.
> If a thearch [merely] embodies yin and yang, [his throne] will be usurped.
> If a king [merely] models himself on the four seasons, [his territory] will be seized.
> If a hegemon [merely] regulates himself by the six standards, he will be disgraced.
> If a prince neglects the level and the marking cord, he will be eradicated.
> If [a person of] small [standing] carries out great [affairs], the results will be turbulent, insubstantial, and uncongenial.
> If a great [person] carries out petty [matters], the results will be narrow, cramped, and unpleasing.

If [the] honorable and mean do not lose their [proper] embodiments, then the world will be [properly] governed.

## 8.9

Generally speaking, disorder arises from profligate indolence. The sources of profligate indolence are fivefold:
> [erecting] great roof beams and framing timbers;
> building palaces and halls;
> courtyard buildings, storied towers, and covered walkways;
> aviaries and well houses;

    with pillars and planks of fruitwood;
    all joined together in mutual support;
    masterpieces of skillful carpentry;
    carved into twists and coils;
    overflowingly engraved and carved and polished;
    adorned with peculiar patterns and spiraling waves;
    [with ornamentation] dripping, floating, billowing, subsiding;
    water chestnut and dwarf oak twining and enfolding;
    extensive, profuse, disordered, fecund;
    cleverly artificial, joined together in apparent confusion;
    each [effect] exceeding the last:
Such is profligate indolence based on wood.
    The depths of excavated ponds and lakes;
    the distance of aligned dikes and embankments;
    the flow of diverted [streams] through gorges and valleys;
    the straitness of ornamental zigzag channels;
    the piling up of stone slabs and the strewing about of stones
    in order to make borders and set out stepping-stones;
    the placing of barriers and dampers in the furious rapids
    so as to stir up the surging waves;
    the making of angles and riffles, bends and meanders
    to imitate the rivers of [Fan]yu and [Cang]wu;
    the augmenting of lotus and water-chestnut plantings
    so as to feed turtles and fish,
    swans, geese, kingfishers,
    fed with leftover rice and sorghum;
    dragon boats with prows carved like water birds,
    wafted along by the breeze for pure pleasure:
Such is profligate indolence based on water.
    High pounded-earth city walls and fortifications,
    plantings of trees [as barriers] in passes and defiles;
    the impressiveness of lofty belvederes and observation posts;
    the immensity of extravagant gardens and walled parks,
    the sight of which satisfies every desire and wonder,
    the height of lofty gate towers that ascend to the clouds and blue [sky];
    great mansions rising tier upon tier,
    rivaling the height of Kunlun;
    the construction of barrier walls and enclosures,
    the making of networks of roads,

    the leveling of highlands and filling in of depressions,
    the piling up of earth to make mountains,
    for the sake of easy passage to great distances;
    the straightening of roads through flatlands and hills,
    so that [drivers] may ceaselessly gallop and race
    without [fear] of stumbles or falls:
Such is profligate indolence based on earth.
    Great bells and tripods,
    beautiful and heavy implements,
    engraved all over with floral and reptilian designs,
    all twisting and intertwined,
    with recumbent rhinos and crouching tigers,
    coiling dragons interlacing together;
    blazingly bright and confusingly contrived,
    shiningly dazzling, brilliantly glittering,
    topsy-turvy, convoluted, luxuriant, tangled,
    [with] overall fretwork and written inscriptions,
    [with] engraved and polished ornamentation;
    cast tin-alloy decorated mirrors,
    now dark, now bright,
    rubbed minutely, every flaw removed;
    frost patterns and deep-cut inlay work,
    resembling bamboo matwork, basketry, or netting,
    or brocade wrappings, regular or irregular,
    the lines numerous but each one distinct:
Such is profligate indolence based on metal.
    Frying, boiling, roasting, grilling,
    the quest to blend, equalize, and harmonize [flavors],
    trying to capture every permutation of sweet and sour in the manner
      of Jing and Wu;
    burning down forests in order to hunt,
    stoking kilns with entire logs,
    blowing through *tuyères* and puffing with bellows
    in order to melt bronze and iron
    that extravagantly flow to harden in the mold,
    not considering an entire day sufficient to the task.
    The mountains are denuded of towering trees;
    the forests are stripped of cudrania and catalpa trees;
    tree trunks are baked to make charcoal;

>    grass is burned to make ash,
>    [so that] open fields and grasslands are white and bare
>    and do not yield [vegetation] in season.
>    Above, the heavens are obscured [by smoke];
>    below, the fruits of the earth are extinguished:
> Such is profligate indolence based on fire.
>   Of these five, [even] one is sufficient for [a ruler] to lose control of the world.
> For this reason, in ancient times the making of the Mingtang was such that
>    below, mud and dampness should not rise up [in the walls];
>    above, drizzle and fog should not enter into [the building];
>    and on all four sides, the wind should not come in.
>    The earthen [walls] were not patterned;
>    the woodwork was not carved;
>    the metal fittings were not ornamented.
>    Clothing [was made] with untrimmed corners and seams;
>    hats were designed without fancy corners and folds.
>    The [Ming]tang was sufficiently large for the movement of [those who] arranged the liturgies;
>    it was sufficiently quiet and clean for sacrifices to the high gods and for ceremonies [directed at] the spirits and deities.
> This was to show forth to the people knowledge, simplicity, and economy.

## 8.12

In ancient times, the Son of Heaven had his royal domain, and the Lords of the Land each had the same [domains as called for by their rank]; each took care of his own portion, and none was permitted to usurp another. If there was one who did not follow the kingly Way,
>    who was cruel and oppressive to the masses,
>    who fought over land and tried to usurp territory,
>    who disrupted the government and violated prohibitions,
>    who when summoned [to the king's court] would not come,
>    who when given commands would not carry them out,
>    who when forbidden [things] would not desist,
>    who when admonished would not alter,
then [the Son of Heaven] raised an army and went forth to punish him,
>    executing the prince,
>    getting rid of his supporters,
>    shutting his ancestral tombs,

    sacrificing at their altars of the soil,
[and] then selecting by divination one of his sons or grandsons to replace him.
  But in later ages, [rulers]
    endeavored to enlarge their lands and encroach on the territory of others,
      forming alliances ceaselessly,
    raised armies for unrighteous causes and mounted punitive expeditions
      against the guiltless;
    killed innocent people and cut off the lineages of the former sages.
    Large countries set off to attack [others];
    small countries built fortifications to defend themselves.
    [Such rulers] confiscated people's oxen and horses,
    took captive their sons and daughters,
    destroyed their ancestral temples,
    carried off their weighty treasures,
    [so that] streams of blood flowed for a thousand *li*,
    and sun-bleached skeletons choked the wild lands.
To satisfy the desires of greedy lords—this is not how armies should be managed.
    Now the purpose of armies is to punish cruelty, not to commit cruelties.
    The purpose of music is to bring forth concord [in human relations], not
      to create licentiousness.
    The purpose of mourning is to bring about a consummation of grief, not to
      create what is meretricious.
Thus,
    there is a Way of serving close relations, and love is the principal means of
      serving them.
    There is substance in the [rituals of] attendance at court, and respect is its
      highest expression.
    There are rituals for the implementation of mourning, and grief is their
      principal quality.
    There are techniques for the use of arms, and Rightness is their foundation.
    If the foundation is established, then the Way can be implemented;
    if the foundation is harmed, then the Way will be abandoned.

# Nine

## THE RULER'S TECHNIQUES

"The Ruler's Techniques" [addresses] the affairs of the ruler of humankind. It provides the means by which to adapt tasks [to individuals] and scrutinize responsibilities so as to ensure that each of the numerous officials exerts his abilities exhaustively.
[It] illuminates
>how to wield authority and manage the handles of governance
>and thereby regulate the multitudes below;
>how to match official titles with actual performance
>and investigate them [with the techniques of] threes and fives.

It is what enables the ruler of men to
>grasp techniques and sustain essentials
>and not act recklessly based on happiness or anger.

Its techniques
>straighten the bent and correct the crooked,
>set aside self-interest and establish the public good,

enabling the one hundred officials to communicate in an orderly fashion
>and gather around the ruler like the spokes of a wheel,
>each exerting his utmost in his respective task,
>while the people succeed in their accomplishments.

Such is the brilliance of the ruler's techniques.

"An Overview of the Essentials" (21.2)

"The Ruler's Techniques" begins by stating: "The ruler's techniques [consist of] establishing non-active management and carrying out wordless instructions." This serves notice that the chapter is not a handbook of tips and tricks for an energetic bureaucrat but a comprehensive plan for achieving the kind of effective self-cultivation, charismatic appeal, and radiant moral force required for a person to be a true universal monarch, a "Son of Heaven." The ruler's non-active orientation is made possible by time-tested techniques that have proved efficacious in creating a harmonious and just society in which the common people flourish and officials support their ruler as spokes of a wheel joined to the hub. The ruler's ability to instruct and yet remain silent as he does so lies in the wondrous power of vital energy (*qi*), which, through self-cultivation, he possesses in quintessential form. By means of this Quintessential *qi*, which in its most refined state is referred to in this chapter interchangeably as the "Utmost Essence" or "spirit," the ruler can avail himself of the Way of Heaven above and transform the people below. In this manner, the ruler achieves a kind of profound and pervasive resonance with his subjects. Stirring their hearts as a fine melody would, such "wordless instructions" are infinitely more persuasive, far-reaching, and influential than any verbal command or purposeful act could be.

True to the *Huainanzi*'s claim to synthesize the best of all previous schools of thought, "The Ruler's Techniques" draws on a very wide range of pre-Han and early Han statecraft literature. Significantly, while it is possible to find in this chapter numerous parallels and allusions to such works as the *Laozi*, the *Hanfeizi*, the *Xunzi*, the *Lüshi chunqiu*, and the *Guanzi*, direct quotations from those works are relatively rare, and "The Ruler's Techniques" clearly represents a new synthesis rather than a simple rehash of old ideas.

This is the longest chapter in the *Huainanzi*, and it is also one of the most wide-ranging. Topics addressed include non-action, positional advantage, sincerity, Potency and Moral Potency, following the natural propensity of things, and laws, taxes, officials, and administrative methods, among others—all of which fall under the capacious rubric of "techniques."

# Nine

## 9.1

The ruler's techniques [consist of]
>establishing non-active management
>and carrying out wordless instructions.
>Quiet and tranquil, he does not move;
>by [even] one degree he does not waver;
>adaptive and compliant, he relies on his underlings;
>dutiful and accomplished, he does not labor.

Therefore,
>though his mind knows the norms, his savants transmit the discourses of the Way;
>though his mouth can speak, his entourage proclaims his words;
>though his feet can advance, his master of ceremonies leads;
>though his ears can hear, his officials offer their admonitions.[1]

Therefore,
>his considerations are without mistaken schemes;
>his undertakings are without erroneous content.
>His words [are taken as] scripture and verse;

---

1. Because this sentence breaks the parallelism of the whole passage, we suspect that the text might have originally read, "his officials receive the admonitions [of others]."

his conduct is [taken as] a model and gnomon for the world.
> His advancing and withdrawing respond to the seasons;
> his movement and rest comply with [proper] patterns.
> His likes and dislikes are not based on ugliness or beauty;
> his rewards and punishments are not based on happiness or anger.
> Each name names itself;
> each category categorizes itself.
> Affairs emerge from what is natural;

nothing issues from [the ruler] himself.

> Thus kings in antiquity wore caps
> > with strings of pearls in front so as to mask their vision
> > and silk plugs in their ears so as to obstruct their hearing.

The Son of Heaven surrounded himself with screens so as to isolate himself. Thus,
> what the ruler patterns himself on is far away, but what he grounds himself in is nearby;
> what he governs himself with is great, but what he preserves is small.

Now,
> if his eyes looked recklessly, there would be profligacy;
> if his ear listened recklessly, there would be delusion;
> if his mouth spoke recklessly, there would be disorder.

One cannot fail to guard carefully these three gateways.
> If you wish to regulate them, that is in fact to distance yourself from them;
> if you wish to embellish them, that is in fact to injure them.

## 9.2

> Heavenly *qi* becomes your ethereal soul;
> earthly *qi* becomes your substantive soul.
> > Return them to their mysterious dwelling place, so that each resides in its proper place.
> > Preserve and do not lose them, so that above you communicate with the Grand One, for the essence of the Grand One communicates with Heaven,
> > and the Way of Heaven is mysterious and silent, shapeless and without pattern.
> > Heaven's limit cannot be reached;
> > its depths cannot be plumbed.

Still it transforms together with humans, [though] knowledge cannot grasp it.

## 9.10

Now,
>for boats to float on water
>and carts to go on land

is their natural propensity. If
>a carriage hits a tree and breaks an axle,
>or if a boat runs aground and shatters the hull,

there is no reason for people to bear resentment against the tree or the rock; they will blame the lack of skill [of the carriage driver or the boatman]. They know that [trees and stones] possess no [conscious qualities]. Thus
>when the Way includes wisdom, there is confusion;
>when Potency includes the mind, there is danger;
>when the mind includes the eyes, there is bedazzlement.
>No weapon is more powerful than awareness and the will. Even the great sword Moye is inferior to them.[2]
>No brigand is as strong as yin and yang. The drumsticks and drums [signaling attack] are inferior to them.

Now the weight and the balance beam, the compass and the square, once fixed do not change.
>Their calibrations are not altered for the sake of Qin or Chu;
>their form does not change for the Hu or the Yue [tribes].

Constant and unswerving, going straight and not meandering, taking form in a single day and passed down for ten thousand generations, they act through non-action.
Thus,
>states have rulers who perish, but no era can see the destruction of the Way.
>People have distress and poverty, but principles never fail to be passed on.

From this standpoint, non-action is the Ancestor of the Way. Attaining the Ancestor of the Way, one responds to things without limit. When one relies [merely] on human talents, the highest kind of statecraft is difficult.

## 9.23

Law is the standard of measurement for the world, the level and the marking cord of the ruler.

---

2. The precious sword Moye, mentioned several times in the *Huainanzi*, took its name from Mo Ye, wife of the legendary swordsmith Gan Jiang and herself a superlatively skilled smith.

[He who] proclaims the laws does so to [impose] law on the lawless;
[he who] sets up rewards does so to reward those who deserve rewards.
After the laws are set,
> those who obey the laws are rewarded,
> and those who fall short of the marking cord['s line] are punished.
> For the honorable and noble, the punishments are not decreased,
> and for the lowly and base, the punishments are not increased.
> If someone disobeys the law, even if he is [otherwise] worthy, he must be punished.
> If someone meets the standard, even if he is [otherwise] unworthy, he must be found innocent.

Thus the Way of the public good will be opened up, and that of private interest will be blocked.

In ancient times,
> a system of responsible officials was established so as to restrain the people and thus prevent them from doing just as they pleased.
> The position of ruler was set up to control the officials so that they could not carry out [policy] on their own.

Laws, records, propriety, and Rightness were used to restrain the ruler so that he could not exercise absolute authority.
> When none of the people could blindly follow their own desires, the Way was triumphant.
> When the Way was triumphant, Patterns were apparent.

Thus government returned to non-action. Non-action does not mean [that the ruler] froze and was inert but that nothing any longer emanated from the ruler personally.

Now the inch comes from the millet grain; the millet grain comes from physical forms. Physical forms come from shadows; shadows come from the sun. This is the root of standards of measurement.

Music comes from the [pentatonic] notes; the notes come from the pitch-pipe tones; and the pitch-pipe tones come from the wind. This is the ancestry of sound.

Law comes from Rightness. Rightness comes from what is appropriate for the people. What is appropriate for the people accords with the human heart. This is the sine qua non of government.

Thus,
> those who penetrate to the root are not confused about the branches.
> Those who see the fundamental are not confused about the details.

Law is

not a gift of Heaven,
not a product of Earth.

It was devised by humankind but conversely is used [by humans] to rectify themselves. Thus,

> what you have in yourself you must not criticize in others;
> what you lack in yourself you must not seek in others;
> what is established for inferiors must not be disregarded by superiors;
> what is prohibited to the people must not be practiced by [the ruler] himself.

A country that can be said to be lost is not one without a ruler but one without laws.

To twist the law does not mean to have no laws [at all] but, rather, that the laws are not employed. That is equivalent to not having laws. Thus when the ruler first establishes laws, he begins by making himself an example and a standard; thus the laws are implemented in the world. Confucius said,

> "If the ruler himself is upright, even though he does not issue orders, they are carried out;
> if he is not upright, though he issue orders, they are not followed."

Thus when the prohibitions apply to [even the ruler] himself, then his orders will be carried out among the people.

## 9.26

Holding on to the handles of authority and positional advantage makes it easy to transform the people.

> That the ruler of Wey took into service [Confucius's disciple] Zilu was because [the ruler's] authority was heavy.
> That Dukes Jing and Huan of Qi made ministers of Guan Zhong and Yan Ying was because [the rulers'] positions were exalted.

That [sometimes]

> the timid can subdue the brave
> and the unintelligent can control the wise

is because they can use positional advantage successfully. Now,

> the limbs of a tree cannot be larger than its trunk,
> the stem cannot be stronger than the root.

So it is said that light and heavy, large and small, have that by which they mutually control each other. It is like the way the five fingers are attached to the arm. They can grasp, extend, snatch, or grab, and none [happens] other than as we wish it. This is to say, the small are appendages of the large. Thus to have the benefit of positional advantage means that what you hold is very small but what you manage is very large; what you guard is very compact, but what you control is vast. Thus a tree trunk ten [hand] spans [in circumference] can support a roof weighing a thousand *jun*, and a key five inches long can control the opening and closing [of a door]. How can this small amount of material be sufficient for the task? The position they occupy is the important thing.

Confucius and Mo Di cultivated the techniques of the former sages and had a penetrating understanding of the theories of the six arts. Their utterances adhered to their doctrines, and their personal actions embodied their will. [Yet] those who, admiring their Rightness and following their influence, submitted to them and served them did not amount to more than a few tens of individuals. But if they had occupied the position of Son of Heaven, everyone in the world would have become Confucians or Mohists.

King Zhuang of Chu was distressed because Wen Wuwei was killed in [the state of] Song. He pushed up his sleeves in anger and arose [to invade Song]. [Officials] in robes and caps fell in with him at every stage along the road so that at last they formed a whole army beneath the walls of Song. [His grasp of] the handles of authority was weighty.

King Wen of Chu liked to wear a cap of *xie* fur,[3] and the people of Chu imitated him. King Wuling of Zhao attended court wearing a belt [decorated with] shells and a cap [plumed] with pheasant feathers, and the [entire] state of Zhao transformed [their dress] along with him. Yet if an ordinary person were to go to court wearing a *xie*-fur hat, a belt of shells, and a cap [plumed] with pheasant feathers, he could not avoid being laughed at by others.

There is not one in ten thousand among the common people who loves goodness, rejoices in uprightness, and, without waiting to hear what is forbidden or punishable, naturally stays within the scope of the laws and standards. But if [the ruler] hands down commands that must be followed, so that those who obey them benefit and those who disobey them suffer, then before the sun [dial's] shadow has moved, no one within the Four Seas will fail to toe the line.

Thus, grasping a sword or a glaive by the blade and [advancing to fight] — not even Beigongzi or Sima Kuaikui could be used to respond to an enemy attack [in that manner]. But if he were to grasp the hilt and raise the tip of the blade, then even an ordinary person might prevail. If [even] Wu Huo [or Jie Fan] were to pull on an ox's tail from behind, even though the tail might break off, still

---

3. The *xie* is identified as a mythical single-horned bovine animal said to be able to distinguish between people who told the truth and those who did not. A cap supposedly made from the animal's fur was popular for a time in Chu and was adapted for use at the Qin court.

the ox would not go where they wanted it to [because] that would be working against [its natural propensities]. But if you put a mulberry stick through [the ox's] nose, even a five-foot-tall child could lead it anywhere within the Four Seas, [because] that would be complying with [its natural propensities].

With a seven-foot oar you can steer a boat to the right or to the left because it uses the water [itself] to assist it. The Son of Heaven issues commands. His orders are implemented and his prohibitions observed because he uses the people [themselves] as his positional advantage.

If the ruler defends the people against what does them harm and opens [a way] for the people to have what brings them benefit, then his awesomeness will spread like the bursting of a dike or the breaking of a dam. Thus if you follow the current and head downstream, it is easy to reach your goal; if you gallop with your back to the wind, it is easy to go far.

When Duke Huan of Qi set up his government, he got rid of meat-eating animals, [got rid of] grain-eating birds, and took down snares and nets. With these three undertakings, he pleased the common people.

When [Tyrant] Djou murdered his uncle, Prince Bi Gan, his blood relatives grew resentful. When he cut off the legs of people who were crossing the river in the early morning, tens of thousands of people rebelled. With these two undertakings, he lost the world.

Now,
> [a ruler's] Rightness cannot be relied on to benefit everyone in the world, but if it benefits one person, the world will follow his example.
> [A ruler's] cruelty might not be enough to harm everyone in the world, but if it harms one person, the whole world might rise in rebellion.

Thus,
> Duke Huan made three undertakings and [subsequently presided over] nine gatherings of the Lords of the Land.
> Djou performed two undertakings, and [subsequently] he could not live even as a commoner. Thus one cannot but be careful of one's actions.

## 9.27

When the ruler levies taxes on the people, he must first calculate what the harvest will bring in, weigh what the people have in storage, and find out, [in anticipation of] abundance or dearth, the numbers of people who have a surplus or a shortage. Only after this should he use [tax revenues to pay for] chariots, carriages, clothing, and food to satisfy his desires.

High terraces and multistoried pavilions, serried rooms, and linked chambers—it is not that they are not elegant, but when the people do not even have hollowed-out caves or wattle huts in which to shelter themselves, an enlightened ruler does not enjoy them.

Rich [food], strong wines, and sweet pastries—it is not that they are not good, but when not even husks of the grain or beans and peas make it to the mouths of the people, then the enlightened ruler does not find [such delicacies] sweet.

A well-made bed and finely woven mats—it is not that these are not restful, but when the people live in frontier walled towns, braving danger and hardship, dying in the meadowlands [leaving] sun-bleached bones, an enlightened ruler does not [lie] peacefully [in his fine bed].

Thus those who ruled over humanity in antiquity felt such sorrowful despondency for [the troubles of] the people that
> if some went hungry in the state, his food would not be heavily seasoned;
> if some people were cold, in winter he would not wear furs.

When the harvest was abundant and the people prosperous, only then would the ruler set up the bells and drums and display the shields and axes [used in ceremonial dances]. Ruler and ministers, superiors and subordinates, then with one mind took pleasure in them, so that there was not a single sorrowful person in the state.

Thus people in ancient times created
> [instruments of] metal, stone, bamboo, and strings to express their joy;[4]
> weapons, armor, axes, and halberds to display their anger;
> wine cups and libations, [sacrificial] meat stands and platters, pledges and toasts, to verify their happiness;
> unbleached mourning garments and straw sandals, breast-beating and gyrating, crying and weeping, to communicate sorrow.

These all are cases of things that swell up internally and then become manifest externally. [But] coming down to [the times of] disorderly rulers,
> in taking from the people, they did not calculate their strength;
> in seeking [taxes] from those below, they did not measure their savings.

Men and women were not able to pursue their callings of farming and weaving because they had to supply the demands of their superiors. Their strength was exhausted and their resources were depleted. Rulers and ministers despised one another. Thus [if just when] the people reached the point that, with parched lips and agitated livers, they had only enough for the moment with nothing put aside, the rulers began to have the great bells struck, the drums beaten, the reed pipes played, and the *qin* and *se* plucked, it would have been just like descendants donning armor to enter the ancestral temple or wearing silk gauze to go

---

4. Here "joy" includes the concept of "music." Both words are written with the same character, which means "joy" when pronounced *le* and "music" when pronounced *yue*.

on a military campaign. [One could say that] they had lost sight of that from whence joy in music rises.

Now as people pursue their livelihoods, if a single man follows the plow, he can till no more than ten *mu* of land. The yearly harvest from fields of middling quality would not exceed four *dan* per *mu*. His wife and children and the elderly and infirm must also rely on this. Sometimes there are diverse calamities such as floods, droughts, and natural disasters. He also has to pay the taxes to the ruler for the expenses of chariots and horses, and soldiers and armor. From this point of view, the life of commoners is pitiful indeed! Now over the great [expanse] of Heaven and Earth, [on average] a three-year period of farming should produce a surplus of one year's grain. Thus roughly

> over nine years, there should be three years' savings,
> six years' accumulation in eighteen years,
> and nine years' reserve in twenty-seven years.

Even if there were floods, droughts, or natural disasters, none of the people would become distressed and impoverished and be left to wander about in utter destitution.

Thus if the state does not have

> a reserve of nine years' production, it is called "insufficient."
> Without six years' accumulation, it is called "pitiful."
> Without three years' surplus, it is called "impoverished."

Thus humane princes and enlightened rulers are restrained in what they take from those below; they are measured in supporting themselves. As a result, the people can receive the bounty of Heaven and Earth and not encounter the difficulties of hunger and cold. But if there are greedy rulers and violent princes, they vex those below, plundering and confiscating [goods] from the people to gratify their insatiable desires. Consequently, the people have no means to avail themselves of Heaven's Harmony or tread the path of Earth's Bounty.

## 9.29

Generally people say that you want

> your heart to be small [cautious] and your will to be large [expansive];
> your wisdom to be round [comprehensive] and your conduct square [proper];
> your abilities to be many and your affairs few.

"The heart should be cautious" means that you should consider difficulties before they arise, prepare for calamities before they occur, guard against transgressions and be careful about small matters, and not dare to give rein to your desires.

"The will should be expansive" means that you should bring together and embrace the myriad states, unify and standardize diverse customs, ally and shelter the commoners as if uniting them as a single people, and act as the hub when [opinions about] right and wrong converge like the spokes of a wheel.

"Wisdom should be round" means that you turn like a circle with no distinction between beginning and end, and flow to the four directions like a deep and inexhaustible spring. When the myriad things arise together, there is nothing to which you fail to turn your attention and respond.

"Conduct should be square" means that you should be straight and unswerving, pure and uncorrupted. Even if you are destitute, you never change your patterns, and when successful, you never force your will [on others].

"Abilities should be many" means that you must be competent in both civil and military matters, and adhere to proper deportment both in movement and at rest. In your actions, in promoting and demoting, you always do what is appropriate. You meet with no opposition, and so nothing is incomplete or inappropriate.

"Affairs should be few" means that you grasp the handles and wield the techniques [of governance], get what is important so as to respond to the multitudes, grasp the essence so as to govern widely, dwell in quietude and stay centered, revolve at the pivot, and use the one to bring together the myriads, like bringing together [the two halves of] a tally.

Thus,
> if your heart is cautious, you can put a stop [to problems] in their incipient stages.
> If your will is great, there will be nothing you do not embrace.
> If your knowledge is round, there will be nothing you do not know.
> If your conduct is square, you will not act in certain instances.
> If your abilities are many, there will be nothing you cannot put in order.
> If your affairs are few, the essence will be what you grasp.

In ancient times when the Son of Heaven held court, he arranged for
> lords and ministers to present forthright admonitions,
> scholars of wide learning to chant the *Odes*,
> music masters to sing critiques of government,
> and the populace to offer their opinions.
> Secretaries recorded the ruler's misconduct;
> chefs cut down on his delicacies.

But still this was not considered sufficient, so
> Yao put in place a drum [at the palace gate] for anyone wishing to admonish [him];
> Shun set up a board on which to post criticisms;

Tang had a superintendent of rectitude;
King Wu set up a small drum to remind him to be careful.
[Thus], when mistakes were still trivial, there already were precautions taken against them.
> According to the sage's concept of goodness, no act [of goodness] is so small that it should not be carried out.
> According to his concept of misconduct, no act [of misconduct] is so trivial that it should not be corrected.

Yao, Shun, Yu, Tang, King Wen and King Wu confidently faced south and ruled the world. In those times,
> when a gong was struck, they ate;
> when the [musical composition] "Concord" was played, the table was cleared.

After finishing their rice, they offered a sacrifice to the stove god. In their conduct, they did not make use of shamans' invocations.
> Ghosts and spirits did not dare to work black magic on them;
> mountains and rivers did not dare to harm them.

They could be said to be [truly] noble. Yet they were
> preoccupied and fearful,
> daily more and more careful.

From this point of view, then, the sage's heart is cautious. The *Odes* says,
> "Indeed this King Wen
> was cautious and reverent;
> illustriously he served the High God,
> thus securing good fortune."

Is this not what is referred to here?

When King Wu of Zhou attacked the Shang dynasty, he
> disbursed the grain from the Zhuqiao granaries,
> distributed the money from the Lutai treasury,
> built a mound over Bi Gan's tomb,
> designated as exemplary the [ancestral] village of Shang Rong,
> brought under royal control the ancestral temple of Cheng Tang,
> and freed Ji Zi from prison.

He let people of all sorts remain in their own homes and till their own fields.
> He did not distinguish between old and new [friends]
> but drew near only to those who were worthy.
> He made use of those who had not previously served him
> and employed those who were not [previously] his own men,

comfortably treating the newcomers as if they had long been in his employ. From this point of view, then, the sage's will is expansive.

King Wen of Zhou
> comprehensively surveyed successes and failures
> and everywhere investigated right and wrong.
> [He considered] what made Yao and Shun glorious
> and [why] Jie and Djou perished,

then recorded all [his findings] in the Mingtang. Thereby he increased his wisdom and expanded his erudition so he could respond to anything that departed from the foursquare. From this point of view, then, the sage's wisdom is round.

King Cheng and King Kang
> carried on the task of Kings Wen and Wu,
> preserved the institution of the Mingtang,
> looked into the traces of [ancient states] that endured or perished,
> and observed the alterations of success and failure.

If something
> contravened the Way, they would not say it;
> contravened Rightness, they would not do it.
> Their words were not spoken heedlessly;
> their actions were not carried out heedlessly.

They selected what was good, and only then would they pursue a course of action. From this point of view, then, the conduct of the Superior Man is square.

Confucius's penetrating qualities [were such that]
> in wisdom he surpassed Chang Hong;
> in bravery he was superior to Meng Ben.
> His feet were quicker than an agile rabbit;
> his strength could lift a city gate.

His abilities certainly were many. Nevertheless,
> his bravery and strength were not heard about;
> his skills and mastery were not known.

It was only through carrying out filial piety and the Way that he became an "uncrowned king." His affairs certainly were few.

In the 242 years of the Spring and Autumn period, fifty-two states perished and thirty-six rulers were assassinated. Confucius
> upheld goodness and condemned wickedness, [thereby]
> perfecting the Way of [the True] King.

His discussions certainly were broad. Nevertheless,
> when he was besieged in Kuang,
> his expression and complexion did not alter.
> He plucked [his *qin*] and sang without pausing.
> When it came to the point that his life was in danger,
> when he encountered calamities and dangerous difficulties,

he clung to Rightness and practiced his principles, and his will was fearless. His sense of discrimination [between life and death] certainly was clear.

Thus, [in serving] as minister of justice in Lu, when he heard cases, he invariably came to a decision. In compiling the *Spring and Autumn Annals*, he did not give accounts of ghosts and spirits, nor did he dare to [inject] his personal opinions.

Now the wisdom of sages certainly embraces many things; what they preserve gets to the essence. Thus when they take some action, the outcome is invariably glorious. The wisdom of a foolish person certainly is very little, yet the things he tries to do are numerous. Thus when he acts on something it is certain to fail. In wisdom, Wu Qi and Zhang Yi did not compare with Confucius and Mo Di, yet they contended with rulers of ten-thousand-chariot states. This is why they eventually had their bodies torn apart by chariots and their lineages wiped out. Now

> if [the ruler] uses uprightness to transform [the people] by teaching, that is easy and he will certainly succeed.
>
> If he uses depravity to manipulate society, that is difficult and he will certainly fail.

Now, if you are going to establish a pattern of conduct and make it general throughout the world, to abandon the easy route that is sure to succeed and to follow the difficult way that is bound to fail would be the height of stupidity and confusion.

The six opposites must, without fail, be scrutinized carefully.

# Ten

## PROFOUND PRECEPTS

"Profound Precepts"
> parses and analyzes [various] assessments of the Way and its Potency,
> ranks and puts in sequence [diverse] differentiations of Humaneness and Rightness,
> summarizes and juxtaposes the affairs of the human realm,

generally bringing them into conformity with the Potency of spirit illumination.
> It proposes similes and selects appositions
> to match them with analogies and illustrations;
> it divides into segments and forms sections
> to respond to brief aphorisms.

It is what makes it possible to find fault with persuasions and attack arguments, responding to provocations without error.

"An Overview of the Essentials" (21.2)

"Profound Precepts" posits that the ruler must follow the promptings of his inner heart and honor his innermost feelings as the basis of his rule, rather than relying on laws, rituals, institutions, or the advice of worthies. "Profound Precepts" thus evinces a deep commitment to concepts of moral autonomy and moral agency. In turn, these echo the radical optimism of the celebrated Confucian philosopher Mencius, who centuries earlier had argued passionately for the power of human emotions to uplift the world. The ideal ruler accordingly seeks goodness within himself and thereby brings goodness to the world. He is able to do so because the intrinsic moral inclinations of his heart, expressed in such feelings as Humaneness and Rightness, are shared by all humanity. Guided by his own feelings, he is able to connect in a profound way with his people, leading them by means of a kind of empathetic resonance that is more powerful than any commands he might utter. Through vigilant introspection, the ruler establishes a close communion with the stirrings of his inner heart, relying on his personal Humaneness and Rightness to establish a government under which the people are loved and benefited as a father loves his son. Ruler and ruled are in perfect accord, and by cultivating his inherent feelings, the ruler sets the world in order.

Transcending ordinary human emotions—such as sorrow, joy, happiness, and anger—for a deeper level of inner experience, sage rulers respond to others with a profound sense of equanimity and transform the hearts of the people by projecting the moral force of their deeply rooted feelings. Much of this chapter outlines how human resonance works, demonstrating the central importance of the human heart and how its feelings evoke sympathetic and resonant responses from others. Of particular relevance is the concept of inner sincerity, an emotion identified with a person's deepest psychic self. In this chapter, it is portrayed as preceding speech and actions and enabling the expression of other emotions.

Of all the chapters in the *Huainanzi*, chapter 10 may fairly be called the most strongly Confucian in orientation. It draws its ideas and themes (although seldom its exact language) from the whole pre-Han and early Han Confucian corpus, including the *Lunyu* (*Analects of Confucius*), the *Liji* (*Record of Rites*), the *Mengzi* (*The Book of Mencius*), the *Zisizi* (*The Book of Master Zisi*), the *Zhong yong* (*Doctrine of the Mean*, chapter 32 of the *Liji*), and the archaeologically recovered text the *Wuxingpian* (*The Five Kinds of Conduct*). The chapter's title, "Profound Precepts," refers to both its content and literary form. Most of the 118 brief moral assertions are followed by a few lines of explication. Such "precepts" would be well suited for use in various oral contexts (such as court debates) to argue against false opinions, precisely as the summary in chapter 21 suggests.

# Ten

### 10.1

> The Way at its highest has nothing above it;
> at its lowest it has nothing below it.
> It is more even than a [carpenter's] level,
> straighter than a marking cord,
> rounder than a compass,
> and more square than a [carpenter's] square.

It embraces the cosmos and is without outside or inside. Cavernous and undifferentiated, it covers and supports with nothing to hinder it.

Therefore, those who embody the Way
> are not sorrowful or joyful;
> are not happy or angry.
> They sit without disturbing thoughts,
> and sleep without dreams.
> Things come, and they name them.
> Affairs arise, and they respond to them.

### 10.5

> The Way is what guides things;
> Potency is what supports nature.

Humaneness is visible proof of accumulated kindness. Rightness is what comports with the human heart and conforms to what is appropriate for the majority of humankind.
Thus
> when the Way was extinguished, Potency was employed.
> When Potency declined, Humaneness and Rightness were born.

Thus
> the earliest era embodied the Way but did not have Potency.
> The middle period had Potency but did not cherish it.

The latter-day era was anxious and fearful lest even Humaneness and Rightness be lost.

## 10.6

> If not for Humaneness and Rightness, the Superior Man would have nothing to live for.
> If he loses Humaneness and Rightness, he will lose the reason for his existence.
> If not for cravings and desires, the petty man would have nothing to live for.
> If he loses his cravings and desires, he will lose his reason for living.

Thus
> the Superior Man fears losing Rightness.
> The petty man fears losing what is valuable to him.

When we look at what people fear, we understand how different they are.

The *Changes* says,
> "Chasing a deer without a guide.
> It goes into the forest.
> For the Superior Man to follow it would not be so good as to abandon it.
> Should he follow it, he would encounter difficulty."

## 10.10

> When the Superior Man sees [the ruler's] transgressions, he forgets about punishment [for pointing it out]. Thus he is able to remonstrate.
> When he sees a worthy, he forgets about [the worthy's low] rank. Thus he is able to yield modestly.

When he sees others who do not have enough, he forgets [his own] poverty. Thus he is able to give charitably.

## 10.16

There is nothing that does not have some use.

> *Tianxiong* and *wuhui* are the [most] virulently poisonous of herbs, but a good physician uses them to save people's lives.
> Dwarves and blind musicians are the troubled invalids of humankind, but the ruler of men uses them to perform music.

For this reason, the sage prepares even the shavings from the timber. There is nothing that he does not use.

## 10.17

With one shout, a brave warrior can cause the Three Armies to retreat. What disperses them is his complete sincerity.

Thus
    if you command, but [the troops] do not [comply] harmoniously;
    if you have intentions, but [the troops] do not support you,
it surely is the case that something is not in accord with your inner heart.
    Thus the reason that Shun, without descending from his mat, [was able to] preserve the world was because he sought it within himself. Thus if the ruler makes more and more excuses, the people will practice more and more deceit. To have a body that is crooked and a shadow that is straight—such a thing has never been heard of.

## 10.24

> The essence of the heart can transform [others] like a spirit, but it cannot point out things to them.
> The essence of the eye can cut through obscurities, but it cannot give clear warning.

What lies within the dark and obscure cannot be verbalized to others.

Thus,
>Shun did not descend from his mat, and the world was ordered.
>
>[The tyrant] Jie did not leave his throne, and the world was disordered.

Certainly, feelings are deeper than spoken commands. To seek from others what one lacks in oneself—such has never been heard of from ancient times to the present.

## 10.25

> If the speech is identical but the people trust it [in some cases], it is because trust preceded the speech.
>
> If the command is identical but the people are transformed by it [in some cases], it is because sincerity lay beyond the command.

When sages rule above and the people are moved and transformed, it is because their feelings have paved the way for them. When there is movement above and no response below, it is because feelings and orders are at variance with one another.

Thus the *Changes* says,
>"The overbearing dragon will have [reason to] regret."

## 10.26

A three-month-old infant does not yet understand the distinction between benefit and harm, but the love of a kind mother is conveyed to the infant because of her feelings.

> Thus, the usefulness of what is spoken—how manifestly tiny it is!
> The usefulness of what is not spoken—how vastly great it is!

## 10.29

> Rightness is more exalted than a ruler.
> Humaneness is more intimate than a father.

Thus
> the ruler in relation to his ministers [has the power to] kill them or let them live, but he cannot force them to do their jobs with negligent unconcern.
>
> A father in relation to his children [has the power to] reject them or raise them, but he cannot force them to be without anxious concern.

Thus
> when Rightness transcends the ruler himself,
> and Humaneness transcends the father himself,
> the ruler is exalted and his ministers are loyal;
> the father is compassionate and his children are filial.

## 10.31

Actions undertaken near at hand cause a civilizing influence to spread far away. Now when he examined his evening gait, the Duke of Zhou was embarrassed by his shadow.[1]

Thus the Superior Man scrutinizes [himself] in solitude. To abandon what is close at hand in expectation of what is far-off is to obstruct [one's path].

## 10.42

> If you turn to goodness, even if you err, you will not be censured.
> If you do not turn to goodness, even if you are loyal, you will invite calamity.

Thus
> being censorious toward others is not so good as being censorious toward yourself.
> Seeking it [i.e., goodness] in others is not so good as seeking it in yourself.

## 10.51

The actions of the sage
> are not joined with anything
> and are not separated from anything.
By analogy, it is like a drum.
> There is no instrument that is in tune with it,
> and no instrument that cannot be accompanied by it.

---

1. Because he was walking with poor posture, which was a violation of ritual correctness even if there was no one else around to observe it.

## 10.54

Culture is the means by which we connect to things.
>  Feelings bind inwardly,
>  but desires manifest themselves externally.
>  If you use culture to obliterate feelings, feelings will be lost.
>  If you use feelings to obliterate culture, culture will be lost.

When the guiding patterns of culture and feelings interpenetrate, the phoenix and the *qilin* will roam extensively. That is to say, the embrace of your Utmost Potency will be far-reaching.

## 10.56

> The ruler wills it.
> The people fulfill it.

This is because of his inner sincerity.
>  Before saying a word, he is trusted;
>  without being summoned, they come.

Something precedes it.

## 10.65

The Way of the Superior Man is
>  close but cannot be attained,
>  low but cannot be ascended,

contains nothing inside it, but cannot be filled. It is
>  enduring yet brilliant,
>  far-reaching yet illustrious.

To understand this and so follow the Way is something that cannot be sought in others but only attained from the self. If you abandon the search within yourself and seek it in others, you will have strayed far from it.

## 10.79

> In an age that has the Way, a man is given to the state.
> In an age that does not have the Way, the state is given to a man.

When Yao ruled the world as king, his anxiety did not abate. When he conferred [his rulership] on Shun, his anxiety disappeared. Anxiously he watched over it; joyfully he gave it to a worthy. To the end he did not consider the benefit [of rulership] to be his private possession.

## 10.83

> The sprouts of good fortune are flossy and fine,
> and the birth of bad fortune is tiny and trifling.

Since the beginnings of good and bad fortune are tiny as a sprout, people overlook them. Only sages see their beginnings and know their ends.

Thus a chronicle says,
> "The wine of Lu was weak and Handan was surrounded;
> the lamb broth was not poured, and the state of Song was endangered."[2]

## 10.87

> One whose Rightness includes a sense of appropriateness is called a Superior Man.
> One whose appropriateness abandons a sense of Rightness is called a petty man.

> Penetrating wisdom achieves [its goals] without exertion;
> the next best kind exerts itself without becoming worn out;
> the lowest kind becomes worn out without exerting itself.
> Men of antiquity tasted [the food offered in sacrifice] but did not covet it.
> Men of today covet [the sacrificial food] but do not care about its taste.

## 10.101

The Superior Man does not say,
> "Small [acts of] goodness are not important enough to do" and therefore sets them aside. Small [acts of] goodness accumulate to become great goodness.

[He also does not say],

---

2. Both these lines refer to incidents in which minor errors in protocol led to major military confrontations.

"Small [acts of] misconduct do not do any harm" and therefore does them. Small [acts of] misconduct accumulate to become great misconduct.

For the same reason,
> a pile of feathers can sink a boat;
> lots of light things can break an axle.

Thus the Superior Man observes prohibitions [even] regarding minutiae.

## 10.102

> A single pleasing act is not sufficient to constitute goodness. Accumulate pleasing acts and they become Moral Potency.
> A single hateful act is not sufficient to constitute wrong. Accumulate hateful acts and they will become evil.

Thus
> the [reputation for] goodness of the Three Dynasties [Xia, Shang, and Zhou] [reflects] the accumulated praise of a thousand years;
> the [reputation for] evil of Jie and Djou [reflects] the accumulated condemnation of a thousand years.

## 10.106

The Superior Man is sincere in Humaneness.
> When he acts, it is out of Humaneness;
> when he does not act, it is also out of Humaneness.

The petty man is sincere in his own inhumaneness.
> When he acts, it is out of inhumaneness;
> when he does not act, it is [also] out of inhumaneness.

[Someone whose] goodness comes from the self, rather than coming from others, is [a person] in whom Humaneness and Moral Potency flourish.

Thus,
> if your feelings overcome your desires, you will flourish.
> If your desires overcome your feelings, you will perish.

## 10.111

> Good fortune is born of non-action;
> bad fortune is born of many desires.

> Harm stems from not preparing;
> weeds stem from not hoeing.

Sages do good as if afraid they will not attain it; they prepare against disaster as if afraid they cannot avoid it.

## 10.113

The sage does not seek praise, nor does he avoid condemnation. He corrects his person and acts with rectitude, and the various evils dissipate of their own accord.

Now were he to
> abandon rectitude and follow the crooked,
> turn his back on truth and follow the crowd,

this would be to consort with the vulgar and to internalize acting without standards. Thus the sage reverts to himself and does not take [the lead from others].

# Eleven

## INTEGRATING CUSTOMS

"Integrating Customs" provides the means by which to
> unify the weaknesses and strengths of the various living things,
> equate the customs and habits of the nine Yi [tribes],
> comprehend past and present discourses,
> and thread together the patterns of the myriad things.

[It]
> manages and regulates the suitability of Ritual and Rightness
> and delineates the ends and beginnings of human affairs.

"An Overview of the Essentials" (21.2)

The title of chapter 11, "Qi su," is strongly evocative of the title of chapter 2 of the *Zhuangzi*, the "Qi wu lun" (On Treating All Things as Equal). Because *Qi* means to "bring together," or "to put on a par," the title of chapter 11 of the *Huainanzi* has been translated as "Equalizing Customs" or "Putting Customs on a Par." Indeed, one of the chapter's main themes is the equivalence of all cultural norms through time and space: the ancient rites of the imperial court are not ultimately more normative than the current folkways of "barbarians" living on the fringe of the empire. As the chapter summary just quoted demonstrates, however, the *Huainanzi* evokes further dimensions of the term *qi*. Just as the Way of the *Zhuangzi* does for all things in the universe, the sage of the *Huainanzi* integrates all customs of the world into a dynamic harmony.

"Integrating Customs" is the *Huainanzi*'s focused treatment of the subject of Ritual, a topic that was of urgent importance to statecraft thinkers of the Warring States and early empire. In both ancient Chinese thought and the text of the *Huainanzi*, "Ritual" encompassed all forms of symbolic action from the most austere to the most mundane, ranging from the grand sacrifices of the imperial cult to the small courtesies (such as bowing) that transpired between people at a chance meeting. "Integrating Customs" thus evinces many parallels with the ritual texts of the classical age, especially the *Liji* (*Record of Rites*). The opening lines of "Integrating Customs," for example, echoes the famous dictum of the *Zhong yong* (*Doctrine of the Mean*, chapter 32 of the *Liji*) that "following nature is called the Way." Both the *Liji* and *Huainanzi* were obviously engaged in a contemporaneous discourse about the nature of ritual, although it is not clear which text was the source for the other.

"Integrating Customs" agrees with Confucian texts like the *Liji* that ritual is an indispensable tool for rulers in the current age, but it breaks from them in viewing ritual as having only contingent rather than ultimate value. At one time, there were sages but no rituals. Now, however, ritual has become necessary to the task of government because the Han live in latter days of decline. Moreover, "Integrating Customs" breaks with the *Liji* in insisting that the current power of ritual does not derive from the wisdom of the sages of antiquity but from the penetrating insight of the sage-ruler of today. Only the monarch whose level of cultivation has given him a perfect reading of the patterns of the cosmos and body politic can fashion rituals appropriate to the current cultural and social conditions of the empire.

# Eleven

## 11.1

> Following nature and putting it into practice is called "the Way";
> attaining one's Heaven[-born] nature is called "Potency."
> Only after nature was lost was Humaneness honored;
> only after the Way was lost was Rightness honored.

For this reason,
> when Humaneness and Rightness were established, the Way and Potency receded;
> when Ritual and Music were embellished, purity and simplicity dissipated.
> Right and wrong took form, and the common people were dazzled;
> pearls and jade were revered, and the world set to fighting [over them].

These four were the creations of a declining age and are the implements of a latter age.

> Now Ritual
>> distinguishes the revered and the lowly,
>> differentiates the noble and the base.

Rightness is what unites sovereign and minister, father and son, elder brother and younger brother, husband and wife, friend and friend.

> What the current age considers Ritual [demands] reverence and respect yet [causes] jealousy.
> What it considers Rightness is boastful and condescending yet [is deemed] potent.

126 INTEGRATING CUSTOMS

[Because of them,]
> ruler and minister oppose each other;
> blood kin become resentful of one another.

This is to lose the basis of Ritual and Rightness. Thus [government] is confused and complicated.
> When water accumulates, it generates fish that eat one another;
> when earth accumulates, it generates beasts that [devour] one another's flesh;
> when Ritual and Rightness are embellished, they generate false and hypocritical scholars.
> To blow on ashes yet not to want to get a mote in one's eye,
> to wade through water yet not to want to get soaked:

these [things] are impossible.

In antiquity, the people were naive and ignorant, [and] they did not know west from east. The [expressions on] their faces did not exceed their feelings [within], [and] their words did not outstrip their deeds.
> Their clothes were warm and without pattern;
> their weapons were blunt and had no edge.
> Their songs were joyful yet without warbling;
> their sobbing was mournful yet without shouting.
> They dug wells and drank,
> plowed fields and ate.

They had nothing with which to adorn their beauty, nor did they grasp for acquisitions.
> Kinsmen did not praise or deprecate one another;
> friends did not resent or revere one another.

Upon the creation of Ritual and Rightness and the valuation of goods and wealth, deception and falsehood sprouted, [and] blame and praise proliferated together; resentment and reverence arose in concert. Because of this,
> there was the perfection of Zeng Can and Xiao Ji,
> the perversity of Robber Zhi and Zhuang Qiao.

Thus where there is the Great Chariot and the Dragon Banner, the feathered canopy and hanging straps, teams of horses and columns of riders, there must be the wickedness of drilling [peep]holes and removing crossbars,[1] digging up graves and climbing over walls. Where there are cunning patterns and complex embroidery, fine cloth and gossamer silk, there must be clomping along in straw sandals and those whose short coats have unfinished hems. Thus it is clear that

---

1. These were means to spy on or fraternize with the opposite sex outside marriage.

high and low depend on each other, the short and the long give form to each other.

Now the frog becomes the quail, [and] the water scorpion becomes the dragonfly. These all give rise to what is not of their own kind. Only the sage understands their transformations.

> When the Hu [northern "barbarians"] see hemp, they do not understand that it can be used to make cloth.
> When the Yue [southern "barbarians"] see fleece, they do not know that it can be used to make a [felt] rug.

Thus with one who does not comprehend things, it is difficult to discuss transformation.

In ancient times, Grand Duke Wang and Duke Dan of Zhou met with each other after receiving fiefs.

> Grand Duke Wang asked the Duke of Zhou, "How will you govern Lu?"
> The Duke of Zhou said, "I will exalt the noble and draw close to my kindred."
> The Grand Duke said, "Henceforward Lu will grow weaker!"
> The Duke of Zhou asked the Grand Duke, "How will you govern Qi?"
> The Grand Duke said, "I will raise up the worthy and promote those of merit."
> The Duke of Zhou said, "In later generations, there will certainly be a ruler who rises through assassination."

Afterward, Qi grew daily larger, to the point of becoming hegemon. After twenty-four generations, [the ducal house] was replaced by the Tian clan. Lu grew daily smaller, being destroyed in the thirty-second generation. Thus the *Changes* says,

> "Treading on frost, hard ice descends."

The sages' perception of outcomes at their origin is [truly] subtle! Thus the "mountain of dregs" originated with the use of ivory chopsticks; the "roasting beam" originated with a hot ladle.[2]

## 11.5

If the original nature of human beings is obstructed and sullied, one cannot get at its purity and clarity—it is because things have befouled it. The children of the Qiang, Dii, Bo, and Dee ["barbarians"] all produce the same sounds

---

2. "Mountain of dregs" and "roasting beam" refer to the extravagant feasts given by Tyrant Djou, last king of the Shang dynasty, and the cruel punishments he meted out to his enemies.

at birth. Once they have grown, even with both the *xiang* and *diti* interpreters,[3] they cannot understand one another's speech; this is because their education and customs are different. Now a three-month-old child that moves to a [new] state after it is born will not recognize its old customs. Viewed on this basis, clothing and ritual customs are not [rooted in] people's nature; they are received from without.

> It is the nature of bamboo to float, [but] break it into strips and tie them in a bundle and they will sink when thrown into the water—it [i.e., the bamboo] has lost its [basic] structure.
> 
> It is the nature of metal to sink, [but] place it on a boat and it will float—its positioning lends it support.
> 
> The substance of raw silk is white, [but] dye it in potash and it turns black.
> 
> The nature of fine silk is yellow, [but] dye it in cinnabar and it turns red.

The nature of human beings has no depravity; having been long immersed in customs, it changes. If it changes and one forgets the root, it is as if [the customs one has acquired] have merged with [one's] nature.

Thus

> the sun and the moon are inclined to brilliance, but floating clouds cover them;
> 
> the water of the river is inclined to purity, but sand and rocks sully it.
> 
> The nature of human beings is inclined to equilibrium, but wants and desires harm it.

Only the sage can leave things aside and return to himself.

Someone who boards a boat and becomes confused, not knowing west from east, will see the Dipper and the Pole Star and become oriented. Nature is likewise a Dipper and a Pole Star for human beings.

> If one possesses that by which one can see oneself, then one will not miss the genuine dispositions of things.
> 
> If one lacks that by which one can see oneself, then one will be agitated and ensnared.

It is like swimming in Longxi:[4] the more you thrash, the deeper you will sink.

Confucius said to Yan Hui, "I serve you by forgetting [you], and you also serve me by forgetting [me]. Although it is so, even though you forget me, there

---

3. The *xiang* and *diti* were interpreters employed to facilitate interactions between the Chinese Central States and their "barbarian" neighbors. Their exact functions are unknown.

4. Longxi was a commandery in the northwestern territory of the Han Empire (in present-day Gansu Province). "Swimming in Longxi" evidently was or became a recognizable trope for a dangerous or foolhardy activity, but if there was an antecedent text that helped explain why, it has been lost.

is still something that has not been forgotten that persists."⁵ Confucius understood the root of it.

The actions of one who gives free rein to desires and loses his nature have never been correct.

> Controlling one's person [in this way leads to] danger;
> controlling a state [in this way leads to] chaos;
> leading an army [in this way leads to] destruction.

For this reason, those who have not heard the Way have no means to return to nature. Thus the sage-kings of antiquity were able to attain it in themselves, and their orders were enacted and their prohibitions were binding. Their names were carried down to later ages, [and] their Potency spread throughout the Four Seas.

## 11.6

For this reason, whenever one is about to take up an affair, one must first stabilize one's intentions and purify one's spirit.

> When the spirit is pure and intentions are stable,
> only then can things be aligned.

It is like pressing a seal into clay:

> if it is held straight, [the impression] will be straight;
> if it is held crookedly, [the impression] will be crooked.

Thus

> when Yao chose Shun, he decided simply with his eyes;
> when Duke Huan chose Ning Qi, he judged him simply with his ears.

If on this basis one were to give up technique and measurements and rely on one's ears and eyes, the [resulting] chaos would certainly be great. That the ears and eyes can judge is because one returns to feelings and nature.

> If one's hearing is lost in slander and flattery
> and one's eyes are corrupted by pattern and color,

if one then wants to rectify affairs, it will be difficult.

> One who is suffused with grief will cry upon hearing a song;
> one suffused with joy will see someone weeping and laugh.
> That grief can bring joy
> and laughter can bring grief—

---

5. The meaning here is not completely transparent in either the *Huainanzi* or the parallel passage in the *Zhuangzi*. The sense seems to be that true personal advancement depends on "forgetting" the constituents of individual identity. Thus Confucius teaches best when he forgets Yan Hui, and Hui studies best when he forgets Confucius. What "persists" in the wake of such forgetting is pristine nature, which is merged with the Way.

being suffused makes it so. For this reason, value emptiness.

> When water is agitated, waves rise,
> when the *qi* is disordered, the intellect is confused.
> A confused intellect cannot attend to government;
> agitated water cannot be used to establish a level.

Thus the sage-king holds to the One without losing it, and the genuine dispositions of the myriad things are discovered, the four barbarians and the nine regions all submit. The One is the supremely noble; it has no match in the world. The sage relies on the matchless; thus the mandate of the people attaches itself [to him].

> One who practices Humaneness must discuss it [in terms of] grief and joy;
> one who practices Rightness must explain it [in terms of] grasping and yielding.
> If the human eye does not see beyond ten *li* and one wants to comprehensively reach all people within the [four] seas, grief and joy will not suffice.
> If one does not have the amassed wealth of the world and wants to comprehensively supply the myriad people, [material] benefit cannot be enough.

Moreover, pleasure, anger, grief, and joy arise spontaneously from a stimulus. Thus,

> a cry issues from the mouth,
> tears flow from the eyes—
> all burst forth within
> and take form externally.

It is like

> water flowing downward
> or smoke rising upward:

What compels them? Thus,

> though one who forces oneself to cry feels pain, he does not grieve;
> though one who forces intimacy will laugh, there is no harmony.

Feelings come forth within, and sounds respond externally. Thus,

> the jug of food of Xi Fuji was better than the Chuiji jade of Duke Xian of Jin,
> the bound meat-strips of Zhao Xuanmeng were more worthy than the great bell of Earl Zhi.[6]

---

6. For these anecdotes, see the "Glossary of Personal Names."

Thus [though] ritual may be elaborate, it does not suffice for effecting love, yet a sincere heart can embrace [those at] a great distance.

## 11.8 (in part)

Ritual is the patterning of substance.
Humaneness is the application of kindness.
Thus Rites accord with human feeling and make for them an ordered pattern, and Humaneness bursts forth as a blush that appears in one's countenance.
When Ritual does not surpass substance
and Humaneness does not surpass [the proper degree of ] kindness,
this is the Way of ordering the world.
The three-year mourning period[7] forces a person to what he cannot reach; thus he supplements his feelings with pretense.
The three-month observance breaks off grief, coercing and hacking at nature.
The Confucians and the Mohists do not [find the] origin [of their doctrines] in the beginnings and ends of human feelings and are committed to practicing mutually opposed systems [for] the five grades of observance. Sorrow and grief are contained in feelings; burial and interment correspond to nurturing.
Do not force people to do what they are incapable of;
do not interrupt what people are able to complete.

## 11.9

Rightness is following the patterns and doing what is appropriate;
Ritual is embodying feelings and establishing a design.
Rightness is appropriateness;
Ritual is embodiment.
Of old,
the Youhu clan acted with Rightness and perished; they understood Rightness but did not understand appropriateness.[8]

---

7. The Confucians advocated elaborate mourning rituals extending over twenty-five months, whereas the Mohists advocated simple and austere mourning rituals lasting only three months. The *Huainanzi* criticizes both positions.
8. In legendary times, the Youhu clan rebelled against Qi, son of Yu the Great (tamer of the Great Flood) because they objected to Yu's bequeathing the throne to Qi by hereditary succession. (They contended that he should have followed the example of Yao and Shun and handed over the throne to a virtuous commoner.) The rebellion failed.

Lu instituted Rites and was pared down; they understood Rites but not embodiment.

In the rites of Youyu, the altar was made of earth; sacrifices were to the central eaves; the tombs were one *mu* square; his music was the "Pool of Xian," the "Bearing Clouds," and the "Nine Harmonies." His clothing gave prominence to yellow.

The altar of the lords of Xia was made of pine; they sacrificed to the door [god]; their tombs were walled; and their coffins were shrouded. Their music was the nine movements of the "Pipes of Xia," the "Six Dance Troops," the "Six Lines," and the "Six Blossoms." Their clothes gave prominence to green.

In the rites of the Yin [i.e., Shang], their altar was made of stone; they sacrificed to the gate; [and] their tombs were planted with pines. Their music was the "Great Melody" and "Morning Dew." Their clothing gave prominence to white.

In the rites of the Zhou, their altar was made of chestnut; they sacrificed to the stove; their tombs were planted with cypress; their music was the "Grand Martiality," the "Three Elephants," and the "Beneath the Mulberry." Their clothing gave prominence to red.

Their Ritual and Music were contradictory; their clothes and regulations were opposed; yet none lost the affection [appropriate to] kinship and remoteness, the discipline of superior and inferior. Now to seize on one ruler's methods and statutes while rejecting the customs transmitted from ages [past] is like tuning a *se* and [then] gluing the bridges in place.[9]

Therefore the enlightened ruler clothes himself with rites and propriety [and] girdles himself with discipline and conduct. His clothes suffice

> to cover his frame,
> to follow the ancient canons,
> to accommodate bowing and bending,
> to convenience his body and frame,
> to ease his movement and steps.

He does not strive for an extraordinary or beautiful appearance or a cornered, diagonal cut.

---

9. The syntax of the original text is convoluted, but this seems to be the sense of the metaphor: Chinese zitherlike instruments, such as the twenty-five-string *se*, had wooden bridges that could be moved back and forth along the strings to adjust their pitch. A Three Kingdoms (220–265 C.E.) text contains this anecdote: "A man of Qi went to a man of Zhao to study the *se*. He relied on [the teacher] to first tune it, then glued the bridges in place and went home. For three years, he could not play a single melody."

His belt suffices
> to tie a knot and gather the flaps,
> to bind tightly and cinch fast.

He feels no urgency that [it be made of] round and square patterned [embroidery].

Thus he institutes Rites and Rightness; he acts with utmost Moral Potency, but he is not fixated on the Confucians and the Mohists.

# Twelve

## RESPONSES OF THE WAY

"Responses of the Way"
    picks out and draws together the relics of past affairs,
    pursues and surveys the traces of bygone antiquity,
    and investigates the reversals of bad and good fortune, benefit and harm.
    It tests and verifies them according to the techniques of Lao and Zhuang,
    thus matching them to the trajectories of gain and loss.
                           "An Overview of the Essentials" (21.2)

This chapter describes the qualities of the ideal ruler through fifty-six anecdotes, each capped with a citation from the *Laozi* that supports the anecdote's didactic claims. These anecdotes and many others of the same kind appear to have circulated in various forms (written, oral, or both) during the Warring States and Han periods and may be considered a distinctive genre of early Chinese prose. Those collected in "Responses of the Way" contain everything from recondite accounts of mystical wandering to moralizing speeches, ethical prescriptions, and practical political counsel. They illustrate how the Way can be understood by the ruler and be used to ensure the success and prosperity of his reign. The *Laozi* here is vested with canonical authority, showing how the anecdotes should be interpreted so as to support the vision of empire and sage-rulership promoted in the *Huainanzi* more generally.

As is true of several other chapters of the *Huainanzi* consisting of many short sections (for example, chapters 10, 14, 16, 17, and 18), "Responses of the Way" begins with an establishing anecdote that sets the theme for the chapter as a whole. Section 12.1 features short dialogues between Grand Purity and Inexhaustible, Non-action and Non-beginning, concerning the nature of the Way. These dialogues affirm the ineffable unity of the Way and are reinforced by two quotations from the *Laozi*. The first states that "when all the world recognizes good as good, there is ill," and the second is the famous affirmation that "those who know do not speak; those who speak do not know." The reader thus is prepared to read the following anecdotes as a discourse on the nature of the Way, with interpretations backed by the authority of the *Laozi*.

These anecdotes depict crucial moments and dilemmas in a wide range of political contexts, discussing the principles to be implemented and attributes to be embodied by the ideal ruler to ensure the success of his regime. As is true of the *Huainanzi* generally, this chapter draws on and synthesizes a wide range of philosophical principles and political techniques. The ideal ruler depicted here is not only a self-cultivated Daoist sage but also a compassionate moralist and a hard-headed realist. Filtered through the lens of the *Laozi*, these anecdotes illustrate the applicability of the Way to a variety of human affairs.

# Twelve

### 12.1

Grand Purity asked Inexhaustible, "Do you know the Way?"
Inexhaustible responded, "I don't know it."
[Grand Purity] then asked Non-action, "Do *you* know the Way?'
Non-action replied, "I know it."
[Grand Purity said,] "Does this Way that you know have norms?"
Non-action responded, "Yes, the Way that I know has norms."
[Grand Purity] inquired, "What are the norms, then?"
Non-action responded, "The Way that I know

> can be weak or strong;
> it can be soft or hard;
> it can be yin or yang;
> it can be dark or bright;
> it can embrace or contain Heaven and Earth;
> it can respond to or await the Limitless.

These are the norms by which I know the Way."

Grand Purity then asked Non-beginning, "Earlier, I asked Inexhaustible about the Way and Inexhaustible replied, 'I don't know it.' I then asked Non-action and Non-action responded, 'I know it.' So I asked him, 'Does this Way that you know have norms?' Non-action then responded, 'Yes, the Way that I know has norms.' When I asked him whether he could [name] the norms, he responded, 'I know that the Way

> can be weak or strong;
> it can be soft or hard;
> it can be yin or yang;
> it can be dark or bright;
> it can embrace or contain Heaven and Earth;
> it can respond to or await the Limitless.

These are the norms by which I know the Way.' This being so, between Inexhaustible's not knowing and Non-action's knowing, which is right and which is wrong?"

Non-beginning answered,

> "Not knowing it is deep while knowing it is shallow;
> not knowing it is internal while knowing it is external;
> not knowing it is refined while knowing it is coarse."

Grand Purity then gazed up at the heavens and said with a long sigh,

> "Then is not knowing, in fact, knowing?
> And is knowing, in fact, not knowing?
> Who knows that knowing it is not knowing
> and that not knowing it is knowing?"

Non-beginning responded,

> "The Way cannot be heard, for what is heard is not the Way;
> the Way cannot be seen, for what is seen is not the Way;
> the Way cannot be spoken, for what is spoken is not the Way.
> Who knows the formlessness of what gives form to form?

Therefore the *Laozi* says:

> "When all the world recognizes good as good,
> there is ill."

Therefore

> those who know do not speak;
> those who speak do not know.

## 12.3

Huizi drafted the state laws on behalf of King Hui [of Wei]. When he had completed them, he showed them to the elders, all of whom praised them. He then submitted them to King Hui. King Hui was elated by them and showed them to Zhai Jian. Zhai Jian exclaimed, "Excellent."

King Hui inquired, "Since they are excellent, can we implement them?"

Zhai Jian responded, "We cannot."

King Hui then asked, "If they are excellent, why can we not implement them?"

Zhai Jian answered, "Now take those who haul heavy logs: those in front call, 'Heave!' while those behind respond, 'Ho!' This is a chant to encourage the strength of those who haul heavy loads. Could it really be that they do not know either the melodies of Zheng and Wey or the [tune called] 'Whirling Chu'? Although they know such melodies, they do not use them because they do not suit the circumstance as well as this chant does. Governing a state is a matter of ritual and not a matter of literary eloquence." Therefore the *Laozi* says:

"The more detailed the laws and edicts,
the more thieves and robbers there are."

This is what is meant here.

## 12.5

When the Duke of Bo won possession of the state of Jing [i.e., Chu], he could not [bring himself to] distribute among the people the grain [kept in] the storehouses. On the seventh day [after the conquest], Shi Qi entered [the capital] and said [to the Duke of Bo]: "You obtained this wealth through unrighteous means. Moreover, you could not [bring yourself to] share it. Calamity is sure to arrive. If you are incapable of giving [this wealth] to the people, it would be best to burn it so as not to give them cause to harm us." The Duke of Bo did not heed his advice.

On the ninth day [after the conquest], the Duke of She entered [the capital]. He brought out the goods from the Supreme Storehouse in order to distribute them to the multitudes. He then removed the weapons from the Lofty Repository in order to distribute them to the common people. Thereafter he attacked the Duke of Bo, and on the nineteenth day [after the conquest] he captured him.

To desire the state when one does not yet possess it may be called the utmost avarice. To be incapable of acting on behalf of others, not to mention being incapable of acting on behalf of oneself, may be called utmost foolishness. How is the Duke of Bo's stinginess any different from the cannibal owl's love for its offspring? Therefore the *Laozi* says:

"Rather than holding it upright and filling it to the brim,
better to have stopped in time.
Hammer it to a point,
and the sharpness cannot be preserved forever."

## 12.8

Viscount Xiang of Zhao dispatched an attacking force against [the "barbarian" state of] Dee and defeated it. When the inhabitants of [the two cities of] Zuo and Zhong had been captured, a messenger arrived to report the victory to Viscount Xiang, who was just about to eat his meal. When Viscount Xiang heard the news, an anxious expression appeared on his face. His attendants asked: "Capturing two cities in one morning is a cause for celebration. Why, then, do you appear so anxious?"

Viscount Xiang replied: "The swelling of the Yangzi and Yellow rivers does not last more than three days; wild winds and violent rains do not last a morning; the sun at high noon lasts for less than a moment. Now the virtuous conduct of the Zhao clan has not yet amounted to anything, and yet in one morning two cities have been captured. Our demise is imminent!"

When Confucius heard about this, he said: "The Zhao clan will surely prosper!"

> Anxiety leads to prosperity;
> happiness leads to ruin.

Winning is not difficult, but preserving victory presents real challenges. The worthy ruler relies on his sense of anxiety to preserve victory, and so his good fortune extends to his descendants. The states of Qi, Chu, Wu, and Yue all were victorious for a time, yet eventually their rulers were captured and ruined because they did not understand how to preserve victory. Only the ruler who possesses the Way can preserve victory. Confucius had enough strength to draw back the bolted gate of the capital, but he did not want to become known for his strength. Mozi engaged in defensive warfare that forced Gongshu Ban to submit to him, yet Mozi did not want to be known as a warrior. Those who are skilled at preserving victory consider their strength as weakness.

Therefore the *Laozi* says:
> "The Way is empty,
> yet when you use it, you need not refill it."

## 12.13

Marquis Wu of Wei asked Li Ke: "Why did the state of Wu perish?"

Li Ke responded: "Countless battles and countless victories."

Marquis Wu retorted: "But countless battles and countless victories are the good fortune of the state and its ruling family. How could such things be the sole cause of Wu's downfall?"

Li Ke replied:
> "With countless battles, the populace grows exhausted;
> with countless victories, the ruler grows arrogant.

Rare indeed is the state that does not perish when an arrogant ruler governs an exhausted populace!

Arrogance leads to recklessness, and recklessness depletes material resources.

Exhaustion leads to resentment, and resentment drives the people to their wits' end.

Given that both superior and subordinate were depleted, the demise of Wu appears to have occurred rather late. This is why King Fuchai [of Wu] took his own life after [his defeat at the battle of] Gansui."

Therefore the *Laozi* says:

> "To withdraw when merit is achieved and reputation established is
> the Way of Heaven."

## 12.18

Duke Huan [of Qi] was reading in the upper part of his hall while Wheelwright Flat was hewing a wheel in the lower part. Setting aside his hammer and chisel, the wheelwright asked Duke Huan, "I venture to ask what books you are reading?"

"The books of the sages," said the duke.

"Are the sages still alive?"

"They already are dead," said the duke.

"Then what you are reading are merely the lees and dregs of the sages."

Flushing in anger, Duke Huan replied, "How dare you, a wheelwright, presume to criticize the books I am reading? If you can explain yourself, all right. If you cannot explain yourself, you shall die."

"Yes, I can explain. I will put it in terms of my occupation as a wheelwright," said Wheelwright Flat. "If [the blows of the mallet] are too hard, [the chisel] will bite and not budge; if they are too gentle, [the chisel] will slide and not take hold. To make the chisel neither slide nor stick is something you can sense with your hand and feel with your heart. Then you can get it down to the utmost subtlety. But I have not been able to teach it to my son, and my son has not been able to learn it from me. That's why I am an old man still hewing wheels after sixty years. Now what the sages have said contains some truth, but since they are dead and long gone, all that remains is the lees and dregs [of their teachings]."

Therefore the *Laozi* says:

> "The Way that can be spoken
> is not the constant Way;
> the Name that can be named
> is not the constant Name."

## 12.19

Previously, when Sicheng Zihan acted as minister to the state of Song, he said to the lord of Song, "The danger or safety of this state and the orderliness or disorderliness of its people depend on how you execute rewards and punishments. Now the gifts of rank and reward are what the people love—these you should carry out personally. The punishments of execution and mutilation are what the people hate—may I ask that I administer them?"

The lord of Song responded: "Excellent! I will enjoy the peoples' praises while you will suffer their resentments. This way I'll be sure to know how to avoid being the laughingstock of the Lords of the Land."

The lord of Song then carried out the rewards while Zihan [implemented] the punishments. When the people of the state came to understand that the regulations concerning executions and amputations rested solely with Zihan, the grand ministers of state treated him with affection, and the hundred surnames [i.e., the common people] feared him. Before a year had passed, Zihan had murdered the lord of Song and usurped his government. Therefore the *Laozi* says:

> "The fish must not be allowed to leave the deep;
> the efficacious instruments of state must not be revealed to anyone."

## 12.24

Viscount Jian of Zhao died and had not yet been buried when the people of Zhongmou shifted their allegiance to the state of Qi. When Viscount Jian of Zhao had been buried for five days, Viscount Xiang [his son] raised troops to attack and encircle them. The encirclement was not yet complete, when a one-hundred-foot section of the city wall suddenly crumbled. Viscount Xiang then beat the gong and withdrew his troops. An official of his army remonstrated with him, saying, "When you were punishing the crimes of Zhongmou, its city walls crumbled. This is a sign that Heaven supports us. Why, then, should we abandon the attack?"

Viscount Xiang replied, "I heard that Shuxiang once said: 'A Superior Man does not impose on others when they profit, nor does he attack others in distress.' Let the people of Zhongmou repair their walls. Only when the walls have been repaired, will we attack them." When the people of Zhongmou heard of the viscount's [sense of] justice, they asked to surrender.

Therefore the *Laozi* says:

> "Now,
> it is because he alone does not contend
> that no one can contend with him."

## 12.31

When Duke Wen of Jin attacked the city of Yuan, he agreed with his grand ministers on [a period of] three days [to capture the city]. When three days passed and Yuan did not surrender, Duke Wen ordered a retreat. A military officer said: "Yuan is sure to surrender in another day or two."

The ruler responded: "I did not realize that it would not be possible to defeat Yuan in three days and so agreed with the grand ministers on [a period of] three days to capture the city of Yuan. Now if we do not end this campaign, even though the designated time has elapsed, it would mean forfeiting my trustworthiness to obtain Yuan. I will not do it."

When the people of Yuan heard about this, they said: "With a ruler like this, how could we refuse to surrender?" They promptly surrendered. When the people of Wen heard about this, they also asked to surrender.

Therefore the *Laozi* says:

> "How dim! How obscure!
> Yet within it is the Quintessence.
> This essence is profoundly genuine,
> for what lies within is trustworthy.
> Therefore beautiful words can buy honor,
> [but] beautiful deeds can raise a man above others."

## 12.36

King Cheng [of Zhou] questioned Yin Yi about governing. "What kind of virtuous conduct will inspire the people to feel affection for their ruler?" he asked.

Yin Yi replied: "Employ them according to the proper seasons. Treat them with respect and compliance."

King Cheng inquired: "To what extent should one practice such things?"

Yin Yi responded: "Practice them as if you were facing a deep abyss or treading on thin ice."

King Cheng said: "How frightening to be a king!"

Yin Yi replied: "Those between Heaven and Earth and within the Four Seas who are good are loved by the people; those who are not good are despised by the people. In ancient times, the subjects of the Shang and Xia reversed their allegiances; they came to despise [the tyrants] Jie and Djou and submitted to the rulership of Kings Tang and Wu. The people of Susha all took it upon themselves to attack their lord and shift their allegiance to the Divine Farmer. Such things are well understood in our age. How could you not be frightened!"

Therefore the *Laozi* says:

"What others fear
you also must fear."

## 12.41

The queen consort of the king of Qi died. The king wanted to appoint a new queen consort but had not yet decided who it would be, so he directed his ministers to deliberate the issue. The Duke of Xue, hoping to discover the king's choice, presented him with ten pairs of earrings, one of which was especially beautiful. The next morning he asked about the whereabouts of the most beautiful pair of earrings and urged that the woman who now had them should be appointed queen consort. The king of Qi was delighted by this and thereafter respected and valued the Duke of Xue even more. Thus, if the intentions and desires of the lord are visible on the outside, he will fall subject to the control of his underlings.

Therefore the *Laozi* says:
"Block the openings,
shut the doors,
and all your life you will not labor."

## 12.43

Mizi had governed Shanfu for three years when Wuma Qi changed his appearance by wearing tattered clothes and a short hemp jacket so that he could [secretly] observe what transformations had taken place there. He saw a night fisherman catch a fish and let it go. Wuma Qi asked him: "You sir, being a fisherman, want to catch fish. Why then do you catch them and let them go?"

The fisherman replied: "Mizi does not want us to catch small fish. Since all the fish I caught were small ones, I let them go."

Wuma Qi returned home and reported his findings to Confucius: "Mizi is the most Morally Potent of all! He is able to inspire people to conduct themselves in the dark of the night as if they were facing a strict punishment for their actions. How is Master Mi able to achieve such things?"

Confucius replied: "I, Qiu, once asked him about governing. He replied, 'Sincerity in this takes shape in that.' Mizi must be practicing this technique."

Therefore the *Laozi* says:
"He discards that and takes this."

# Thirteen

## BOUNDLESS DISCOURSES

"Boundless Discourses" provides the means by which to
    stitch up the spaces in ragged seams and hems
    and plug up the gaps in crooked and chattering teeth.[1]
    It welcomes the straightforward and straightens out the devious,
    in order to extend the Original Unhewn and thereby anticipate
    the alternations of success and failure
    and the reversals of benefit and harm.
It is what enables you to
    not be foolishly immersed in the advantages of political power,
    not be seductively confused by the exigencies of affairs,
    and so tally with constancy and change
    to link up and discern timely and generational alterations,
and extend and adjust [your policies] in accordance with transformations.
                      "An Overview of the Essentials" (21.2)

Using numerous examples, "Boundless Discourses" shows that change has always been a part of human history, from remote antiquity to the present

---

1. "Ragged seams and hems" and "gaps in crooked and chattering teeth" are metaphors for the various shortcomings of the age, the consequences of persistent decline from the primordial era of sage-rulership.

day. It argues that successful rulers do not resist change in a futile attempt to uphold the policies and standards of the past but instead modify their actions to suit changing customs and circumstances. Sages, on whom rulers are urged to model themselves, are portrayed as having a unique insight that allows them to see the enduring reality behind superficial qualities. That, in turn, enables them to adapt to change and to innovate while following diverse strategies to realize the Way under varying circumstances.

The vision of primordial antiquity presented here is somewhat different from that found in chapter 8, "The Basic Warp." In that chapter, the society of the remote past is presented as a kind of communitarian ideal that, regrettably but inevitably, is no longer available to us in more complicated modern times. Chapter 13, in contrast, acknowledges that primitive society was peaceful and innocent but also describes it as poor, inconvenient, and dangerous. Therefore, to ease the lives of the people, the sages contrived inventions: houses, agricultural implements, and much more. Chapters 8 and 13 do agree, however, that every change begets more change and that the ruler's role is managing change and adapting to new circumstances.

As is true of many chapters in the *Huainanzi*, and in keeping with the text's claim for itself, this chapter draws on a wide range of earlier texts and intellectual lineages to create its own distinctive synthesis. Of particular importance to its emphasis on the inevitability of change are the *Mozi* and the *Hanfeizi*, both of which affirm that not only is it impossible to return to the simple ways of the remote past but if it were possible, it still would not be desirable. This underscores the basic stance of the *Huainanzi* as a whole: that it is a practical blueprint for successful government in its own time.

# Thirteen

### 13.1

In ancient times, those who wore [plain] caps and [simple] rolled collars ruled the world. Their Potency was of life, not death, of giving, not usurping. None in the world rejected their service; all embraced their Potency. In those times,
> yin and yang were harmonious and tranquil;
> the winds and rains were timely and moderate.
> The myriad things prospered and flourished;
> nests of birds and owls could be inspected on bended knee;
> wild animals could be ensnared and kept compliant.

What need was there for official costumes, wide sashes, buckled collars, grand insignia?

### 13.2

In ancient times, the people lived in humid lands, hollowing out caves again and again.
> In the winters, they could not bear the frost, the snow, the fog, the dew;
> in the summers, they could not bear the oppressive heat, the sultry days, the mosquitoes, the flies.

The sages therefore created for them the pounding of earth and the cutting of trees to make houses. Above they placed ridgepoles, and below they placed rafters

to protect against the winds and rain
and to keep out the cold and heat.
The common people were put at ease.

Bo Yu was the first to make clothing. He spun the hemp, working the warp with his hand, suspending it through his fingers, and forming it like netting. Later generations [of sages] made looms for doubled weaves to increase their usefulness. The people were thus able to protect their bodies and drive off the cold.

In ancient times, [the people]
sharpened sticks to plow,
polished clam shells to weed,
cut firewood to make fuel,
and hauled jars to draw water.

The people labored, but their gains were few. Later generations [of sages] made them plows, plowshares, and hoes; axes for cutting firewood; and well sweeps for drawing water. The people were at ease, [and] their gains multiplied.

In ancient times, the great rivers and famed waterways cut across the roads and impeded the comings and goings of the people. Consequently, [the sages] hollowed logs and squared timbers to make rafts and boats. Therefore, according to a place's circumstances of plenty or dearth, things could be exchanged and transported.

They made shoes from hides and traversed a thousand *li*,
they endured the labor of carrying loads on their backs.

[The sages] thus created for them
the bending [of wood] into wheels and the constructing of carts,
the hitching of horses and the yoking of oxen.

The people could thus go great distances without tiring.

Since ferocious beasts would injure people and there was nothing with which to stop them, [the sages] created for them the casting of metal and the forging of iron to make weapons and arms. The animals could harm them no more.

Thus,
pressed by difficulties, [the sages] searched for what was advantageous;
bound by adversity, they created what was necessary.

In each case, the people used what they had come to know [from the sages]
to eliminate what harmed them
and to seek what benefited them.

If the unchanging past cannot be followed, if the martial implements [of the past] cannot be relied on, then there will be [occasions when] the laws and standards of the former kings must be adjusted to changing [circumstances].

## 13.6

In antiquity,
> the people were pure, the artisans skillful,
> the merchants straightforward, the women simple.

This is why
> governance and education were easily transformed [in response to circumstances],
> and habits and customs were easily adjusted [to suit changing times].

In the present age, Moral Potency is declining more and more, and the customs of the people are becoming more and more stingy. Wanting to use straightforward and simple laws to put in order a people already corrupted is like wanting to control a horse without a bit and a whip.

In ancient times, the Divine Farmer used no regulations or commands, yet the people followed. Tang [i.e., Yao] and Yu [i.e., Shun] had regulations and commands but no punishments.

> The Xia used no false words;
> the Shang made oaths;
> the Zhou made covenants.

When one comes down to the present time, people accept shame and think lightly of being disgraced; they value taking and belittle giving. Wanting to use the way of the Divine Farmer to put things in order would only make chaos inevitable. When Bocheng Zigao resigned from being a Lord of the Land and simply tilled the fields, the world exalted him. Now, those who resign from office and become hermits occupy the bottom [rung] of their locales. How can this be considered the same?

The armies of antiquity had bows and swords; their lances had no sharp points; their halberds, no tips.

The armies of the later ages have siege weapons and battering rams with which to attack, spiked balls with which to defend, arrays of crossbows with which to shoot, and iron chariots with which to fight.

When states fought in ancient times, they did not kill the young, [and] they did not capture the old.

What in antiquity was proper is today laughable; what was taken to be honorable in antiquity is taken to be disgraceful today; what was taken to be order in antiquity is taken to be chaos today.

Now,
> the Divine Farmer and Fuxi did not give out rewards and punishments,
> yet the people did no wrong; but those who govern [today] are unable to dispense with laws and rule the people.

> Shun grasped a shield and axe and brought the Miao rulers to submission, yet those who lead campaigns [today] are unable to use arms to reduce the violence.

Looking at the issue from this perspective, it is clear that laws and standards are the means to assess the customs of the people and regulate relaxation and work; instruments and implements accord with the alterations of the times and are regulated to fit what is suitable. Now,

> the sages created laws and the myriad people were regulated by them;
> the worthies established rituals and the ignorant were restrained by them.
> [But] people who are regulated by laws cannot propose far-reaching initiatives;
> those who are restrained by rituals cannot effect responsive alterations.
> An ear that does not know the difference between high and low [tones] cannot order tunes and notes;
> a mind that does not understand the source of order and disorder cannot impose regulations and laws.

It is necessary to have

> an ear that uniquely hears,
> discernment that uniquely sees;

for only then can you take personal responsibility for implementing the Way.

> Now,
> the Yin replaced the Xia;
> the Zhou replaced the Yin;
> the Spring and Autumn period replaced the Zhou.

The rites of the Three Dynasties were not the same. Why should antiquity be followed?

## 13.13

When [a ruler] causes the world to be desolate and chaotic,

> Rites and Rightness are cut off;
> bonds and ties are dispensed with.
> The strong take advantage of the weak;
> attackers force the submission of the vanquished;
> minister and ruler lack hierarchical distinction;
> the noble and the humble lack deferential order;
> armor and helmets become infested with lice and fleas;
> swallows and sparrows roost in the tents and canopies;

so that the soldiers never get any rest. At that point, he may begin to adopt a cautious demeanor and [conduct] reverent rites, but [it will be too late and] he will invariably be destroyed with no possibility of being restored.

When [a ruler causes] the world to be secure and peaceful,
> administration and instruction are harmonious and equitable;
> the one hundred names [i.e., the common people] are reverent and affable;
> superiors and subordinates are mutually affectionate.

At that point, [the ruler] might begin to establish an atmosphere of leniency. [If so,] he will embolden the courageous and strong and so will be unable to avoid falling subject to the laws of those who have authority.

For this reason,
> sages can be yin, and they can be yang;
> they can be weak, and they can be strong;
> in tempo with the times, they are active or still;
> in accordance with the inner substance of things, they establish merit.
> When things become active, they know their reversions;
> when affairs sprout forth, they anticipate their alterations;
> when things transform, they act in their image;
> when things move, they respond to them;

this is why to the end of their days, they are effective and free of troubles.

## 13.20

With regard to actions,
> there are some that you want to carry out, but circumstances warrant that you abandon them;
> there are some that you want to avoid, but circumstances warrant that you pursue them.

There was a man of Chu who boarded a boat and encountered a typhoon. The waves were upon him, and in his fright he threw himself into the water. It is not that he did not covet life and fear death but that sometimes in fearing death, you commit the contradiction of being forgetful of your life. Thus human lusts and desires are also like this.

Among the people of Qi was someone who stole gold. Just when the market was most crowded, he arrived, grabbed it, and fled. When held by force and asked: "Why did you steal gold from the market?" He responded: "I did not see anyone, I only saw gold." When the mind is preoccupied with desires, it forgets what it does. For this reason, sages
> scrutinize the alterations of movement and rest,
> accord with the due measures of receiving and giving,
> order the feelings of liking and loathing,
> and harmonize with the occasions of happiness and anger.

When [the distinctions of] movement and rest are attained, calamities will not be encountered;
> when receiving and giving are in accord, crimes will not accumulate;
> when liking and loathing are ordered, anxiety will not come near;
> when happiness and anger are in [proper] occasion, resentment will not encroach.

Thus, those who have achieved the Way are not indifferent to obtaining [things] but are not ravenous for wealth;
> what they have, they do not abandon,
> but what they do not have, they do not seek.
> They are constantly full but not overflowing;
> they persevere in emptiness but are easily satisfied.

Now the rain that drips from the eaves is sufficient to fill to overflowing a *hu* vessel, but the waters of the Yangzi and Yellow Rivers cannot fill a leaking *zhi* cup.[1] Thus the human heart is like this. If you make yourself conform to the Techniques of the Way in measurement and limitation, food will fill the emptiness; clothes will block the cold; and it will suffice to care for the body of one seven feet tall.[2] But if you lack the Techniques of the Way in measurement and limitation and try to practice restraint and moderation on your own, the positional advantage of ten thousand chariots will not suffice to make you honored, and all the wealth in the world will not suffice to make you happy.

---

1. A *hu* is a large storage vessel, and a *zhi* is a small drinking cup.
2. A Han "foot" (*chi*) was about nine inches long, so, in modern terms a person "seven feet tall" in Han measure would have been about five feet, three inches.

# Fourteen

## SAYINGS EXPLAINED

"Sayings Explained" provides the means by which to
> compare through analogy the tenets of human affairs
> and elucidate through illustration the substance of order and disorder.
> It ranks the hidden meanings of subtle sayings,
> explaining them with literary expressions that reflect ultimate principles.
> Thus it patches up and mends deficiencies due to errors and oversights.
>
> — "An Overview of the Essentials" (21.2)

"Sayings Explained" is a collection of gnomic sayings (set off in italics in our text), most of which are followed by a few lines of commentary that explicate and clarify their significance. Although at first glance, the sayings and explications may seem to be merely conventional statements of received wisdom, taken as a whole they recapitulate and reinforce important concepts and themes addressed elsewhere in the *Huainanzi*: What are the essential attributes of the sage? How does the sage bring order to his intrinsic self and, by extension, to the world? The sayings collected in this chapter address these central concerns, and the truths they are intended to express are explained through various analogies and illustrations.

Many, perhaps most, of the sayings collected here would have been familiar to educated people in the early Han, as analogous passages can be found in a wide range of earlier texts. The distinctive contribution of the *Huananzi*'s treatment of these sayings lies in the explications, which consistently address the attributes of sage-rulership and how they may be attained through self-cultivation. The sayings and explications depict several ideal human types that illustrate what a sage-ruler can and should be. The Genuine Person embodies a pristine, primeval time before the emergence of time, when there was perfect unity. He identifies completely with the Grand One—that is, the divine embodiment of primal nondifferentiation. The Sage is fundamentally, although not exclusively, associated with the empty, nameless, formless, non-active, non-striving, nonintervening attributes of the Way. His ability to embody these aspects of the Way empowers him to sustain an inner equanimity in his person and a harmonious unity in his governance. Thus in ordering his person, the sage avoids the various external distractions that can entangle the mind and disturb the nature. In ruling, the sage's qualities enable him to have to suffer neither the malice of his underlings nor the resentment of the common people. The Superior Man is more deeply engaged with the differentiated world of affairs but nevertheless rises above petty concerns. The Genuine Person, the Sage, and the Superior Man all have profound lessons to teach real-world rulers about the nature and practice of rulership.

# Fourteen

## 14.1

Cavernous and undifferentiated Heaven and Earth, chaotic and inchoate Uncarved Block, not yet created and fashioned into things: this we call the "Grand One." Together emerging from this unity, so that each acquired its distinctive qualities, there were birds, there were fish, there were animals: this we call the "differentiation of things."

Regions became distinguished according to their categories;

things became differentiated according to their groupings.

Their natures and destinies were dissimilar; all acquired their physical forms in the realm of "Being."

Separate and not interconnected, differentiated as the myriad things, none could return to their Ancestor. Thus,

when animated, things are said to be alive;

when dead, things are said to be expired.

In both cases, they are things. It is not that there was nothing that made things into things; rather, what made things into things is not among the myriad things.

In antiquity, at the Grand Beginning, human beings came to life in "Nonbeing" and acquired a physical form in "Being." Having a physical form, [human beings] came under the control of things. But those who can return to that from which they were born, as if they had not yet acquired a physical form, are called the "Genuine." The Genuine are those who have not yet begun to differentiate from the Grand One.

## 14.2

*The sage*
>*does not for the sake of a name become a corpse;*
>*does not for the sake of stratagems store things up;*
>*does not for the sake of affairs take on responsibility;*
>*does not for the sake of wisdom become a ruler.*

[The sage]
>dwells in the Formless,
>moves in the Traceless,
>and wanders in the Beginningless.
>He does not initiate things for the sake of good fortune,
>nor does he begin things to deal with misfortune.
>He remains in Emptiness and Non-being
>and moves when he cannot do otherwise.
>For those who desire good fortune, sometimes suffer misfortune,
>and those who desire benefit, sometimes suffer harm.

Thus,
>those who are secure through non-action become endangered when they lose that by which they are secure [i.e., non-action].
>Those who are well ordered through nonintervention become disordered when they lose that by which they are well ordered.

## 14.5

*Those who trust themselves cannot be swayed by slander or flattery.*
*Those whose knowledge is sufficient cannot be enticed by power or profit.*

Thus,
>those who fully comprehend the genuine qualities of their nature do not strive to accomplish what their nature cannot accomplish.
>Those who fully comprehend the genuine qualities of their destiny do not concern themselves with what their destiny cannot control.

For those who fully comprehend the Way, things are not enough to disorder their inner harmony.

## 14.8

*Trace to the source Heaven's decree,*
*cultivate the techniques of the mind,*
*regulate likes and dislikes,*
*follow your disposition and nature,*
*and the Way of governing [oneself] will come through.*

> If you trace to the source Heaven's decree, you will not be deluded by bad or good fortune.
> If you cultivate the techniques of the mind, you will not be unrestrained in your happiness and anger.
> If you regulate your likes and dislikes, you will not covet what is useless.
> If you follow your disposition and nature, your desires will not exceed the appropriate limits.
> If you are not deluded by bad or good fortune, your movement and stillness will comply with the inherent principles of things.
> If you are not unrestrained in your happiness and anger, your rewards and punishments will not be partial.
> If you do not covet what is useless, you will not allow your desires to harm your nature.
> If your desires do not exceed the appropriate limits, you will nurture your nature and know contentment.

As a general rule, these four things cannot be sought after in what is outside the self nor can you bestow them on others. You can obtain them only by returning to the self.

## 14.9

*The world*
> *cannot be acted on by knowledge;*
> *cannot be discerned through perceptiveness;*
> *cannot be governed by intervening;*
> *cannot be subjugated through humaneness;*
> *and cannot be vanquished through strength.*

These five are all aspects of human talent. If your Potency does not flourish, you will not be able to perfect even one of them. Where Potency is established, these five will not be endangered. But where these five appear, Potency will not be established.

Thus,
> if you grasp the Way, stupidity will be more than sufficient;
> if you lose the Way, knowledge will be insufficient to the task.

## 14.11

> *The root of governance lies in bringing security to the people.*
> *The root of bringing security to the people lies in using them sufficiently.*
> *The root of using them sufficiently lies in not taking them from their seasonal tasks.*
> *The root of not taking them from their seasonal tasks lies in decreasing what they need to attend to.*
> *The root of decreasing what they need to attend to lies in moderating their desire.*
> *The root of moderating their desire lies in returning to their nature.*
> *The root of returning to their nature lies in eradicating [what] burdens [their mind].*

If you eradicate [what] burdens [their mind], they will become empty. Being empty, they will become balanced.
> Balance is the beginning of the Way.
> Emptiness is the abode of the Way.

## 14.17

> *If you disregard the Way and rely on knowledge, invariably you will be endangered.*
> *If you abandon technique and employ talent, invariably you will encounter difficulties.*
> *There have been those who perished because their desires were numerous;*
> *there have never been those who were endangered because they were free from desires.*
> *There have been those who desired order but suffered disorder;*
> *there have never been those who preserved what is constant and yet lost their state.*

Thus,
> while knowledge [alone] will not suffice for you to avoid trouble,
> stupidity [alone] will not suffice to jeopardize your peace.
> If you preserve these distinctions

and act in accordance with these principles,
when you lose, you will not feel vexed,
and when you succeed, you will not feel happy.
For when you accomplish something, it is not because you have acted deliberately,
and when you acquire something, it is not because you have sought after something.
What you receive, you take without [consciously] accepting;
what you give, you confer without [consciously] distributing.
If you [nourish] life in accordance with spring,
and you kill in accordance with autumn,
those to whom you grant life will not view you as exerting Moral Potency,
and those whom you subject to death will not view you as expressing anger.
[Thus] you will have come close to the Way.

## 14.18

*The sage does not do things that are wrong*
*yet does not hate those who do wrong to him.*
*He cultivates Moral Potency worthy of praise*
*yet does not seek the praise of others.*
*He cannot prevent ill fortune from arising*
*yet trusts that he personally will not summon it.*
*He cannot assure that good fortune will invariably befall him*
*yet trusts that he personally will not yield to it.*

[Thus,]
if misfortune befalls him, because it is not something he sought to bring about, should he fail, he feels no anxiety.
If good fortune befalls him, because it is not something he sought to bring about, should he succeed, he feels no pride.
He knows that what determines bad and good fortune is beyond his control.
Thus, he is joyful abiding at his leisure and governs through non-action.

## 14.22

*The sage has no conscious deliberations;*
*he has no fixed ideas.*

> *He neither welcomes what arrives*
> *nor sends off what departs.*
> *Though others occupy positions north, south, east, and west,*
> *he alone is established at the center.*

Thus, he encounters various crooked ways, but he does not lose his rectitude; the world flows to and fro, but he alone does not leave his [ancestral] shrine and walled city.

Thus,
> he does not encourage what he likes,
> nor does he avoid what he dislikes;

he simply follows Heaven's Way.
> He does not initiate,
> nor does he personally assume authority;

he simply complies with Heaven's Principles.
> He does not make plans in advance,
> nor does he miss the opportune moment;

he simply complies with Heaven's Times.
> He does not seek to obtain things,
> nor does he shun good fortune;

he simply goes along with Heaven's Patterns.
> He does not seek after what he does not possess,
> nor does he lose what he has obtained.
> Inwardly he experiences no unexpected misfortune;
> outwardly he experiences no unexpected good fortune.

Since neither ill fortune nor good fortune arises, how can others harm him?

## 14.35

> *The Way of Rulership is not the means by which one acts;*
> *it is the means by which one does not act.*

What does "non-action" mean? [It means that]
> the wise do not avail themselves of their position to intervene;
> the courageous do not avail themselves of their position to engage in violence;
> and the humane do not avail themselves of their position to confer kindness.

This may be called "non-action." Through non-action, you can grasp the One. The One is the root of the myriad things. It is the Way that is unopposed.

## 14.39

*To regulate your body and nourish your nature,*
  *moderate your sleep and rest,*
  *be appropriate in your food and drink,*
  *harmonize your happiness and anger,*
  *and make suitable your movement and stillness.*

When you achieve the [ability to] carry out these things within the self, noxious *qi* will have no means to be produced. Is not this similar to one who, fearing an asthmatic attack might occur or a skin ulcer burst forth, takes the proper precautions in advance?

## 14.49

   *The clothing of the sage is neither long nor short.*
   *His conduct is neither extraordinary nor unusual.*

   His clothing does not arouse notice.
   His conduct does not elicit observation,
   and his speech does not incite criticism.
   When successful, he is not ostentatious.
   When impoverished, he is not afraid.
   When honored, he is not showy.
   When ignored, he is not bereft.
   He is extraordinary yet does not appear unusual.
   He is always appropriate yet identifies with the multitudes.
There are no means to name him. This is what is called "Great Merging."

## 14.53

   *Too many deals impoverish the merchant.*
   *Too much artistry exhausts the craftsman.*

It is because their minds are not [focused on] one thing.
   Thus,
      *when the span of a tree is great, its height is compromised.*
      *When the flow of a river is wide, its depth is compromised.*
   If you possess knowledge but lack technique, though you bore with an awl you will never get through anything.

If you possess a hundred different kinds of skills but lack a single Way, though you achieve things you will not be able to sustain [your achievements].

Thus the *Odes* states:
> "The good man, the Superior Man,
> his propriety is one.
> His propriety is one.
> His heart is as if bound."

How bound by oneness is the Superior Man!

## 14.56

*Non-action is the substance of the Way.*
*Following behind is the outward form of the Way.*

Those who do not act control those who act; this is [called] technique.
Those who follow behind control those who take the lead; this is [called] the proper sequence of things.
If you rely on technique, you will be strong.
If you understand the proper sequence of things, you will be calm.

Now when it came to giving away Mr. Bian's jade disk,[1] when he had not yet obtained it, [Mr. Bian] was ahead. When he pleaded to present it and would not give up despite his indignation, he was behind.

If three men live together and two begin to quarrel, each will think he is right, and neither will listen to the other. Though the third man is a fool, he will invariably resolve the dispute from the sidelines. This is not due to his intelligence but is because he was not fighting.

If two men begin to fight and a weakling stands at their side, if he helps one man, that man will win. If he aids the other man, that man will avoid defeat. Though the two fighters are strong, invariably [the outcome is] controlled by the single weakling. This is not due to his courage, but due to the fact that he does not fight.

Looking at it from this perspective,
> that those who follow behind control those who take the lead
> and that those who are still defeat those who are excitable

---

1. Mr. Bian's jade disk, also known as Mr. He's jade disk, was a fabulous precious object discovered by Bian He, a man of Chu, in the mountains of that state. When the jade was presented to King Li of Chu as an uncut matrix, the king suspected Bian He of fraud and had his left foot cut off as punishment. When King Li died and Bian He tried to present the jade to his son, King Wu, the king ordered that his right foot be cut off. When King Wu finally had the stone cut and polished, its precious nature was revealed.

is due to following the proper sequence of things.
>    To defy the Way and abandon the proper sequence of things, hoping thereby to encounter good luck;
>    to alter constant norms and change precedents, relying on your intelligence in your desire to cover up for yourself;
>    to pass over your own errors and to take credit when you hit the mark;
>    to conduct yourself from a position of darkness and recklessly change things;
>    to remain throughout your life unaware;

such actions are called "reckless."
>    To be dissatisfied with misfortune and satisfied with good fortune,
>    to regret committing errors and feel satisfied when you achieve merit,
>    to push ahead and not know to return,

this [too] is called "reckless."

## 14.67

*When the sage encounters things in the world amid their thousand alterations and myriad evolutions, he invariably relies on what never transforms to respond to what is always transforming.*

Cold and heat stand in opposition to each other.
>    During the season of intense cold, the ground cracks and water freezes, yet fire's capacity to burn is not diminished as a consequence.
>    During the season of intense heat, stones melt and metal fuses, yet fire's capacity to burn is not enhanced as a consequence.

The alterations of cold and heat neither harm nor benefit his person, for his inner substance is unchanging.

## 14.71

>    *When the Superior Man does good, he cannot ensure that it will bring good fortune;*
>    *when he refuses to do evil, he cannot ensure that it will not bring bad fortune.*

>    If good fortune arrives, since it is not something he sought, he does not proclaim his achievements;
>    if bad fortune arrives, since it is not something he elicited, he does not regret his actions.

If he should cultivate himself inwardly to the utmost and still adversity and bad fortune arrive, it is due to Heaven and not the person. Therefore, within himself his mind is constantly tranquil and still, and his Moral Potency is unencumbered. Even the barking of a dog cannot startle him because he naturally trusts his genuine responses.

Thus,
> *those who understand the Way are not confused;*
> *those who understand fate are free from anxiety.*

# Fifteen

## AN OVERVIEW OF THE MILITARY

"An Overview of the Military" provides the means by which to illuminate
>    the techniques of battle, victory, assault, and capture;
>    the force of formations and movements;
>    and the variations of deception and subterfuge
>    embodying the Way of Adaptation and Compliance
>    and upholding the Theory of Holding Back;

it is what [enables you] to
>    know that when you form for battle or deploy to fight contrary to the
>        Way, it will not work;
>    know that when you assault and capture or fortify and defend contrary
>        to Moral Potency, it will not be formidable.
>    If you truly realize its implications,
>    whether advancing or retreating, moving right or left,
>    there will be no place to be attacked or endangered.
>    It takes relying on force as its substance
>    and clarity and stillness as its constant.
>    It avoids fullness and follows emptiness,
>    as if driving forward a flock of sheep.

Such are the means to discuss military affairs.

"An Overview of the Essentials" (21.2)

One possible translation for the title of chapter 15, "Bing lue," is "Military Strategies." As the chapter summary makes clear, however, chapter 15 deals with all dimensions of military affairs, from tactics and strategy to basic military organization, the role of the military in state and society, and the ethics of war. Moreover, in section 21.3, the *Huainanzi* compilers make clear that chapter 15 was designed to exemplify the "overview" as a genre of writing. Thus we translate the title as "An Overview of the Military."

True to its title, chapter 15 surveys and draws on an expansive corpus of military writings inherited from the Warring States period (such as, but not limited to, the famous *Master Sun's Arts of War* (*Sunzi bingfa*). By the Han, the once-new outlook of these texts had become authoritative, and the *Huainanzi* treats their concepts and terminology as self-evidently normative. Thus battlefield outcomes are not determined by valor or divine favor but by the shifting dynamics of *shi*, or "force," a purely material measure of potential combat effectiveness. Victory is not secured by physical strength or bravado but by skillful manipulation of the "usual" and "extraordinary" tactical responses in order to confuse the opponent and gain the advantage of surprise.

Chapter 15 does bring its own original perspective to military affairs, however. The *Huainanzi* insists that human society had once (albeit briefly) existed in the complete absence of arms or conflict. Thus, although military affairs were indispensable to imperial rule (and national security) in the current age, they did not hold the key to ultimate power and authority. Moreover, although the authors acknowledge the importance of skill and knowledge, they insist that victory could be achieved only by the commander who had acquired transcendently penetrating insight through mystical self-cultivation. Finally, in keeping with Liu An's interests, "An Overview of the Military" emphasizes that the military could never be used to routinize power throughout the imperial domain. Military offensives might be undertaken only to "sustain those who [were] perishing, revive those [lineages] that had been cut off," that is, to protect the hereditary prerogatives of vassal princes like Liu An himself. The chapter ends with a description (15.26) of an extraordinary ritual in which the successful commanding general atones for his "treason" in wielding state power (which properly belongs to the ruler alone) during the course of the campaign.

# Fifteen

## 15.1

In antiquity, those who used the military did not value expanding territory or covet the possession of gold and jade. They sought to sustain those who [were] perishing, revive those [lineages] that had been cut off, pacify the chaos of the world, and eliminate harm to the myriad people.

All beasts that have blood and *qi*,
> are equipped with teeth and horns.
> They have claws in front and paws behind.
> Those with horns gore;
> those with teeth bite;
> those with poison sting;
> those with hooves kick.
> When they are happy, they play with one another;
> when they are angry they injure one another;

this is their Heaven[-born] nature.

Humans have instincts for clothing and food, yet [material] things are lacking. Thus they settle together in various locations. If the division is not equal, if demands are not fulfilled, they fight. When they fight, the strong threaten the weak and the brave attack the cowardly.

> People do not have strong muscles and bones or sharp claws and teeth, thus
>> they cut leather to make armor;
>> they forge iron to make blades.

Greedy and cruel people brutalize and rob the world. The myriad people are shaken; they cannot rest in tranquillity with what they possess. The sage rises up vehemently, punishing the strong and the violent [and] pacifying the chaotic age. He suppresses danger and eliminates disorder.

> He makes the sullied pure;
> he makes the imperiled calm.

Thus people are not cut off in mid[life].
The origins of the military are distant!

> The Yellow Emperor once warred with Yan Di;
> Zhuan Xu once fought with Gong Gong.
> The Yellow Emperor warred in the wilds of Zhuolu;
> Yao warred on the banks of the River Dan;
> Shun attacked the Youmiao;
> Qi attacked the Youhu.

Since the time of the Five Thearchs, [no one] has been able to ban [the military], much less in a declining age!

## 15.3

In regard to the military of later ages, although rulers may be without the Way, none do not dig moats, build battlements, and defend [them]. Those who attack do not do so to curtail violence or eliminate harm; they want to invade the land and expand their territory. For this reason, the bodies pile up and the blood flows; they face one another all day, yet the achievement of a hegemon does not appear in the age. It is because they act selfishly.

> One who wars for territory cannot become a king;
> one who wars for himself cannot establish his merit.
> One who takes up a task on behalf of others will be aided by the multitude;
> one who takes up a task on his own behalf will be discarded by the multitude.
> One who is aided by the multitude must [become] strong even if he is weak;
> one who is discarded by the multitude must perish even if he is great.

The military is
> weak if it loses the Way;
> strong if it obtains the Way.

The commander is
> inept if he loses the Way;
> skillful if he obtains the Way.

The State will
> survive if it obtains the Way;
> perish if it loses the Way.

## AN OVERVIEW OF THE MILITARY

What is called the Way
    embodies the circle and is modeled on the square,
    shoulders the yin and embraces the yang,
    is soft on the left and hard on the right,
    treads in the obscure and carries illumination.
It alters and transforms without constancy; it obtains the source of the One and thereby responds limitlessly. This is called spirit illumination.
    The circle is Heaven;
    the square is earth.
    Heaven is circular and without terminus, thus one cannot view its form;
    the earth is square and without boundaries, thus one cannot see its gateway.
    Heaven transforms and nurtures yet is without form;
    Earth generates and rears and yet is without measure.
Vague, hazy, who knows their capacity?
    All things have that which defeats them; only the Way is invincible. It is invincible because it has no constant shape or force. It cycles ceaselessly, like the motion of the sun and moon.
    Just as summer and autumn alternate,
    just as the sun and the moon have day and night,
    it reaches an end and begins again;
    it illuminates and becomes dark again.
None can attain its pattern.
    It controls form yet is formless;
    thus its merit can be complete.
    It objectifies things yet is no object;
    thus it triumphs and does not submit.

## 15.4

Form/punishment[1] is the ultimate of the military. Arriving at being without form/punishment may be called the ultimate of the ultimate. For this reason,

---

1. This is a deliberate pun. The character translated (*xing*) means both "form" and "punishment," and both meanings are being invoked here. The latter sense is that punishing wrongdoing is the ultimate end of the military but that the ultimate fulfillment of this end is achieved when punishments are no longer necessary. The former sense is that "form" (the formation of the army in battle, the form of plans and operations) is the ultimate arbiter of success for the military but that achieving a state of "formlessness" (or accessing the power of the Formless) is the ultimate embodiment of martial skill.

the great military does no injury; it communicates with the ghosts and spirits. It does not brandish the five weapons, [yet] none in the world dares oppose it. It sets up its drums [but] does not open its arsenal, and none of the Lords of the Land do not freeze in terror. Thus

> one who wars from the temple becomes emperor;
> one who [effects] spirit transformation becomes king.

What is called "warring from the temple"[2] is modeling [oneself] on the Way of Heaven.
Spirit transformation is modeling [oneself] on the four seasons.

> He cultivates governance within his borders and those afar long for his Potency;
> he achieves victory without battle, and the Lords of the Land submit to his might.

It is because internally his government is ordered.
In antiquity those who obtained the Way

> in stillness modeled [themselves] on Heaven and Earth,
> in motion complied with the sun and moon.
> In delight and anger they corresponded to the four seasons;
> in calling and answering they were comparable to the thunder and lightning.
> Their voice and breath did not oppose the eight winds;
> their contracting and extending did not exceed the five standards.
> Below to those [creatures] that have armor and scales;
> above to those that have fur and feathers;

all were ordered from first to last. Among the myriad creatures and the hundred clans, from beginning to end, none was without its proper place.
For this reason, [the Way]

> enters what is small without being pressed,
> lodges in what is vast without being exposed.
> It seeps into metal and stone;
> it washes over grasses and trees.

[From] something that expands to fill the limits of the six coordinates to the end of a single hair, nothing does not cleave to it. The penetration of the Way

---

2. "Warring from the temple" alludes to the first chapter of the *Sunzi bingfa*, which discusses the calculations made in the ancestral temple before battle has been joined. The basic notion here is that victory is achieved in the careful preparation before the battle, not in heroics on the battlefield itself.

suffuses what is [most] subtle. There is nowhere it does not reside; this is why it triumphs over the powerful and the many.

## 15.6

The military has three foundations:
> In ordering the kingdom, regulate within the borders.
> In effecting Humaneness and Rightness, spread Moral Potency and Benevolence.
> In establishing correct laws, block deviant paths.

[When]
> the collected ministers are intimately close,
> the common people are harmonious,
> superiors and inferiors are of a single mind,
> ruler and minister unite their efforts.
> The Lords of the Land submit to your might and the four directions cherish your Moral Potency;
> you cultivate governance in the temple hall and extend control beyond one thousand *li*;
> you fold your hands, issue commands, and the world responds as an echo.

This is the highest use of the military.

[When]
> the territory is broad and the people numerous;
> the ruler is worthy and the commanders loyal;
> the kingdom is rich and the military strong;
> covenants and prohibitions are trustworthy;
> pronouncements and orders are clear.
> The two armies oppose each other;
> the bells and drums face each other;

yet the enemy flees before the soldiers meet or blades clash. This is the middling use of the military.

[When]
> you understand what suits the terrain,
> practice the beneficial [use of] narrow and obstructed [positions],
> discern the alterations of the extraordinary and the usual,
> investigate the rules for marching and formation, dispersion and concentration;
> bind the drumsticks [to your forearms] and roll the drums.
> White blades meet;

flying arrows are exchanged;
you wade through blood and tread through guts;
you cart the dead away and support the wounded;
the blood flows for a thousand *li*;
exposed corpses fill the field;

thus victory is decided. This is the lowest use of the military. Now everyone in the world

knows to work at studying its branches,
and none knows to resolve to cultivate its root.

This is to discard the root and plant the limbs.

Those things that assist the military in victory are many; those that ensure victory are few.

If armor is sturdy and weapons sharp,
chariots are solid and horses excellent,
rations and equipment sufficient,
officers and men numerous,

these are the great foundations of the army, yet victory is not [found] here. If one is clear about

the movements of the stars, planets, sun, and moon;
the rules of recision and accretion[3] and the occult arts;
the advantages of the rear, front, left, and right;

these are aids to warfare, yet completeness is not [found] here.

That by which the excellent commander is ensured victory is his constant possession of a knowledge without origin, a Way that is not a Way. It is difficult to share with the multitude.

## 15.17

There is no spirit nobler than Heaven;
there is no force more versatile than Earth;
there is no motion more swift than time;
there is no resource more advantageous than people.

These four are the pillars and trunks of the military, yet they must rely on the Way to operate because [the Way] can unite their functions.

The advantage of terrain overcomes Heaven and time;
clever tactics overcome the advantage of terrain;
force overcomes people.

Thus,

---

3. That is, the annual waxing and waning of the yin and yang forces in the universe.

one who relies on Heaven can be led astray;
one who relies on Earth can be trapped;
one who relies on time can be pressured;
one who relies on people can be fooled.

Humaneness, courage, trustworthiness, and incorruptibility are the most excellent qualities among people. However,

the brave can be lured;
the humane can be robbed;
the trustworthy are easily cheated;
the incorruptible are easily schemed against.

If the commander of a host has even one of these [flaws], he will be taken captive.

Seen from this perspective, it also is clear that victory in arms is produced by the Pattern of the Way, not by the worthiness of human character.

Thus, deer and elk can be seized by snares;
fish and turtle can be taken by nets;
geese and swans can be collected with the dart and line.

Only to the Formless may nothing be done. For this reason, the sage

lodges in the Sourceless, so his feelings cannot be grasped and observed;
moves in the Formless, so his formations cannot be attained and traced.
He has no model and no protocol;
he does what is appropriate [for what] arrives;
he has no name and no shape;
he fashions [a new] image for [each] alteration.
How deep!
How distant!
Through winter and summer,
through spring and fall,
above reaching the highest branch,
below fathoming the deepest depth,
altering and transforming,
never hesitating or halting,
he sets his mind in the Field of Profound Mystery
and lodges his will in the Spring of the Nine Returns.

Though one has acute eyes, who can detect his feelings?

## 15.26

Whenever the kingdom has difficulty, from the palace the ruler summons the commander, charging him: "The fate of the altars of the soil and grain are on your person. The kingdom faces a crisis, I wish you to take command and respond to it."

When the commander has accepted his mandate, [the ruler] orders the Supplicator and Great Diviner to fast, sequestered for three days. Going to the Great Temple, they consult the Magic Tortoise to divine a lucky day for receiving the drums and flags.

The ruler enters the temple portal, faces west, and stands. The commander enters the temple portal, rushes to the foot of the platform, faces north, and stands.

The sovereign personally grasps the *yue* ax. Holding it by the head, he offers the commander its handle, saying, "From here up to Heaven is controlled by [you,] the commander." [The ruler] again grasps the *fu* ax. Holding it by the head, he offers the commander its handle, saying, "From here down to the Abyss is controlled by [you,] the commander."[4]

When the commander has accepted the *fu* and *yue* axes, he replies,

"[Just as] the kingdom cannot be governed from without,
the army cannot be ruled from within.
[Just as] one cannot serve the ruler with two minds,
one cannot respond to the enemy with a doubtful will.

Since [I,] your minister, have received control from you, I exclusively [wield] the authority of the drums, flags, and *fu* and *yue* axes. I ask nothing in return. I [only] hope that Your Highness likewise will not hand down one word of command to me.

If Your Highness does not agree, I dare not take command.
If Your Highness agrees, I will take my leave and set out."

[The commander] then trims his fingernails, dons funeral garb, and exits through the "ill-augured" portal.[5] He mounts the commander's chariot and arrays the banners and axes, tied as if not [yet] victorious. On meeting the enemy and committing to battle,

he pays no heed to certain death;
he does not have two minds.

For this reason,

he has no Heaven above;
he has no Earth below;
he has no enemy in front;

---

4. The *yue* and *fu* axes are the ruler's military regalia. The conferring of these symbols on the commander represents the transfer of sovereign authority to him for the duration of the campaign.
5. That is, the commander symbolically prepares himself for his own funeral and leaves by the ill-omened northern door of the palace. These acts signify his willingness to die in the ruler's service.

he has no ruler behind;
he does not seek fame in advancing;
he does not avoid punishment in retreating;
he [seeks] only to protect the people;
his benefit is united with that of the ruler.

This is the treasure of the kingdom, the Way of the superior commander.

If he is like this,
the clever will plan for him;
the brave will fight for him;
their *qi* will scrape the azure clouds;
they will be swift as galloping [steeds].

Thus before weapons have clashed, the enemy is terrified.

If the battle is victorious and the enemy flees, [the commander] thoroughly dispenses rewards for merit. He reassigns his officers, increasing their rank and emolument. He sets aside land and apportions it, making sure it is outside the feudal mound.[6] Last, he judges punishments within the army.

Turning back, he returns to the kingdom, lowering his banners and storing the *fu* and *yue* axes. He makes his final report to the ruler, saying, "I have no further control over the army." He then dons coarse silk and enters seclusion.

[The commander goes] to ask pardon of the ruler. The ruler says, "Spare him." [The commander] withdraws and dons fasting garb. For a great victory, he remains secluded for three years; for a middling victory, two years; for a lesser victory, one year.

That against which the military was used was surely a kingdom without the Way.

Thus
one can triumph in battle without retribution,
take territory without returning it;
the people will not suffer illness;
the commander will not die early;
the five grains will flourish;
the winds and rains will be seasonable;
the battle is won without;
good fortune is born within.

Thus one's reputation will be made, and afterward there will be no further harm.

---

6. In other words, the commander ensures that land given as rewards lies outside the sacred mound used to perform sacrifices to the ancestors of the defeated ruler, in order to avoid angering those ancestral spirits and turning them into malevolent ghosts.

# Sixteen and Seventeen

A MOUNTAIN OF PERSUASIONS
*AND* A FOREST OF PERSUASIONS

"A Mountain of Persuasions" and "A Forest of Persuasions" demonstrate how to
    skillfully and elegantly penetrate and bore open the blockages and
        obstructions of the many affairs
    and thoroughly and comprehensively penetrate and pierce the barriers and hindrances of the myriad things,
    proposing analogies and selecting similes,
    distinguishing categories and differentiating forms,
they thereby
    lead and order your awareness,
    loosen and untie what is knotted up,
    and unravel and unwind what is wound up,
so as to illuminate the boundaries of affairs.

                                  "An Overview of the Essentials" (21.2)

As their similar titles suggest, chapter 16, "A Mountain of Persuasions," and chapter 17, "A Forest of Persuasions," are collections of brief, persuasive utterances that share the same literary form and didactic function in the text. Given these similarities, we have chosen to treat these chapters together as a pair, following the example of *Huainanzi* 21, "An Overview of the Essentials," which similarly summarizes these chapters together. Their purpose seems to be to provide a kind of repository of aphorisms (which we refer to here as "persuasions") that could be used in a variety of settings to which the performative aspects of language were crucial, such as in oral deliberation, instruction, and debate. These "talking points" then would give a person engaged in oral argument or instruction a kind of arsenal of well-turned phrases with which to reinforce the rhetorical force of his arguments.

These chapters of the *Huainanzi* are modeled to some extent on the similarly titled chapters 22 and 23, "Shui lin shang" and "Shui lin xia" (A Forest of Persuasions, parts 1 and 2), in the *Hanfeizi*. Another example of the genre is Liu Xiang's slightly later compilation the *Shuoyuan* (*A Garden of Sayings*), particularly chapter 16, "Tan cong" (A Thicket of Remarks). Some of the persuasions found in these two *Huainanzi* chapters may also be found, in only slightly different form, in the *Hanfeizi* and the *Shuoyuan*. This suggests that such compilations of talking points for would-be public speakers may have been a widespread and highly appreciated Han literary genre.

# Sixteen

### 16.1

The *po* [substantive soul] asked the *hun* [ethereal soul], "How does the Way take physical form?" The *hun* replied, "It takes Nothing There as its physical form." The *po* asked, "Does Nothing There have a physical form, then?" The *hun* replied, "It does not." The *po* asked, "If there is Nothing There, how can one apprehend it and be informed about it?" The *hun* replied, "I only have ways to encounter it, that is all. When we look at it, it has no form; when we listen to it, it has no sound. We call it 'the Dark Mystery.' The Dark Mystery can be used to refer to the Way, but it is not the Way." The *po* said, "Now I get it." Thereupon he turned his gaze inward and reverted to himself. The *hun* said, "Those who have attained the Way have forms that cannot be seen and names that cannot be expressed. *You* still have 'form' and 'name.' How can you attain the Way?" The *po* said, "What use is speech, then? I shall return to my Ancestor." The *po* turned to look, and suddenly the *hun* could not be seen. The *po* then turned and got a grip on himself and also entered the formless.

### 16.8

Sages spend their lives talking about governing. What is of use is not their words [as such] but what they have to say. Singers use lyrics, but what people really enjoy hearing is not the lyrics themselves. A parrot can speak, but it cannot engage in meaningful discourse. Why is this? It has the power of speech but does not have anything to say.

Thus if someone follows you and walks in your tracks, he cannot produce fresh footprints of his own.

## 16.10

The four directions are the gates and doors, windows and back gates of the Way; which one you go through [determines] how you view things. Thus
> fishing can be used to teach someone horseback riding;
> horseback riding can be used to instruct a person in charioteering;
> and charioteering can be used to teach someone how to pole a boat.

## 16.18

> Orchids grow in dark valleys. They are no less fragrant just because no one [happens to] wear them.
> Boats ply rivers and oceans. They are no less buoyant just because no one [happens to] ride in them.
> The Superior Man practices Rightness. He does not stop doing so just because no one [happens to] know about it.

## 16.22

> Those who are in prison consider a day a long time.
> Those who are about to be executed in the marketplace consider a day to be very short.

The length of a day has a set standard, but
> from where one person stands it is short
> and from where another stands it is long.

This is because their center is not balanced. Thus when one uses what is not balanced to consider what is balanced, then what one takes to be balanced will not be balanced.

## 16.28

> A good archer shoots and does not miss the target. That is good for the archer, but not good for the target.

> A good fisherman never loses a fish. That is good for the fisherman, but not good for the fish.

Thus where there is that which is good, there also is that which is not good.

## 16.34

If you
> grasp a crossbow and call a bird
> or brandish a club and beckon a dog,

then what you want to come will surely go away instead. Thus,
> a fish cannot be hooked without bait;
> an animal cannot be lured with an empty trap.

## 16.46

A hundred men trying to lift a gourd is not as good as one person grabbing it and running off. Thus there certainly are situations in which a crowd is not as good as a few people.

Two people pull a cart, and six more push behind. Thus there certainly are affairs in which mutual cooperation is necessary for success.

If two people are drowning, they cannot rescue each other, but if one is on shore, he can [save the other]. Thus identical things cannot set each other in order. It is necessary to depend on difference; only then there will be a good outcome.

## 16.51

> When the ruler wants a plank, his officials cut down a tree.
> When the ruler wants a fish, his officials dry up a valley.
> When the ruler wants an oar, his underlings give him a whole boat.
> When the ruler's words are like threads, his underlings' words are like rope.
> When the ruler likes one thing, his underlings praise it twice.
> When the ruler faults three [people], his underlings kill nine.

## 16.67

Someone who wanted to put a stop to slander went from door to door saying, "I really did not have an affair with my elder sister-in-law!" The slander increased more and more.

> Trying to stop words with more words
> or affairs with more affairs
> is like making piles of dirt to ward off dust
> or using armloads of firewood to douse a fire.

Spouting words to expunge slander is like using black dye to clean something white.

## 16.77

In a family to the east, the mother died. Her son cried but was not sorrowful. A son from a family to the west saw this and returned home to his mother, saying, "Mother, why don't you die right away? I would certainly cry very sorrowfully for you!"

Now if someone really wants his mother to die, if she did die, he certainly would not be able to cry sorrowfully for her.

[Likewise,] if someone says, "I have no free time to study," even if he had free time, he would still not be able to study.

## 16.96

> When the majority are crooked, they cannot tolerate the straight;
> when the majority are bent, they cannot tolerate the upright.

Thus,
> when people are in the majority, they eat wolves;
> when wolves are in the majority, they eat people.

## 16.103

> When birds are about to arrive, people spread out nets to await them. What catches the bird is a single eye of the net, but a single-eyed net will never catch a bird.
> Now a person who dons armor prepares for an arrow to strike him. If he knew for sure where the arrow would hit, he could wear just one tiny scale of armor.
> Matters sometimes cannot be measured beforehand;
> things sometimes cannot be foreseen.

Thus sages cultivate the Way and await the right time.

## 16.114

> When you give someone a horse but [first] take off the harness,
> when you give someone a chariot but [first] detach the yoke rings,
> what you have kept is [worth] little,
> and what you have given away is [worth] a lot.

Thus the peasants have a saying: "If you boil beef without salt, you defeat the purpose."

## 16.145

A man from Ying was going to sell his mother. He said to a [prospective] buyer, "This mother is old. Please feed her well and don't let [her life] be bitter." This is to carry out a large offense against Rightness while hoping to perform a small act of Rightness.

# Seventeen

### 17.1

To apply the standards of a bygone era in governing the world [today] is like a passenger in a boat who lost his sword in midstream. Right away he made a mark on the boat, intending to come back at night to look for the sword. His lack of knowledge of how to sort things out was certainly profound! Now to follow the footprints in one small corner [of the world] and not to know how to wander in accord with Heaven and Earth—no confusion can be greater than that. Just because something is suitable for a particular time is not enough to make it valuable [always]. It can be compared with making earthen dragons in time of drought or making [sacrificial] straw dogs during an epidemic. They are sovereign only at a particular time.

### 17.15

> The best flavor does not satiate;
> the highest language does not embellish.
> The highest joy does not [elicit] laughter;
> the loftiest sound does not call out.
> The greatest artist does not chop;
> the greatest cook does not carve;
> the greatest hero does not fight.

When you attain the Way, its Potency follows. This is like the correspondence of the [pitch-pipe] note Yellow Bell and the [pentatonic] note *gong*, or the correspondence of the [pitch-pipe] note Great Budding and the [pentatonic] note *shang*—their consonance cannot be altered.[1]

## 17.32

>The purveyor of coffins desires human illness and plague;
>the hoarder of grain desires yearly drought and famine.

## 17.42

>Metal overcomes wood, but it is not possible to destroy a forest with a single knife.
>Earth overcomes water, but it is not possible to plug the Yangzi with one clod of earth.

## 17.48

Suppose the stride of a rabbit were made as big as that of a horse. It could keep up with the sun and pursue the wind. If [a rabbit] actually became [as big as] a horse, though, it would not be able to run at all.

## 17.49

>In winter there might be thunder and lightning,
>and in summer there might be frost and snow.

Nevertheless, the inherent tendencies of heat and cold do not change. Small differences are not enough to hinder constant principles.

## 17.64

>A nursing bitch will bite a tiger;
>a brooding hen will peck a fox.

When their [maternal] concern has been aroused, they do not take account of [relative] strengths.

---

1. Yellow Bell and *gong* and Great Budding and *shang* are pairs of identical notes.

## 17.84

> The markings of tigers and leopards attract archers;
> the agility of monkeys and apes brings hunters.

## 17.122

> When you see an elephant's tusk, you know he was bigger than an ox.
> When you see a tiger's tail, you know it was bigger than a fox.

One portion appears, and the remaining one hundred portions are known.

## 17.132

With the wheel hub [properly] set up, each of its thirty spokes makes full use of its strength but does not detract from the others. If you take one spoke alone and set it into the hub, discarding all the others, how would it be possible to go ten thousand *li*?

## 17.151

Skillfully using others is like the feet of a millipede; though numerous they do not harm one another.

Or like the lips and the teeth, the hard and the soft rub up against each other but do not overcome each other.

## 17.190

> When the traveler thinks [of his loved one] on the road,
> the one at home dreams in her bed.
> When the kindly mother sighs in Yan [in the north],
> her son misses her in Jing [in the south].

These are [cases of] Essence going back and forth.

## 17.205

To take the immensity of the world and entrust it to the talent of a single person is like hanging a weight of a thousand *jun* on a single branch of a tree.

## 17.219

    Bows must first be adjusted; later you can seek out the strong ones.
    Horses must first be trained; later you can seek out the fine ones.
    People must first prove trustworthy; later you can seek out the able ones.

## 17.226

    You do not carve a pure white jade;
    you do not inscribe a beautiful pearl.
The basic material is more than enough [already].
Thus,
    if it strides forth without resting, even a lame turtle can go a thousand *li*;
    if you pile things up without stopping, you can amass a great heap.

# Eighteen

## AMONG OTHERS

"Among Others" provides the means by which to
> observe the alterations of bad and good fortune,
> discern the reversals of benefit and harm,
> diagnose the symptoms of success and failure,
> and mark out and hold up to view the boundaries of ends and
>     beginnings.

[It]
> differentiates and distinguishes the subtleties of the one hundred
>     affairs

and discloses and reveals the mechanisms of preservation and loss, enabling you to know
> bad fortune as good fortune,
> loss as gain,
> success as failure,
> and benefit as harm.

If you truly grasp [its] utmost implications, you will possess the means to move to and fro and up and down among the vulgar of the age, while remaining unharmed by slander, abuse, venom, or poison.

"An Overview of the Essentials" (21.2)

Chapter 18 of the *Huainanzi* shares its title, "Ren jian," with chapter 4 of the *Zhuangzi* and could also be translated as "Among Human Beings" or "The Human Realm." As the opening section of the chapter explains, here we have left the internal domain of the mind and nature and entered the multidimensional world of time and space populated by *ren*, "other people," or, simply, "others." For this reason, we translate the title of chapter 18 as "Among Others."

"Among Others" is made up of the same kind of short units of anecdotal prose that constitute chapter 12, "Responses of the Way," most of which are also found in other early anthologies such as the *Lüshi chunqiu*, the *Hanfeizi*, and the *Zhanguo ce* (*Intrigues of the Warring States*). It is not clear whether the *Huainanzi* (and later Han anthologies) drew from these earlier works or whether all these texts borrowed from a stock of anecdotal lore that circulated in various written and oral forms. Even though chapter 18 shares its composite pieces with these other texts, it uses them quite distinctively.

"Among Others" consists almost entirely of pairs of anecdotes set into a generic framework. Each section of the chapter is set off by a motif composed of two parallel and (typically) opposing propositions, for example, "some [things] are increased by being decreased, some [things] are decreased by being increased" (18.2). The text then presents two anecdotes, the first illustrating the first leg of the motif and the second illustrating the second.

The purposes of chapter 18 were multifold. The *Huainanzi* compilers included it as both an example of elegant literary parallelism and a commentary on the uses and effectiveness of logical disputation (a subject that also informs other chapters, especially 10, 16, and 17). On the one hand, chapter 18 demonstrates that a skillful orator may deploy elegant examples to support almost any side of a question. Thus the efficacy of logical argumentation cannot be completely discounted in the current age. On the other hand, the vagaries of affairs "among others" are so complex and contradictory that "no one who is not a spirit or a sage" can distinguish the origins of "calamity and good fortune." Thus the means to assess the products of logic or literary artistry must be found in more fundamental realms accessible only through mystical self-cultivation.

# Eighteen

### 18.1

    The nature of humans is pure, clear, peaceful, and content.
    The regulators of affairs are models, gnomons, the compass, and the square.
    If you understand the nature of humans, you will not err in nurturing yourself.
    If you understand the regulators of affairs, you will not be confused in your taking and giving.
        When one end emerges,
        it comprehends limitlessly.
        Roaming the eight limits,
        it gathers it all into a single straw.
It is called "the mind."

    Looking at the root and knowing the branches, observing the finger and seeing the return [path], holding to the One and responding to the many, grasping the essentials and ordering the details. These are called "techniques."

    What the wise are at rest, where the wise go in motion, what the wise wield in affairs, that from which the wise act: this is known as "the Way."

    The Way:
        Place it in front, and [the cart] will not lean forward;
        place it behind, and [the cart] will not lean backward.
        Put in inside a cramped space, and it will not fill it,

Spread it over the world, and it will not be stretched.
For this reason,
> what cause others to exalt and praise you are the strengths of the mind.
> What cause others to denigrate and slander you are the faults of the mind.
> Words that issue from the mouth cannot be halted among others;
> actions that are manifest nearby cannot be kept from afar.
> Affairs are difficult to complete and easily defeated;
> reputation is difficult to establish and easily abandoned.
> A thousand-*li* dike will breach because of a cricket or ant burrow;
> a hundred-*xun* roof will burn because of a spark from a crack in the chimney.

The *Admonitions of Yao* says, "Trembling and shaking, take heed day by day. People do not stumble over a mountain; they stumble over an anthill." This is why those who look lightly on small harms and scorn minor affairs will have many regrets. Worrying about a calamity once it has arrived is like a sick person's searching for a good doctor once he has already become critically ill. Even if [the doctor] has the skill of a Bian Que or a Yu Fu, [the patient] will still not live.
> The arrival of calamity is generated by human beings;
> the arrival of good fortune is effected by human beings.
> Calamity and good fortune share a gateway;
> benefit and harm are neighbors.

No one who is not a spirit or sage can distinguish them.

In all people's undertaking of affairs, none dares set his plans before using his intelligence to reflect and assess. Some lead to benefit, others to harm; this is the difference between the stupid and the wise. Those who thought that they clearly knew the fulcrum of survival and extinction, the portal of calamity and good fortune, and who, having used it, become trapped in difficulty, cannot be counted. If whenever one knew what was right, one's affair would succeed, there would be no unfinished ventures in the world. For this reason,
> intelligence and reflection are the portals of calamity and good fortune;
> motion and stillness are the fulcrums of benefit and harm.

The alterations and transformations of the hundred affairs, the order and chaos of the state and the household, wait [for them] to be effected. [For this reason, one who does not fall into difficulty succeeds.] Thus one cannot but take heed of them.

## 18.7

In olden times, among the people of Song there was [a family] whose [members] were very close. The three generations did not separate. Without warning, the household's black cow gave birth to a white calf. They asked the grandfather and he said, "This is a good omen. Offer it up to the ghosts and spirits." After one year, the father suddenly went blind, and the cow again gave birth to a white calf. The father again sent his son to consult the grandfather. His son said, "Before we listened to grandfather and you lost your sight. If we consult him again now, what will happen?" His father said, "According to the words of the sages, one must first scrutinize and then adopt. The affair is not yet clear; we must still try asking him once more." The son again went to consult the grandfather. The grandfather said, "This is a good omen. I again instruct you to offer it to the ghosts and spirits." [The son] returned to convey these orders to his father. The father said, "Carry out grandfather's instructions." In one year, the son also suddenly went blind. Afterward Chu attacked Song, besieging the city. At this time, people traded their children for food; they cut up corpses and cooked them. The able and strong were dead; the old, sick, and children all had to mount the city walls. They defended them without failing. The king of Chu was furious. When the walls were breached, all those defending them were slaughtered. It was only because the father and son were blind that they did not mount the walls. When the army retired and the siege was lifted, both the father and son [regained] their vision.

As for the revolutions and the mutual generation of calamity and good fortune, their alterations are difficult to perceive. At the near frontier, there was a [family of] skilled diviners whose horse suddenly became lost out among the Hu [people]. Everyone consoled them. The father said, "This will quickly turn to good fortune!" After several months, the horse returned with a fine Hu steed. Everyone congratulated them. The father said, "This will quickly turn to calamity!" The household was [now] replete with good horses; the son loved to ride, [but] he fell and broke his leg. Everyone consoled them. The father said, "This will quickly turn to good fortune!" After one year, the Hu people entered the frontier in force; the able and strong all stretched their bowstrings and fought. Among the people of the near frontier, nine out of ten died. It was only because of lameness that father and son protected each other. Thus,

> good fortune becoming calamity,
> calamity becoming good fortune;
> their transformations are limitless,
> so profound they cannot be fathomed.

## 18.8

Some are correct in word yet not comprehensive in action; some are faulty of ear and stubborn of mind yet accord with substance.

Gaoyang Tui was about to build a house, [so] he consulted a carpenter. The carpenter replied, "It cannot be done yet. The wood is still living. If plaster is applied to it, it will definitely warp. When green material is covered with heavy plaster it may [seem] completed now, [but] it will definitely collapse later." Gaoyang Tui said, "Not so. As the wood dries, it gets harder; as the plaster dries, it gets lighter. When hard material is covered with light plaster, even though it is bad now, it will certainly be better later." The carpenter was out of words, he had no reply. He accepted his orders and built the house. When it was completed, it was apparently fine, but afterward it indeed collapsed. This is what is known as "correct in word yet not comprehensive in action."

What is called faulty of ear [and] stubborn of mind yet according with substance? Lord Jingguo was about to fortify Xue. Most of his guest clients tried to stop him; he did not listen to them. He told his heralds, "Send no word from my guest clients." A man of Qi requested an audience, saying, "I will speak only three words. If I surpass three words, please cook me [alive]." Lord Jingguo heard this and granted him an audience. The guest rushed forward, bowed twice, and rising, said, "Great sea fish," then retreated. Lord Jingguo stopped him, staying, "I want to hear your persuasion." The guest said, "I do not dare die for sport." Lord Jingguo said, "You, honored sir, have paid no heed to distance in coming here, I want you to explain it to me." The guest said, "The great sea fish: nets cannot stop it, hooks cannot catch it. [But] if it beaches and is out of the water, then crickets and ants will have their way with it. Now Qi is your sea. If you lose Qi, do you think that Xue can survive alone?" Lord Jingguo said, "Excellent" and thereby halted the fortification of Xue. This is what is called "being faulty of ear and stubborn of mind, yet attaining the substance in action."

Now using "do not fortify Xue" as a persuasion to halt the fortification of Xue was not as good as "great sea fish."

Thus things
> sometimes are distant yet near to it,
> sometimes are near yet far off the mark.

## 18.27

The juxtapositions of the categories of things so that they are close [to one another] but of a different family are numerous and difficult to recognize. Thus
> some are placed in categories to which they do not belong;
> some are excluded from categories to which they do belong.
> Some seem so and are not;
> some are not and seem so.

A proverb says, "When a hawk dropped a rotten mouse, the Yu clan was lost." What does this mean? It is said that the Yu clan were tycoons of Liang. Their household was replete with riches; they had limitless gold and coins, immeasurable wealth and goods. They raised a lofty tower on the edge of the highway on which they staged musical [performances], served wine, and played games of chess. As some wandering swordsmen passed under the tower together, one of the chess players above moved against his friend's position and laughed as he turned over two pieces. [Just at that moment] a flying hawk dropped a rotten mouse as it passed and hit the wandering swordsmen.

The wandering swordsmen said to one another, "The Yu clan's days of wealth and happiness have been long, and they often are scornful of other people's will. We did not dare to disturb them, yet they insult us with a dead mouse. If this is not avenged, we will not be able to stand and proclaim ourselves to the world. Let us unite our strength to a single purpose, lead all our followers, and resolve to exterminate their house." That night they attacked the Yu clan and exterminated the house. This is what is called "placing it in a category in which it does not belong."

What is called "excluding [it] from a category to which [it] does [belong]"? Qu Jian told Shi Qi, "Duke Sheng of Bo is about to rebel." Shi Qi said, "Not so. Duke Sheng of Bo humbles his person and exalts knights; he would not dare treat the worthy arrogantly. His house lacks the safeguards of keys and locks or the security of crossbars and bolts. He uses oversized *dou* and *hu* [measures] in distributing [grain] and undersized *jin* and *liang* [weights] when collecting [it]. Your assessment of him is inaccurate." Qu Jian replied, "These [conditions] are precisely why he will rebel." After three years, Duke Sheng of Bo indeed did rebel, killing Prime Minister Zijiao and Minister of War Ziqi. This is what is called "being excluded from a category yet belonging to it."

What is called "seeming so and yet not"? Zifa was the magistrate of Shangcai. A common person committed a crime and faced punishment. The case was disputed and the arguments made. When it was decided before the magistrate, Zifa sighed with a pitiful heart. When the criminal had been punished, he did not forget Zifa's kindness. After this, Zifa committed a crime against King Wei and fled. The man who had been punished thus disguised the one who had been kind to him, and the man who had been kind fled with him to a hut below the city walls. When pursuers arrived, [the man] stamped his foot and said angrily, "Zifa oversaw and decided my crime and had me punished; my hatred for him makes my bones and marrow ache. If I could get his flesh and eat it, I could never have enough!" The pursuers all felt he was truthful and did not search the interior, so Zifa survived. This is what is called "seeming so and yet not."

What is called "not yet seeming so"? In antiquity, King Goujian of Yue humbled himself to King Fuchai of Wu. He asked to serve [Fuchai] personally as his minister and to give [Fuchai] his wife as concubine. He supplied the four seasonal sacrifices and remanded tribute every spring and autumn. He took down [his own state's] altars of the soil and grain, exerted his energies [like a] commoner, lived in seclusion, and fought in the front ranks. He was extremely humble in all courtesies and extremely submissive in all speech. He distanced himself far from the mind of a rebel, yet with three thousand men he captured Fuchai at Guxu.

One cannot fail to examine these four cases. What makes it difficult to understand affairs is that [people] hide their origins and conceal their tracks; they establish the selfish in the place of the impartial; they incline toward the deviant over the correct and confuse other people's minds with victory. If one could make what people harbor internally tally perfectly with what they express externally, then the world would have no lost states or broken households. When the fox catches the pheasant, it must first prostrate its body and lower its ears and wait for [the pheasant] to come. The pheasant sees this and believes it, thus it can be enticed and captured. If the fox were to widen its eyes and stare directly [at the pheasant], manifesting its lethal inclination, the pheasant would know to be alarmed and fly far off, thus escaping [the fox's] wrath.

> The mutual deception of human artifice
> is not merely the cunning of birds and beasts.

The resemblances between things and categories that cannot be externally assessed are numerous and difficult to recognize. For this reason, they cannot but be investigated.

# Nineteen

## CULTIVATING EFFORT

"Cultivating Effort" provides the means by which those
    whose entry into the Way is not profound
    and whose appreciation of argumentation is not deep
can, by observing these literary expressions, turn themselves around
    to take clarity and purity as constants
    and mildness and serenity as roots.
[But those who]
    idly and lazily set aside their studies,
    give free rein to their desires and indulge their feelings.
    and wish to misappropriate what they lack,
will be obstructed from the Great Way.
   Now,
    madmen have no anxiety,
    and sages, too, have no anxiety.
    Sages have no anxiety
    because they harmonize by means of Potency,
    whereas madmen have no anxiety
    because they do not know [the difference between] bad and good
       fortune.
   Thus,
    the non-action of those who fully comprehend [the Way]
    and the non-action of those who are obstructed from [the Way]

> are alike with regard to their non-action
>
> but differ with regard to the means by which they are non-active.
>
> Thus, on their behalf, what can be heeded has been brought to the surface, declared, circulated, and explained, thereby inspiring scholars to diligently appropriate [these principles] for themselves.
>
> "An Overview of the Essentials" (21.2)

"Cultivating Effort" offers arguments that can be used to challenge a number of political and philosophical views that seem to have been in vogue at the time the *Huainanzi* was created. Together, these arguments support the general theme of the chapter, that cultivating effort is necessary in a wide variety of contexts and among a wide variety of people, from the sage who tries to bring benefit to the world to the common man who tries to lift himself morally through education and training. Rhetorically, the chapter provides the reader with valuable examples of techniques of assertion and refutation that can be used in oral debate. Accordingly, the chapter is a teaching tool in form as well as in content. Each of the chapter's seven sections lays out a sustained argument that begins by asserting or refuting a particular proposition. In every case, personal effort is seen to be indispensable even when it pertains to the key concept of "non-action" (*wuwei*), advocated throughout the *Huainanzi* as a technique of sagely government. Here "non-action" is redefined to highlight the importance of human agency and human exertion.

The opening lines of this chapter comprise an interesting and unusual case in which the *Huainanzi* seems to directly contradict itself. Chapter 8, "The Basic Warp," begins by stating, "The reign of Grand Purity was harmonious and compliant and thus silent and indifferent." Chapter 19 begins, "Some people say: 'Those who are non-active are solitarily soundless and indifferently unmoving. . . .' I believe this is not so." How can we account for this discrepancy? The answer, we believe, is that these statements must be viewed in context, for when they are, the apparent contradiction tends to disappear. Chapter 8 refers to a simple, remote (and unrecoverable) era in which everyone was so attuned to the Way that a ruler had only to reign in order to rule. Chapter 19, though, refers to a much more complicated contemporary world in which a do-nothing ruler would not stay on his throne for long. The author of "Cultivating Effort" does not deny the principle of *wuwei* (non-action), but he denies that it means doing nothing. Rather, he shows, the great sages of antiquity worked hard. It is just that their efforts were so attuned to the Way that the good consequences of their acts became a cosmic imperative. (In this way, chapter 19 is consistent with chapter 13, which insists that a successful ruler must constantly embrace and respond to change.)

The *Huainanzi* is, above all, intended as a practical guide to good rulership. Here the author makes clear that the ruler's self-cultivation, preparation, education, and hard work all are indispensable elements of good and lasting government.

# Nineteen

## 19.1

Some people say: "Those who are non-active
    are solitarily soundless
    and indifferently unmoving
    Pull them, and they do not come;
    push them, and they do not go.
Only those who are like this give the appearance of having attained the Way."

    I believe this is not so. I might ask them: "Is it possible to refer to such men as the Divine Farmer, Yao, Shun, Yu, and Tang as sages?' [Even] those who hold to this view [of non-action] certainly could not contend otherwise. [But] if you examine these five sages, it is clear that none of them achieved non-action.

    In ancient times,
        the people fed on herbaceous plants and drank [only] water,
        picked fruit from shrubs and trees
        and ate the meat of oysters and clams.
They frequently suffered tribulations from feverish maladies and injurious poisons. Consequently, the Divine Farmer first taught the people to plant and cultivate the five grains.
        He evaluated the suitability of the land,
        [noting] whether it was dry or wet, fertile or barren, high or low.
        He tried the taste and flavor of the one hundred plants
        and the sweetness or bitterness of the streams and springs,

issuing directives so the people would know what to avoid and what to accept. At the time [he was doing this], he suffered poisoning [as many as] seventy times a day.

Yao established filial piety, compassion, humaneness, and love, inspiring the people to become like sons and brothers.
> To the west, he taught the People of the Fertile Lands;
> to the east, he reached the Blackteeth People;
> to the north, he soothed the Yudu People;
> and to the south he made inroads to Jiaozhi.
> He exiled Huan Dou to Mount Chong,
> pursued the Three Miao [tribes] to Three Dangers [Mountain],
> banished Gong Gong to Yuzhou,
> and executed Gun at Feather Mountain.

Shun created homes.
> Constructing walls and thatching roofs,
> opening lands and planting grains,

he directed all the people
> to abandon their caves and
> each to establish a family dwelling.
> These are the practices he initiated.
> To the south he chastised the Three Miao [tribes],
> dying along the way at Zangwu.

Yu,
> bathed by torrential rains
> and combed by violent winds,
> cleared the waterways and dredged the rivers,
> bored through Dragon Gate,
> opened up Yin Pass,

repaired the embankments of Peng Li [i.e., Boyang Lake],
> mounted the four vehicles,[1]
> followed the mountains,
> and marked their trees,
> leveling and ordering the water and land

so as to determine [the boundaries of] the eighteen hundred states.

Tang
> rose early and retired late
> to take full advantage of his perspicacious intelligence;

---

1. Most of the several explanations of the "four vehicles" include boats for water and carts for land. The remaining ones might be a mud sledge, a vehicle or shoes especially useful in climbing mountains, another kind of mud sledge, and a sedan chair.

　　　　reduced taxes and lightened demands
　　　　　to enhance the people's livelihood;
　　　　displayed virtue and bestowed favor
　　　　　to rescue the impoverished and bereft.
　　　　He mourned the dead and inquired about the afflicted
　　　　　to take care of orphans and widows.
[Consequently,]
　　　　the common people grew close to and cleaved to him.
　　　　His policies and directives flowed forth and circulated [everywhere].
Thus he subsequently
　　　　marshaled his troops at Mingtiao,
　　　　surrounded [Jie] of the Xia at Nan Guo,
　　　　punished him for his transgressions,
　　　　and banished him to Mount Li.

　These five sages were rulers who made the world flourish. They labored their bodies and used their minds to the utmost on behalf of the people to bring benefit and eradicate harm, yet they never tired of doing so.

　　　　Now if you raise a beaker of wine,
　　　　　no one would notice [the strain] from your face,
but if you lift a vat [weighing] a *dan*, sweat will flow profusely.
　　　　How much more so will this be the case if you take on the worries of
　　　　　　the world
　　　　　and assume responsibility for all the affairs within the [Four] Seas!
This is far heavier than a vat weighing a *dan*.
　　Moreover, these sages
　　　　were not embarrassed by their humble status
　　　　　but regretted that the Way did not prevail;
　　　　were not anxious about their brief life spans
　　　　　but worried that the people were impoverished.
For this reason,
　　　　when Yu acted on the waterways,
　　　　he used his own body to break through the banks of the Yangxu
　　　　　　[River];
　　　　and Tang, at the time of the great drought,
　　　　　offered himself as a sacrifice at the edge of Mulberry Forest.
If the sages' solicitousness for the people was as clear as this, is it not deluded to accuse them [of being] "non-active"?
　　Furthermore, in ancient times
　　　　when emperors and kings were established, it was not to serve and nourish
　　　　　their [own] desires;

when sages took office, it was not to indulge and delight their own persons.

It was because in the world,
- the strong oppressed the weak,
- the many violated the few,
- the clever deceived the ignorant,
- and the brave dispossessed the timid.
- Those who possessed knowledge did not impart it;
- those who accumulated wealth did not distribute it.

Thus the Son of Heaven was established in order to equalize them.

Since one person's intelligence was not sufficient to shed light on all things within the [Four] Seas, the Three Dukes and the Nine Ministers were established to aid and assist him.

Since inaccessible states with varied customs and remote and secluded locales could not receive and be enriched by the ruler's virtue, Lords of the Land were established to instruct and admonish them.

This made it so that
- no land was untended,
- no season was not [met with its proper] response,
- no official concealed his activities,
- no state neglected to benefit [the people].

By these means, they clothed the cold and fed the hungry, nourished the old and infirm, and gave respite to those wearied from their labors.

[Moreover,] if you look at the sages from the perspective of the common man, then
- [the cook] Yi Yin, with cauldron on his back, sought to serve Tang;
- [the butcher] Lü Wang, with carving knife in hand, entered Zhou [to serve as a high official];

Baili Xi was sold back to [Duke Mu of] Qin;

Guan Zhong was tied and fettered [and taken to the court of Duke Huan of Qi].

Confucius's stove was not black,
and Mozi's mat was not warm.[2]

Thus it is that sages
- do not consider mountains high,
- do not consider rivers wide.

---

2. Confucius's stove was not black and Mozi's mat was not warm because their duties as teachers so often took them away from home.

They withstand insult and humiliation in order to seek to serve a ruler of their age. They do not crave high salaries or covet official posts but instead want to work to advance the world's benefits and eradicate the common people's hardships. In a work that has been transmitted to us it is written:

> "The Divine Farmer was haggard and downcast;
> Yao was emaciated and forlorn;
> Shun was weather-beaten and dark;
> and Yu had calloused hands and feet."

Looking at it from this perspective, the sages' anxious toiling for the common people is profound indeed. Thus from the Son of Heaven down to the common people, when

> the four limbs are not exercised
> and thought and forethought [are] not applied,

yet the tasks of governance are addressed and resolved—such a thing has never been heard of.

## 19.7

> Those who fully comprehend things cannot be startled by the unusual;
> those who are versed in the Way cannot be moved by the strange;
> those who examine words cannot be dazzled by their designations;
> those who investigate into forms cannot be misled by their appearances.

People who follow the conventions of the present age mostly revere the ancient and scorn the present. Thus those who formulate [teachings of] the Way necessarily ascribe them to the Divine Farmer or the Yellow Emperor; only then will they proceed with their discussion. Muddled rulers of chaotic eras venerate what is remote and what proceeds therefrom, so they value such things. Those who study are blinded by their theories and respect [only] what they have heard. Facing one another,

> seated with a dignified air they praise [the ancients];
> stiff-necked they recite [the ancient texts].

This shows that the distinction between what is true and what is false is not clear.

Now,

> without a square and a compass, even Xi Zhong could not determine square and round;
> without a level and a marking cord, even Lu Ban could not straighten the crooked.

Thus,

when Zhongzi Qi died, Bo Ya broke the strings and destroyed his *qin*,
knowing that in his times no one could appreciate his playing.

When Hui Shi died, Zhuangzi ceased to talk, perceiving that there was no
one else with whom he could converse.

At the age of seven, Xiang Tuo became Confucius's teacher. From time to time, Confucius listened to his words. If someone this young were to offer a persuasion to a village elder, though, the child would not have time to duck a blow on the head. How would he be able to illuminate the Way [under such circumstances]?

In the past, Xiezi had an audience with King Hui of Qin, and the king was pleased with him. He asked Tang Guliang about him. Tang Guliang said, "Xiezi is a debater from Shandong who uses clever persuasions to gain the confidence of young princes." King Hui accordingly hid his anger and awaited Xiezi. The next day when Xiezi had a second audience, the king rejected him and would not heed him. It is not that [Xiezi's] persuasion differed but that the way in which the king heard it changed.

If you mistake [the note] *zhi* for [the note] *yu*, it is not the fault of the string;
if you mistake a sweet taste for a bitter one, it is not the mistake of the flavor.

A man from Chu had some boiled monkey meat that he gave to his neighbors. They thought it was dog meat and found its flavor pleasing. Later, when they heard it was monkey, they knelt down and vomited all they had eaten. This was a case of not even beginning to know about flavor.

A music master from Handan made up a new tune and said it was composed by Li Qi. All the people vied to learn it. Later when they discovered it was not written by Li Qi, they all abandoned the tune. This was a case of not even beginning to know about music.

A country fellow found a rough piece of jade. Being pleased by its appearance, he considered it to be precious and hid it away. When he showed it to others, people considered that it was just a stone, so he threw it away. This was a case of not even beginning to know about jade.

Thus when your [views] tally with what is essential, you will value what is true and [give] equal [consideration to] the present and the ancient. If you do not have the means to heed persuasions, then you will value what has come down from the past, [simply] because it is remote. This is why [Bian] He cried so hard that he bled at the foot of Mount Jing.

Now,
a sword may be broken off and bent, thin and scratched, chipped and broken, and warped and twisted, but if it said to have been the sword of King Qingxiang of Chu, then it is prized, and the people will compete to wear it.

A *qin* may be twangy and sharp, crooked and bent, with its resonance gone and its aftertones excessive, but if it is said to have been the *qin* of King Zhuang of Chu, then it is [prized], and the favored will contend to play it.

Although the short-handled spears from Mount Miao and the [cast-iron] spear points of Sheepshead [Mountain] can cut through a dragon boat in the water and pierce armor of rhinoceros hide on land, no one wears them on his belt.

Although *qins* made of mountain *tong* wood with sounding boards of river-valley catalpa wood may sound as pure, lingering and clear as [the music of] Master Tang or Bo Ya, no one plays them.

Those with penetrating discernment are not like this.

> The swordsman hopes for a sharp blade; he does not hope for [the perfection of] a Moyang or a Moye;
>
> the horseman hopes for a thousand *li* [steed]; he does not hope for [the perfection of] Hualiu or Lü'er;
>
> the *qin* player hopes for a pure, lingering, and clear sound; he does not hope for [the perfection of] Lanxie or Haozhong.³

One who [studies by] reciting the *Odes* and the *Documents* hopes to achieve a comprehensive understanding of the Way and a general knowledge of things; he does not hope for [the perfection of] a "Great Plan" or an "Ode of Shang."

Sages perceive what is true and what is false, just as

> what is white and black is distinguished by the eye
>
> and what is high pitched and low pitched is differentiated by the ears.

But most people are not like this. Within themselves they lack a master [by means of which] to make [such] discernments. It is like a man who is born after his father dies. When [in later years] he climbs the tomb mound, he will wail and cry as ceremony demands, but nothing makes [those feelings] cleave to his heart.

Thus,

> when a boy and his twin look alike, only their mother can distinguish them.
>
> When jade and [ordinary] stone are of the same sort, only a fine craftsman can identify them.
>
> When texts and chronicles record strange things, only sages can discuss them.

---

3. Moyang and Moye were famous swords; Hualiu and Lü'er were famous horses; and Lanxie and Haozhong were famous *qin*. Each was an exemplar of perfection.

Now, if we should get a new text from a sage and attribute it to Confucius or Mozi, then those disciples who point to every sentence and accept the text [as genuine] will certainly be numerous. Thus

> a beauty need not be of the same type as Xi Shi;
> a knowledgeable scholar need not be of the same sort as Confucius or Mozi.

If his mind has the perspicacious capacity to penetrate things, then he will write books to illustrate matters, and they will be taken up by the learned. A scholar who truly attains clear-minded understanding, who grasps the profound mirror in his mind, illuminating things brilliantly and not changing his mind on account of [whether something is] ancient or current, will accordingly propound his writings and clearly point out [his views]. Then, even though his coffin might close, he would have no regrets.

Formerly Duke Ping of Jin ordered his officials to make [a set of] bells. When they were finished and presented to Music Master Kuang, the latter said, "The bells are not in tune."

Duke Ping said, "I have shown them to skilled persons, and they all think they are in tune. Yet you think they are not. Why?"

Music Master Kuang said, "If they are for those of later generations who have no knowledge of the notes, then they will do; but for those who know the notes, they will certainly know they are not in tune." Thus Music Master Kuang's wish for well-tuned bells was for those of later generations who knew the notes.

The [people of the] Three Dynasties acted the same as we do, and the Five Hegemons had the same level of intelligence as we. [But] they alone had the reality of sagely knowledge, while we lack even

> the reputation of a country village
> or the common knowledge of a poor lane.

Why? [It is because] they set themselves straight and established their integrity, while we are rude idlers and lazy layabouts.

Now Mao Qiang and Xi Shi were recognized by the world as beauties, but if they were made to

> carry putrid rats in their mouths
> and be wrapped in hedgehog skins,
> and dress in leopard fur,[4]
> with waist sashes of dead snakes,

even cloth-wearing, leather-belted [ordinary] people passing by all would look off to the left or right and hold their noses. But if we were to let them

---

4. In this context, the connotation is of masculinity and perhaps barbarism, not of luxury or feminine elegance.

wear perfume and unguents,
adjust their moth eyebrows,[5]
put on hair clasps and earrings,
dress in fine silk,
and trail [sleeves of] Qi silk gauze,
with white face powder and black mascara,
wearing jade sash-bangles,
walking with gliding steps,
wearing sprigs of fragrant angelica,
with enticing looks,
bewitching smiles,
haunting glances,
speaking delicately and softly,
exposing their beautiful teeth,
twitching the dimples in their cheeks,

then even among the great statesmen of the royal court, whose conduct displays a stern will and haughty air, there would be none who would not court these beauties, long for them, and desire to have sex with them.

Nowadays a person of average talent, benighted by ignorant and deluded wisdom, cloaked in insulting and shameful conduct, who has no training in his own calling or in the techniques that are his responsibility—how could he not make people look askance at him and hold their noses?

Now dancers twirl their bodies like rings of jade. They bend and touch the ground and turn quickly and nimbly. As they move, they twist and turn, lithe and beautiful, imitating spirits.

Their bodies seem as light as wind-borne autumn floss,
their hair like banners flapping in the wind,
their steps are quick as those of a racehorse.

Acrobats, raising poles of *wu* [*tong*] or catalpa wood and grasping crooked tree branches, are as uninhibited as monkeys. Laughing, they pull the leaves toward them; crouching and stretching like dragons, they perch on the branches like swallows. Holding thick tree limbs, they raise them effortlessly. As they dance, they rise like dragons or birds as they gather. They grasp and release; how fast they move!

There is no one among the spectators who does not grow faint at heart and weak in the knees. Meanwhile, the performers continue their act with a smile and then put on the costumes for the feather dance.

---

5. Moth eyebrows were artificial eyebrows applied with makeup.

The dancers do not [inherently] have such supple and nimble [bodies];
the acrobats do not [inherently] have such keenness and strength.
It was the gradual, long-term practice and training that made them so. Thus,
when a tree grows, no one sees its progress; at a certain point, we realize that it has grown tall.
If a hard object is continually [sharpened] on a whetstone, no one sees it diminishing, but at some point we realize that it is thinner.

Pigweed and hyssop grow by leaps and bounds, each day adding several inches. But they cannot be used for the crossbeams of a building. With hardwoods [like] lindera, southernwood, or camphor, only after seven years can their growth be recognized. Then they can be used to make coffins and boats.

Thus, matters
that can be accomplished easily gain small fame for the one who does them;
[those] that are difficult to accomplish gain great merit.
The Superior Man cultivates his good points. Even though there might not be an [immediate] advantage, good fortune will come later. Thus the *Odes* says,
"The days pass and the months proceed;
through study of brightness and brilliance,
I gain radiance and light."
This is what is referred to here.

# Twenty

## THE EXALTED LINEAGE

"The Exalted Lineage"
    traverses the eight end points,
    extends to the highest heights,
    illuminates the three luminaries above,
    and harmonizes water and earth below.
    It aligns the Way of past and present,
    orders the hierarchy of human relationships and patterns,
    summarizes the tenets of the myriad regions,
    and returns them home to a single root,
thereby
    knotting the net of the Way of Governance
    and weaving the web of the affairs of the True King.
[It] then
    traces to the source the techniques of the mind,
    sets in order instinct and nature,
and thereby
    provides a lodging place for the numen of Clarity and Equanimity.
    It clarifies and purifies the quintessence of spirit illumination,
    thereby enfolding and cleaving to the harmony of Heaven.
It provides the means to observe how the Five Thearchs and the Three Kings
    embraced the heavenly *qi*,
    cherished the Heavenly Heart,

and grasped centrality and savored harmony.
Their Moral Potency having taken shape within [them],
it then cohered Heaven and Earth,
issued forth and aroused yin and yang,
ordered the four seasons,
rectified the changeable directions,
calmed things with its tranquillity,
and extended them with its efficaciousness.

[Their Moral Potency] then thereby
fired and smelted the myriad things,
buoyed up and transformed the innumerable life forms,
singing forth, they harmonized,
moving about, they followed along,

so that all things within the Four Seas with a single mind unanimously offered their allegiance.

Thus,
lucky stars appeared,
auspicious winds arrived,
the Yellow Dragon descended,
phoenix nests lined the trees,
and the *qilin* tarried in the open fields.
Had Moral Potency not taken shape within [them],
yet their laws and tributes were implemented,
and their regulations and measures were employed exclusively,
then the spirits and divinities would not have responded to them;
good fortune and blessings would not have returned home to them;
all things within the Four Seas would not have submitted to them;
and subjects would not have been transformed by them.

Thus,
Moral Potency that takes shape within
is the great foundation of governance.

This is [the message of] "The Exalted Lineage" of the *Profoundly Illustrious*.

"An Overview of the Essentials" (21.2)

With this final substantive chapter of the *Huainanzi*, the reader is invited to "knot the net of the Way of Governance and weave the web . . . of the True King," thus rounding off his education. "The Exalted Lineage" reminds the young monarch, who is the intended audience of the entire book and who presumably aspires to sagely rule, that the "Moral Potency that takes shape within is the great foundation of governance." Moreover, this chapter makes clear that such internally generated Moral Potency has far-reaching cosmo-political implications affecting both Heaven above and the people below. In making its case, the chapter identifies for the reader a number of exemplary rulers of both the recent and the remote past who embodied these ideals and thereby brought order and harmony to the wider world.

As the chapter title suggests, these great rulers are seen as being part of a virtual lineage culminating in the rulers of the present Han dynasty, the Liu clan (of which the *Huainanzi*'s sponsor-editor, Liu An, was himself a prominent member). Not surprisingly, whereas many earlier chapters of the *Huainanzi* drew, in various ways, on the whole corpus of pre-Han and early Han literature, the principal source for this chapter is the *Huainanzi* itself. This long and rhetorically rich chapter recapitulates many of the themes and concepts associated with sage-rulership found in earlier chapters of the *Huainanzi*, and so it brings this great work to a close.

# Twenty

### 20.1

Heaven
> established the sun and moon,
> arranged the stars and planets,
> harmonized the yin and yang,
> and displayed the four seasons.
> The day serves to blaze things with sunlight;
> the evening serves to give them respite;
> the wind serves to dry things out,
> and the rain and dew serve to moisten them.
> In giving life to things, no one sees the means by which it nurtures them and yet things reach maturity.
> In taking life away from things, no one sees the means by which it sends them off to death and yet things cease to exist.

This is called "spirit illumination." Sages take it as their model. Thus,
> when they initiate good fortune, no one sees from whence it originates and yet it arises.
> When they eradicate calamity, no one sees the means by which they do so and yet it disappears.
> Move away from it; it nears.
> Approach it; it recedes.
> Search for it; it will not be obtained.

Examine into it; it is not insubstantial.
Reckon it by days; it is incalculable.
Reckon it by years; there is surplus.

## 20.3 (in part)

When the High Ancestors went into mourning, for three years they did not speak, and all within the Four Seas were silent and voiceless. [But] as soon as a single word was uttered, [they] greatly moved the world. This is because they relied on their Heavenly Heart when opening and closing their mouths. Thus, as soon as you stimulate the root, the hundred branches all respond. It is like the spring rains watering the myriad things;

> turbulently they flow,
> copiously they spread out;
> there is no place that is not moistened
> and no plant that does not thrive.

Thus, when the sage embraces his Heavenly Heart, his voice can move and transform the world. Thus, when his Quintessential Sincerity is stimulated within, an embodied *qi* responds in Heaven:

> Lucky stars appear,
> yellow dragons descend,
> auspicious winds arrive,
> sweet springs appear,
> excellent grains thrive,
> rivers do not fill and overflow,
> and the seas do not churn and roil.

Thus the *Odes* says,

> "Nurturing and yielding are the hundred spirits
> even to the rivers and mountain peaks."

When you oppose heaven and oppress the myriad things,

> the sun and moon [suffer] partial eclipses;
> the five planets lose their proper orbits;
> the four seasons overstep one another.
> In the day it is dark and at night it is light;
> mountains crumble and rivers flood;
> in winter there are thunderstorms, and in summer there are frosts.

The *Odes* says,

> "In the first month, frost is abundant;
> my heart is anxious and grieved."

## 20.5

Now with regard to ghosts and spirits,
> we look for them, but they are without form;
> we listen for them, but they are without voice;

yet we perform the Suburban Sacrifice to Heaven and the [appropriate] observances to the mountain and river [spirits].
> With prayer and sacrifice we seek prosperity;
> with invocations and charms we seek rain;
> with tortoise shell and milfoil we decide matters.

The *Odes* says,
> "When the spirits might descend
> cannot be calculated.
> How can you treat them with disdain?"

## 20.10

Heaven, Earth, and the four seasons do not [purposefully] produce the ten thousand things.
> Spirit and illumination join,
> yin and yang harmonize,

and the myriad things are born. When a sage rules the world, he does not change the people's nature but soothes and facilitates the nature that is already present and purifies and cleanses it. Thus following [the nature of things] may be considered great, whereas making [things] may be considered minor.

Yu dredged the Dragon Gate, broke through Yique, demarcated the Yangzi River, and channeled the Yellow River [so that] they ran eastward into the sea, by following the [natural] flow of water.

Lord Millet reclaimed the grasslands and introduced tillage, fertilized the soil and planted grain, enabling each of the five grains to grow appropriately, by following the propensity of the soil.

Tang and Wu, with three hundred armored chariots and three thousand soldiers in armor, quelled the violent and rebellious and brought Xia and Shang under control, by following the people's desire.

Thus if you can follow [the nature of things], you will be matchless in the world.

Now if things first have what is natural to them, afterward human affairs can be governed.

Thus,
> a fine carpenter cannot carve metal,

and a skillful blacksmith cannot melt wood.
The propensity of metal is that it cannot be carved,
and the nature of wood is that it cannot be melted.
You can
mold clay into a vessel,
gouge out wood and make a boat,
forge iron and make a blade,
cast metal and make a bell,
by following their [inherent] possibilities.
You can
drive a horse and lead an ox,
use a rooster to announce night's end,
and tell a dog to guard the gate—
because it follows their natures.
People have a nature that is fond of sex, so there is the ceremony of marriage.
They have a nature that [requires] food and drink, so there is the suitability of a great banquet.
They have a nature that delights in music, so there are the sounds of bells, drums, pipes, and strings.
They have a nature to grieve and be melancholy, so there are the customs of wearing mourning clothes, crying, and jumping about [at funerals].
Therefore, the institutions and laws of the former kings followed what the people liked but [also] established controls and civilizing [restrictions] for them.
Following along with people's fondness for sex, they set up the rites of marriage so men and women could be [properly] separated.
Following along with their delight in music, they rectified the sounds of the "Ya" and "Song" so that habits and customs would not be unrestrained.
Following along with their preference to live as families and find joy in their wives and children, they taught filial piety so that fathers and sons would be affectionate.
Following along with their delight in friendship, they taught brotherly love so that older and younger would be in proper standing with each other.
Only after this did they
use court ceremonies to clarify high rank and low
and use rural libations[1] and archery contests to clarify adulthood and youth.

---

1. "Rural libations" refers to a kind of village festival during which participants drank in order of seniority.

In season, [the youths] held exercises to practice using weapons or entered school according to their station to learn to cultivate the arts of human relations.

These all are cases in which people already possessed [qualities] by nature, which sages fashioned and completed.

Thus if the nature is not there, it is not possible to educate or train [a person]. If the nature is there but has not been nurtured, he cannot follow the Way.

> It is the nature of the silkworm to make silk, but unless you have a skilled female worker to boil the cocoon in hot water and draw its filaments, there can be no silk.
>
> An egg transforms into a chick, but unless you have a mother hen to sit on and warm the egg and brood it for several days, it cannot produce a chick.

Human nature is endowed with Humaneness and Rightness, but unless you have a sage to institute laws and standards to teach and guide them, people will not be able to find the correct path.

Thus the teaching of the former kings was
> to follow what people delight in so as to encourage goodness and
> to follow what people hate so as to prohibit wickedness. Thus,
> punishments and penalties were not used, but awe-inspiring conduct seemed to flow forth [everywhere].
> Policies and ordinances were limited, but their transforming brilliance [pervaded] as if they were spiritlike.

Thus if you follow nature, the whole world will come along with you. If you go against nature, even if you were to publish the laws, it would be of no use.

## 20.13 (in part)

The sage
> covers like Heaven, upholds like Earth,
> illuminates like the sun and moon,
> harmonizes like yin and yang,
> transforms like the four seasons,
> [treats] the myriad things all differently,
> is without precedent or novelty,
> is without stranger or kin.

Thus [the sage] takes Heaven as his model.
> Heaven does not have [only] a single season;
> Earth does not have [only] a single benefit;
> humankind does not have [only] a single affair.

Therefore,
>   various undertakings cannot but have multiple origins;
>   hurried steps cannot but take different directions.
>   The Five Phases are of different *qi*, but all are harmonious.
>   The Six Arts are of different categories, but all are connected.
>   Warmth and kindness, gentleness and goodness, are the influences of the *Odes*;
>   purity and grandeur, nobility and generosity, are the teachings of the *Documents*;
>   clarity and brilliance, perception and penetration, are the norms of the *Changes*;
>   deference and self-control, respect and humility, are the behaviors of the *Rites*;
>   broad-mindedness and magnanimity, simplicity and easiness, are the transforming [qualities] of the *Music*;
>   reprimands and critiques, blame and appraisal, are the polishing cloths of the *Spring and Autumn [Annals]*.

Thus [if relied on exclusively],
>   the shortcoming of the *Changes* is superstition;
>   the shortcoming of the *Music* is lewdness;
>   the shortcoming of the *Odes* is foolishness;
>   the shortcoming of the *Documents* is rigidity,
>   the shortcoming of the *Rites* is stubbornness, and
>   the shortcoming of the *Spring and Autumn* is censoriousness.

The sage uses [all] six in conjunction and both prizes and institutes them.

## 20.18

In governing the self,
>   it is best to nurture the spirit.
>   The next best is to nurture the body.

In governing the state,
>   it is best to nurture transformation.
>   The next best is to correct the laws.
>   A clear spirit and a balanced will,
>   the hundred joints all in good order,

constitute the root of nurturing vitality.
>   To fatten the muscles and skin,
>   to fill the bowel and belly,

>    to satiate the lusts and desires,
>
> constitute the branches of nurturing vitality.
>    If the people
> >    yield to one another and compete to dwell humbly;
> >    delegate benefit and compete to receive scantily,
> >    work at tasks and compete to follow arduously,
>
> daily transformed by their superiors and moved to goodness without realizing the means by which they came to be so, this is the root of government.
> >    With beneficial rewards to encourage goodness
> >    and fearful punishments to prevent misdeeds,
> >    laws and ordinances corrected above
> >    and the common people submitting below:
>
> these are the branches of government.

Earlier generations nurtured the root, but later generations served the branches. This is why Great Peace does not arise. Now a ruler who desires to govern well does not appear in every age, and a minister who can accompany a ruler in initiating good government does not appear once in ten thousand [officials]. To rely on a minister who does not appear once in ten thousand to seek out a ruler who does not appear in every age is the reason why they do not meet once in ten thousand years!

## 20.19

> >    The nature of water
> >    is to be saturating and clear.
> >    In valleys where it is stagnant
> >    and gives birth to green algae,
>
> [that results from] not controlling it [according to] its nature. If you make channels where it flows and deepen the flow or build up where it [threatens to] flood through and raise [its level], you will enable it to move in compliance with its natural propensity, moving along and flowing onward. Though carrion and rotten bones flow and mix with the water, they cannot pollute it. The nature [of water] is not different; it is just a matter of whether it can flow through [a channel] or not flow through.
>    Customs and habits are like this. If [the ruler's] sincerity
> >    floods through to goodness of will,
> >    builds embankments against depravity of heart,
> >    opens up the road to goodness
> >    and blocks the path to wickedness,

then likewise [sincerity] emerges into a single Way, [so that] the people's nature can become good and customs and habits can be beautified.

## 20.23

In ancient times,
    laws were established, but they were not violated;
    punishments were elaborated, but they were not used.
It is not the case that they could punish but did not punish.
  The hundred kinds of artisans adhered to the seasons, and their many achievements were, without exception, brilliant. Propriety and Rightness were cultivated, and the worthy and the virtuous were employed. Thus they promoted
    the loftiest in the world to become the Three Dukes,
    the loftiest in the state to become the Nine Ministers,
    the loftiest in the counties to become the twenty-seven grandees,
    and the loftiest in the prefectures to become the eighty-one functionaries.
    Those whose knowledge surpassed ten thousand men were called "talented";
    those whose knowledge surpassed a thousand men were called "eminent";
    those whose knowledge surpassed a hundred men were called "brave";
    those whose knowledge surpassed ten men were called "prominent."
Those who
    understood the Way of Heaven,
    investigated the patterns of Earth,
    penetrated human feelings,
    whose greatness sufficed to accommodate the multitudes,
    whose Moral Potency sufficed to embrace the distant,
    whose trustworthiness sufficed to unify heterogeneity,
    and whose knowledge sufficed to understand alteration
were the "talented" among men.
  Those whose
    Moral Potency sufficed to transform [the people] through education,
    conduct sufficed to accord with Rightness,
    Humaneness sufficed to win the multitudes,
    and brilliance sufficed to illuminate those below
were the "eminent" among men.
  Those whose
    conduct sufficed to be ceremonious and exemplary,
    knowledge sufficed to resolve deceptive resemblances,
    honesty enabled them to distribute resources,

trustworthiness enabled them to inspire [others] to honor their commitments,
accomplished deeds could be emulated,
and spoken words could be used for guidance

were the "brave " among men.

Those who
held to their duties and did not abandon them,
dwelled in Rightness and were not partisan,
encountered hardships and did not illicitly avoid them,
and perceived advantages and did not illicitly gain from them

were the "prominent" among men.

The "talented," "eminent," "brave," and "prominent" each in accordance with their degree of ability occupied their official position and attained what was appropriate to each.

From the root flowing to the branches, using the heavy to control the light,
when the ruler called, the people harmonized;
when the ruler moved, the lowly followed.

Within the Four Seas, all submitted with a single mind, turning their backs on greed and avarice and turning toward Humaneness and Rightness. In transforming the people, they resembled the wind stirring the grasses and trees, leaving nothing unaffected.

## 20.28

Those who have the ability to accomplish the work of hegemon or king are invariably those who gain victory;
those who have the ability to gain victory are invariably those who are powerful;
those who have the ability to be powerful are invariably those who employ the people's strength;
those who have the ability to employ the people's strength are invariably those who gain the people's hearts;
those who have the ability to gain the people's hearts are invariably those who gain mastery over the self.

Thus,
the heart is the root of the self;
the self is the root of the state.
There has never been a person who gained "the self " and lost the people;
there has never been a person who lost "the self " and gained the people.

Thus, to establish the basis of order, you must exert yourself to secure the people.

> The root of securing the people lies in sufficiency of use;
> the root of sufficiency of use lies in not taking them from their seasonal [work];
> the root of not taking them from their seasonal [work] lies in reducing endeavors;
> the root of reducing endeavors lies in regulating desires;
> the root of regulating desires lies in reverting back to nature.

It has never been possible
> to agitate the root yet calm the branches;
> to pollute the source yet purify the flow.

Thus,
> those who know the essential qualities of nature do not endeavor to make nature do what it cannot do.
> Those who know the essential qualities of fate are not anxious about what fate cannot control.

Thus,
> those who do not [erect] lofty palaces and terraces do not do so because they cherish trees;
> those who do not [cast] massive bells and tripods do not do so because they cherish metal.

They straightforwardly put into practice the essential qualities of nature and fate so that their regulations and measures can be taken to constitute a standard for the myriad people.

Now when
> the eyes delight in the five colors,
> the mouth relishes enticing flavors,
> the ears are enraptured by the five sounds,

the seven orifices struggle with one another and harm [your] nature, daily attracting wicked desires and disturbing its heavenly harmony. If you cannot govern "the self," how can you govern the world? Thus if in nurturing the self you achieve regulation, then in nurturing the people you will win their hearts.

The expression "taking possession of the world" does not refer to holding power and position, accepting hereditary rank, or being referred to by a respectful title. It means
> linking up with the strength of the world
> and winning the hearts of the world.

The territory of [the tyrant] Djou to the left reached the Eastern Sea and to the right reached to the Sea of Sands. Before him lay Jiaozhi and behind him lay Youdu.[2] His armies climbed Rong Pass and reached the Pu River. Their warriors numbered in the tens and hundreds of thousands, but they all shot their arrows backward and fought with their halberds turned [toward the tyrant]. King Wu of Zhou with his left hand held a yellow battle-ax and with his right grasped a white banner to direct his armies, and the enemy were shattered like broken tiles and fled, collapsing like a pile of earth.

[The tyrant] Djou had the title of "the one who faces south" [i.e., the ruler] but lacked the praise of even a single man. This is how he lost the world. Thus Jie and Djou cannot be considered [to have been true] kings, and [Kings] Tang and Wu cannot be considered to have banished them.

The Zhou people dwelled in the lands of Feng and Hao. Their territory did not exceed a hundred *li*, yet they swore an oath against [the tyrant] Djou at Mulberry Field and attacked and occupied the Yin state. They

> held a memorial service at the ancestral temple of Tang the Victorious,
> conferred a plaque at the gates of the village where Shang Rong lived,
> built up the tomb of Bi Gan,
> and released the imprisoned Jizi.

Only then did they

> snap the drumsticks and destroy the drums of war,
> retire the five kinds of weapons,
> release the oxen and the horses,
> gather up the jade insignia tablets,
> and accept the fealty of the world.

The people [lit. the "hundred surnames"] sang ballads to celebrate them while the Lords of the Land, grasping gifts of exotic birds, came calling at their court, for the hearts of the people had been won.

---

2. This description reflects the orientation of Chinese maps, with south at the top of the page. The places named correspond approximately to the Yellow Sea, the Gobi Desert, Vietnam, and the Inner Asian frontier grasslands.

# Twenty-One

## AN OVERVIEW OF THE ESSENTIALS

"Yao lue," or "An Overview of the Essentials," stands somewhat apart from the twenty chapters of the *Huainanzi* that precede it. Although "Yao lue" appears at the end of the work (following the established convention of Chinese works of the late Warring States and early Han periods), it serves as, and apparently was written as, an introduction to the entire work. It explains why the book was written, orients readers to its contents, and makes claims for its value and universal validity. We believe that the chapter was originally written by Liu An himself for oral recitation at the imperial court as an introduction to and description of the *Huainanzi* when the entire text was formally presented to Emperor Wu in 139 B.C.E., shortly after he ascended the throne. Having been recited at court, the "overview" would then have been appended in written form to the twenty substantive chapters of the *Huainanzi*, serving as a postscript to review and summarize its contents.

The chapter consists of four complementary sections. The first introduces the work as a whole and provides a list of the twenty chapter titles that, strikingly, form a rhymed set. The second gives a thoughtful and illuminating summary of each chapter in turn. (We have quoted these summaries in our introductions to each of the chapters.) The next section links the twenty chapters together in a grand design, showing that each chapter builds on those that precede it. The final section argues for the cogency and significance of the work as a whole by placing it in a comparative and historical framework.

The form of this chapter is distinctive and of great interest. It is a *fu* (poetic expression), a type of verse very popular in Han China, and of which Liu An was an acknowledged master. (Another example of the genre in the *Huainanzi* is section 8.9.) As we see in this chapter, works in the *fu* genre tend to be quite long, and to make intricate use of rhyme, shifting meter, and ornate, baroque vocabulary. Apparently, *fu* were usually composed in writing (again as seems to be the case here) for oral recitation. Both the written text and the oral recitation were expected to be virtuoso performances, in which the literary quality of the work increased both its prestige and its persuasiveness. It is inspiring to think of Liu An (or a professional performer reciting on his behalf) intoning this dazzling poetic composition as a way of launching the *Huainanzi* on its long career as a major work of Chinese philosophy.

# Twenty-One

### 21.1 (in part)

We have created and composed these writings and discourses as a means to
> knot the net of the Way and its Potency
> and weave the web of humankind and its affairs,
> above investigating them in Heaven,
> below examining them on Earth,
> and in the middle comprehending them through patterns.

Although they are not yet able to draw out fully the core of the Profound Mystery, they are abundantly sufficient to observe its ends and beginnings. If we [only] summarized the essentials or provided an overview and our words did not discriminate the Pure, Uncarved Block and differentiate the Great Ancestor, then it would cause people in their confusion to fail to understand them. Thus,
> numerous are the words we have composed
> and extensive are the illustrations we have provided,

yet we still fear that people will depart from the root and follow the branches.
   Thus,
> if we speak of the Way but do not speak of affairs,
> there would be no means to shift with the times.

[Conversely],

> if we speak of affairs but do not speak of the Way,
> there would be no means to move with [the processes of] transformation.
>
> Therefore we composed [the book's] twenty essays. . . .

## 21.3

In all, these interconnected writings are the means to focus on the Way and remove obstructions, enabling succeeding generations to know what is appropriate to uphold or abandon and what is suitable to endorse or reject.

> Externally, when they interact with things, they will not be bewildered;
> internally, they will possess the means to lodge their spirit and nourish their *qi*.

They will take ease in and merge with utmost harmony, delighting themselves in what they have received from Heaven and Earth.
Therefore,

> Had we discussed the Way ["Originating in the Way"] and not illuminated ends and beginnings ["Activating the Genuine"],
> you would not know the models to follow.
> Had we discussed ends and beginnings and not illuminated Heaven, Earth, and the four seasons ["Celestial Patterns," "Terrestrial Forms," and "Seasonal Rules," respectively],
> you would not know the taboos to avoid.
> Had we discussed Heaven, Earth, and the four seasons and not introduced examples and elucidated categories,
> you would not recognize the subtleties of the quintessential *qi* ["Surveying Obscurities"].
> Had we discussed the Utmost Essence and not traced to its source the spiritlike *qi* of human beings,
> you would not know the mechanism by which to nourish your vitality ["Quintessential Spirit"].
> Had we traced to their source the genuine dispositions of human beings and not discussed the Potency of the great sages,
> you would not know the [human] shortcomings associated with the Five Phases ["The Basic Warp"].
> Had we discussed the Way of the [Five] Thearchs and not discussed the affairs of the ruler,
> you would not know the proper order distinguishing the small from the great ["The Ruler's Techniques"].

Had we discussed the affairs of the ruler and not provided precepts and illustrations,
you would not know the times for taking action or remaining still ["Profound Precepts"].
Had we discussed precepts and illustrations and not discussed alterations in customs,
you would not know how to coordinate and equate their main tenets. ["Integrating Customs"].
Had we discussed alterations in customs and not discussed past events,
you would not know the responses of the Way and its Potency ["Responses of the Way"].
To know the Way and its Potency but not know the perversions of the age,
you would lack the means to accommodate yourself to the myriad aspects of the world ["Boundless Discourses"].
To know "Boundless Discourses" but not know "Sayings Explained,"
you would lack the means to take your ease.
To comprehend writings and compositions but not know the tenets of military affairs,
you would lack the means to respond to [enemy] troops ["An Overview of the Military"].
To know grand overviews but not know analogies and illustrations,
you would lack the means to clarify affairs by elaboration ["A Mountain of Persuasions" and "A Forest of Persuasions"].
To know the Public Way but not know interpersonal relations,
you would lack the means to respond to ill and good fortune ["Among Others"].
To know interpersonal relations but not know "Cultivating Effort,"
you would lack the means to inspire scholars to exert their utmost strength.

Should you desire
    to forcibly abridge this composition
    by observing and summarizing only its essentials
without traveling its winding paths and entering its subtle domains, this will not suffice to exhaust the meanings of the Way and its Potency.

    Therefore, we composed [these] writings in twenty chapters. Thereby
    the patterns of Heaven and Earth are thoroughly examined;
    the affairs of the human realm are comprehensively engaged;
    and the Way of [the Five] Thearchs and [Three] Kings is fully described.

Their discussions are
> sometimes detailed and sometimes general,
> sometimes subtle and sometimes obvious.
> The tenets advanced in each chapter are different,
> and each has a reason for being expressed.

Now, if we spoke exclusively of the Way, there would be nothing that is not contained in it. Nevertheless, only sages are capable of grasping its root and thereby knowing its branches. At this time, scholars lack the capabilities of sages, and if we do not provide them with detailed explanations,
> then to the end of their days they will flounder in the midst of darkness and obscurity
> without knowing the great awakening brought about by these writings' luminous and brilliant techniques.

Now, the "Qian" and "Kun" [trigrams] of the *Changes* suffice to comprehend the Way and disclose its meanings. With the eight trigrams you can understand the inauspicious and auspicious and know bad and good fortune. Nevertheless, Fu Xi made them into the sixty-four permutations [i.e., hexagrams], and the house of Zhou added six line-texts to each of the hexagrams, and these are the means to
> trace to the source and fathom the Way of Purity and Clarity
> and grasp and follow the Ancestor of the myriad things.

The number of the five notes does not exceed *gong, shang, jue, zhi,* and *yu*. Nevertheless, you cannot play them all on the [unstopped] five strings of a *qin*. You must control and harmonize the fine and thick strings, and only then can you produce a melody.

Now, if you draw only the head of a dragon, those observing it will not be able to identify what animal it is. But if you add the body, there will be no confusion as to the animal's identity.

Now,
> if our references to the "Way" were numerous,
> [but] if our references to "things" were few;
> if our references to "techniques" were extensive,
> [but] if our references to "affairs" were superficial,
> and we extended this [throughout] our discussions,
> we would be left speechless.
> Anyone who intended to study this

and who firmly wished to build on it, would [also] find himself with nothing to say.

Now,
> discussions about the Way are surpassingly profound;

> therefore, we have written many compositions on it [i.e., the Way] to reveal its true qualities.
> The myriad things are surpassingly numerous;
> therefore we have broadly offered explanations of them to communicate their significance.

Though these compositions may be
> winding and endless,
> complicated and slow going,
> intertwined and numerous,
> and distant and dawdling,

in order to distill and purify their utmost meaning and ensure that they are neither opaque nor impenetrable, we have retained them and not discarded them.

Now, although the debris and putrid carcasses floating in the Yangzi and Yellow rivers cannot be surpassed in number, nevertheless those who offer sacrifices draw water from them. [This is because] the rivers are so large.

Although a cup of wine may be sweet, if a fly is immersed in it, even commoners will not drink it. [This is because] the cup is so small.

If you sincerely comprehend the discussions in these twenty chapters, you will thereby
> observe their general patterns and grasp their essentials,
> penetrate the Nine Fields,
> pass through the Ten Gates,
> externalize Heaven and Earth,
> and extend beyond the mountains and rivers.
> Wandering and ambling through the span of a single age,
> governing and fashioning the forms of the Myriad Things,

surely this is an excellent journey! This being the case,
> you will clasp the sun and the moon without being burned,
> and you will anoint the myriad things without drying up.

> How ample! How lucid!
> It is enough to read this [alone]!
> How far-reaching and vast! How boundless!
> Here you may wander!

## 21.4 (in part)

> In this book of the Liu clan [i.e., the *Huainanzi*], [we have]
> observed the phenomena of Heaven and Earth,
> penetrated past and present discussions,

> weighed affairs and established regulations,
> measured forms and applied what is suitable,
> traced to its source the heart of the Way and its Potency,
> and united the customs of the Three Kings,
> collecting them and alloying them.
> At the core of the Profound Mystery,
> the infinitesimal movements of the essence have been revealed.
> By casting aside limits and boundaries
> and by drawing on the pure and the tranquil,

[We have] thereby

> unified the world,
> brought order to the myriad things,
> responded to alterations and transformations,
> and comprehended their distinctions and categories.

We have not

> followed a path made by a solitary footprint
> or adhered to instructions from a single perspective
> or allowed ourselves to be entrapped or fettered by things so that we would not advance or shift according to the age.
> Thus,
> situate [this book] in the narrowest of circumstances and nothing will obstruct it;
> extend it to the whole world and it will leave no empty spaces.

# GLOSSARY OF PERSONAL NAMES

This glossary contains the names of all personages found in the excerpted text, whether mythical, legendary, or historical, with the exception of names such as Grand Purity, Inexhaustible, and Wheelwright Flat that are clearly fanciful. Names are alphabetized by Chinese name. For example, Duke Huan of Qi is found under Huan (Duke Huan of Qi), and Music Master Kuang is found under Kuang (Music Master Kuang).

**BAILI XI** was the prime minister of Qin in the time of Duke Mu (ca. 660–621 B.C.E.). He was captured by Jin forces in Yu and escaped to Chu. Duke Mu told the ruler of Chu that Baili Xi had abandoned his office and offered five sheepskins for his return for prosecution. He thus secured the return of his valuable minister for a trifling amount.

**BEIGONGZI** (also known as Beigong You) was a famous swordsman of Qi, regarded as a paragon of courage.

**BI GAN** (eleventh century B.C.E.) was an upright uncle of Tyrant Djou, last king of the Shang dynasty. King Djou supposedly had his heart torn out to see if the heart of a famous worthy was any different from that of an ordinary person.

**BIAN HE** attempted to present a piece of raw jade to successive kings of Chu. Twice he was accused of fraud and severely punished but ultimately was vindicated.

**BIAN QUE** (fifth century B.C.E.) was a famous physician.

**BO** (Duke of Bo, Duke Sheng of Bo [d. 479 B.C.E.]) was a grandson of King Ping of Chu (r. 528–516 B.C.E.). His father was executed by the ruler of Zheng, and the Duke of Bo urged the prime minister of Chu to attack Zheng. Instead, Chu formed an alliance with Zheng and sent an army to help Zheng repel an invasion by Jin. The Duke of Bo rebelled and killed the Chu prime minister but was himself trapped in a bathhouse and killed.

BO YA was a master musician who famously broke his instrument when Zhongzi Qi, the person who most appreciated his music, died.

BO YU, supposedly a minister of the (mythical) Yellow Emperor, is identified as the inventor of clothing.

BOCHENG ZIGAO, a (mythical) Lord of the Land in predynastic times, was appointed by Yao but resigned his rank on the appointment of Shun to be Son of Heaven, complaining that government had become too burdensome and complex.

CHANG HONG (d. 492 B.C.E.) was an official of the state of Lu, famed for his skill in astronomy, calendrical computations, and divination.

CHENG (King Cheng of Zhou [r. 1043–1021 B.C.E.]) was the third king of the Zhou dynasty. The Duke of Zhou served as his regent until he reached his majority.

CHENG TANG. See Tang (King Tang or Tang the Victorious).

CHONG'ER. See Wen (Duke Wen of Jin).

CONFUCIUS (Kongzi [Master Kong] or Kong Qiu [551–479 B.C.E.]) is regarded as China's first philosopher and is especially revered as a great teacher.

DA BING and QIAN QUE were mythical charioteers of the astral god known as the Grand One (Taiyi).

DAN, DUKE. See Zhou Gong (Duke of Zhou).

DIVINE FARMER. See Shen Nong.

DJOU (Tyrant Djou [r. ?–1046 B.C.E.]), a semi-legendary last king of the Shang dynasty, was known for his extravagance and cruelty.

FU YUE was a (possibly legendary) minister during the Shang dynasty (ca. 1550–1046 B.C.E.). He is said to have ascended to Heaven by riding on certain constellations.

FUCHAI (King Fuchai of Wu [r. 495–477 B.C.E.]) defeated King Goujian of Yue and took him prisoner. He was subsequently defeated, and his state was extinguished, by the resurgent King Goujian with the help of the beautiful concubines Mao Qiang and Xi Shi, who had been sent from Yue to seduce and distract him.

FUXI (Tamer of Beasts) was a mythical culture-hero of predynastic times, credited with domesticating animals and creating the trigrams and hexagrams of the *Changes*. He is associated with his sister-spouse Nüwa, with early images of the pair often depicting them with entwined serpentine bodies.

GAN JIANG was a legendary swordsmith of superlative skill and the husband of the equally renowned swordsmith Mo Ye.

GAOYANG TUI was a grandee of Song, about whom nothing else is known.

GONG GONG was a mythical figure supposed to have lived during the predynastic era of sage-rulers. His name could be translated as "Master Artisan." He fought a titanic battle with Zhuan Xu, during which one of the pillars of Heaven was so damaged that the land tilted upward in the northwest.

GONGNIU AI was what might colloquially be termed a "weretiger." According to one commentator, the ability to transform into a tiger was a hereditary trait of the Gongniu clan.

GONGSHU (also known as Gongshu Ban or Lu Ban [ca. fifth century B.C.E.]) was a legendary artisan of supreme skill. He is said to have invented a "Cloud-Scaling Ladder" with which the king of Chu planned to attack the walled capital of the state of Song, until

Mozi persuaded him that his own disciples, who were defending Song, could defeat this technology.

GOU MANG was a mythical being or deity associated with the planet Jupiter.

GOUJIAN (King Goujian of Yue [r. 496–465 B.C.E.]) was defeated by King Fuchai of Wu and endured the humiliation of becoming his servant, but he later led a Yue army to defeat King Fuchai and extinguish his state.

GRAND ONE (Taiyi) was an astral deity who embodied the unity of the Way.

GRAY WOMAN was a mythical goddess or fairy associated with winter.

GUAN ZHONG was one of the most celebrated statesmen of the Spring and Autumn period. He served as prime minister under Duke Huan of Qi (r. 685–643 B.C.E.). The text known as the *Guanzi* bears his name but was written or compiled several centuries after his lifetime.

GUN was the (mythical) father of Yu the Great. He tried but failed to control the Great Flood and was therefore punished by the sage-ruler Shun.

HAN FEI (d. 233 B.C.E.) was a statecraft theorist during the late Warring States period. The text that bears his name, the *Hanfeizi*, was an important source for the *Huainanzi*.

HOU JI (Lord Millet) was a mythical sage-king of the predynastic era and divine ancestor of the ruling clan of the Zhou dynasty.

HOU TU (Sovereign of the Soil) was a mythical ruler during China's predynastic period.

HUAN (Duke Huan of Qi [r. 685–643 B.C.E.]) was one of the most powerful rulers of the Spring and Autumn period. He was the first to hold the post of hegemon and employed the famous statesman Guan Zhong as his prime minister.

HUAN DOU, a mythical figure who supposedly was a minister under the sage-ruler Yao, was exiled for opposing the accession of Shun to the throne.

HUANG DI, the Yellow Emperor, was a mythical sage-ruler of ancient China, associated with the central regions and the planet Saturn. He was credited with inventing the calendar, metallurgy, and other cultural phenomena.

HUI (King Hui of Qin [r. 337–311 B.C.E.]) was an aggressive ruler who expanded the power of Qin during his tenure as monarch. After taking the throne, he executed the reformer Shang Yang but continued his progressive policies.

HUI (King Hui of Wei, also known as King Hui of Liang [r. 369–319 B.C.E.]) was the first ruler of Wei to assume the title of king. He moved the capital of Wei to Da Liang and oversaw the building of several large-scale public works. At the end of his long reign, after suffering successive defeats by powerful neighbors, he initiated a campaign to attract scholars and drew figures like Mencius to his court.

HUI SHI. *See* Huizi.

HUIZI (Master Hui or Hui Shi [fourth century B.C.E.]) was a sophist who served as chief minister of King Hui of Liang (also known as King Hui of Wei). He is often depicted as having engaged in debates with Zhuangzi.

JI ZI (or Jizi) was a (possibly legendary) loyal official of the Shang dynasty. He was condemned to death by the tyrannical King Djou but escaped execution by feigning madness.

JIAN (Viscount Jian of Zhao, also known as Zhao Yang [d. 475 B.C.E.]), a ministerial vassal of Jin, was the successful leader of the Zhao clan in factional struggles against rival vassal clans. He was a proponent of government reform known for casting the penal laws of Jin onto bronze tripods for public display.

**JIE** (Tyrant Jie [ca. 1550 B.C.E.]), the semi-legendary last king of the Xia dynasty, was known for his cruelty and profligacy. He was overthrown by Tang the Victorious, founding king of the Shang dynasty.

**JIE FAN** was supposedly a strongman of the late Warring States period, about whom nothing else is known.

**JING** (Emperor Jing of the Han Dynasty, personal name Liu Qi [r. 157–141 B.C.E.]) was the fourth emperor of the Han dynasty. He was a grandson of the founding emperor, Liu Bang (Emperor Gao), and son of Emperor Wen. He and Liu An, the sponsor-editor of the *Huainanzi*, were cousins, and much of the book seems to have been written during Jing's reign.

**JING** (Duke Jing of Qi [r. 547–490 B.C.E.]) was placed on the throne by the rebel Cui Zhu. He was reputed to be a harsh and licentious ruler but to have improved somewhat under the edifying influence of Yan Ying.

**JINGGUO** (Lord Jingguo, also known as Tian Ying) was a scion of the Tian clan who became prime minister of Qi in 311 B.C.E. His son attained fame as Lord Mengchang. His fief of Xue is located in present-day Shandong Province.

**KANG** (King Kang of Zhou [r. ca. 1021–996 B.C.E.]) was the fourth king of the Zhou dynasty.

**KUANG** (Music Master Kuang), a semi-legendary figure said to have been Master of Music for the state of Jin during the Spring and Autumn period, was regarded as the greatest authority on music in ancient China. He is mentioned frequently in early texts.

**KONGZI** or **KONG QIU**. *See* Confucius.

**LAO DAN** (sixth century B.C.E.), a possibly legendary figure, has traditionally been identified with Laozi, the "Old Master," the supposed author of the work known as the *Laozi* or the *Daodejing*.

**LI JI, LADY** (seventh century B.C.E.) was a woman of a northern "barbarian" Rong tribe who became the favorite concubine of Duke Xian of Jin. His infatuation with her led to a train of disastrous events.

**LI KE** (also known as Li Kui [ca. 455–395 B.C.E.]) was a statesman and government reformer who served as the prime minister of Wei under Marquis Wen. He is credited with inventing certain techniques of rule, such as using the sale and purchase of state grain reserves to stabilize prices.

**LI QI** was a famous musician in the state of Zhao.

**LI ZHU** was supposedly a minister to the mythical sage-king Huangdi, the Yellow Emperor.

**LIU AN** (179–122 B.C.E.) was the patron, editor, and probable coauthor of the *Huainanzi*. He became king of Huainan in 164 B.C.E., succeeding his father after an interval of some years during which the kingdom was greatly reduced in size. He presided over a highly literary court that became a magnet for writers and intellectuals. Accused of plotting rebellion against the Han imperial throne, he committed suicide in 122 B.C.E.

**LIU BANG** (r. 206–195 B.C.E.) was the founding emperor of the Han dynasty, posthumously known as Emperor Gao.

LIU CHANG (199?–174 B.C.E.) was the father of Liu An, patron of the *Huainanzi*. A son of the Han founder, Liu Bang, he was enthroned as king of Huainan while still an infant but later was accused of rebellion and died on the road to exile.

LIU CHE. *See* Wu (Emperor Wu of the Han dynasty).

LIU QI. *See* Jing (Emperor Jing of the Han dynasty).

LORD MILLET. *See* Hou Ji.

LU BAN. *See* Gongshu Ban.

LÜ BUWEI (d. 235 B.C.E.) was a prime minister of Qin during the late Warring States period. He assembled a group of scholars as his clients and, with their assistance, produced a large and highly syncretic text, the *Lüshi chunqiu*, that served as both a model and an important source for the *Huainanzi*.

LÜ WANG. *See* Wang (Grand Duke Wang).

MAO QIANG and XI SHI were famous beauties from the state of Yue, credited with helping engineer the destruction of the state of Wu by so distracting King Fuchai (r. 495–477 B.C.E.) that he neglected his royal duties. Their names became emblematic of perfect feminine beauty.

MENCIUS (Mengzi [Master Meng], personal name Meng Ke [ca. 390–305 B.C.E.]) was a philosopher and teacher, the leading Confucian disciple of his era. The *Huainanzi* draws to some extent on the text that bears his name.

MENG BEN was a semi-legendary fearless hero of the Warring States period, known for his acute vision.

MIZI (also known as Mi Buqi and Zijian [b. 521 B.C.E.]) was a disciple of Confucius.

MO DI. *See* Mozi.

MO YE was the wife of the legendary swordsmith Gan Jiang and herself a superlative smith. The legendary sword "Moye" is named for her.

MOZI (Master Mo, personal name Mo Di [fl. fifth century B.C.E.]) was a rival of Confucius who advocated "universal love" and opposed offensive warfare. In the *Huainanzi*, Mozi and Confucius are often paired as exemplary philosophers.

MU (Duke Mu of Qin [r. ca. 650–621 B.C.E.]) was a notably effective ruler during the Spring and Autumn period.

MUSIC MASTER KUANG. *See* Kuang (Music Master Kuang).

NING QI, a native of Wei during the Spring and Autumn period, began life in poverty and ultimately rose to succeed Guan Zhong as the prime minister of Qi. He first attracted the attention of Duke Huan with his mournful singing.

PING (Duke Ping of Jin) ruled from 557 to 532 B.C.E.

QI was the son of Yu the Great, the mythical tamer of the Great Flood and legendary founder of the Xia dynasty. When he inherited the throne from his father, the principle of hereditary dynastic succession was established.

QIAN QUE and DA BING were mythical charioteers of the astral god known as the Grand One (Taiyi).

QIN SHIHUANGDI (First Emperor of Qin [259–210 B.C.E.]) became king of Qin in 246 B.C.E. In a series of campaigns, Qin then defeated and absorbed all the other states of the Warring States period by 221, uniting China as a single empire for the first time. When he died in 210, his dynasty quickly collapsed and was succeeded by the Han dynasty in 206 B.C.E.

QINGXIANG (King Qingxiang of Chu) ruled from 299 to 263 B.C.E.

QU JIAN was a grandee of Chu.

QUEEN MOTHER OF THE WEST (Xiwangmu) was a goddess who ruled over a paradise on Mount Kunlun, somewhere to the northwest of China. She was believed to know the recipe for an elixir of immortality.

RU SHOU was a mythical being or deity associated with the planet Venus.

SHANG RONG was a (possibly legendary) Shang dynasty worthy who was put to death by Tyrant Djou for his honest admonitions against the king's abuses.

SHAO HAO was a mythical being or deity associated with the planet Venus.

SHE (Duke of She, also known as Shen Zhuliang [fifth century B.C.E.]) was a grandee and vassal of Chu who led the forces that put down the rebellion of the Duke of Bo.

SHEN NONG (Divine Farmer) was a mythical culture-hero of predynastic times, credited with inventing agriculture.

SHENG (Duke Sheng of Bo). See Bo (Duke of Bo).

SHI QI (d. 479 B.C.E.) was a minister and diplomat in the service of Duke Sheng of Bo. He assisted the duke in his rebellion against the Chu throne. When the rebellion was put down, he was boiled alive as punishment.

SHU HAI was supposedly an official in the service of the semi-mythical ruler Yu the Great, the mythical tamer of the Great Flood and legendary founder of the Xia dynasty.

SHUN (also known as Youyu or Yu [written with a character different from that for the name of Yu the Great]) was a mythical sage-king of the predynastic era. He was given the throne by his predecessor, Yao, and similarly passed over his unworthy son and bequeathed the throne instead to Yu the Great, the mythical tamer of the Great Flood and legendary founder of the Xia dynasty.

SHUXIANG was the nickname of Yangshe Xi, a grand officer of the state of Jin during the Spring and Autumn period who was known for his worthiness and ability.

SICHENG ZIHAN. See Zihan.

SIMA KUAIKUI was a knight of Zhao during the Warring States period, famed for his skill with a sword.

SOVEREIGN OF THE SOIL. See Hou Tu.

SUNZI (Master Sun, personal name Sun Wu [fl. sixth century B.C.E.]) was a famous general who, according to legend, led the armies of Wu to a great victory over Chu in the sixth century B.C.E. A later text that bears his name, the *Sunzi bingfa* (*Master Sun's Arts of War*), is an important source for the military teachings of the *Huainanzi*.

SUPREME THEARCH (Shang di) was the chief deity and celestial ruler of ancient Chinese religion, dating back to at least the Shang dynasty (ca. 1550–1046 B.C.E.).

TAI HAO was a mythical being or deity associated with the planet Jupiter.

TAI ZHANG was supposedly an official in the service of the semi-mythical ruler Yu the Great, the mythical tamer of the Great Flood and legendary founder of the Xia dynasty.

TAIYI. See Grand One.

TANG (King Tang or Cheng Tang [Tang the Victorious] [ca. 1550 B.C.E.]) was the semi-legendary founder of the Shang dynasty.

TANG (Master Tang, also known as Music Master Tang) is said to have instructed Confucius in the art of playing the *qin*.

TANG GULIANG was a minister of Qin in the time of King Hui (r. 337–311 B.C.E.).

TRANQUIL WOMAN was a deity associated with maintaining the harmonious progression of the seasons.

VERMILION THEARCH (Chi di) was a mythical ruler of high antiquity, sometimes equated with Yan di, the Flame Emperor.

WANG (Grand Duke Wang, also known as Lü Wang [eleventh century B.C.E.]) was a commoner who sold meat by the roadside before he came to the attention of King Wu of the Zhou. After being promoted, he became the Zhou military commander at the battle of Muye, when the Zhou dynasty achieved its final victory over the Shang. His descendants, the Ji clan, later ruled the state of Qi until they were overthrown by the Tian clan in 379 B.C.E.

WANG LIANG was a grandee of the state of Jin during the Spring and Autumn Period, known for his skill as a charioteer.

WEI (King Wei of Chu) reigned from 339 to 329 B.C.E.

WEN (Duke Wen of Jin, also known as Chong'er [r. 636–628 B.C.E.]) was a storied ruler who, despite having a crippling physical deformity and being forced to live in exile in early life, rose to become one of the most powerful leaders of the state of Jin and the second Zhou vassal lord to assume the title of hegemon. He figures in many early texts.

WEN (King Wen of Chu [r. 689–677 B.C.E.]) is credited with having established the state of Chu as a major power during the Spring and Autumn period.

WEN (King Wen of Zhou [r. ca. 1099–1049 B.C.E.]) was the founder of the Zhou dynasty.

WEN WUWEI (also known as Shen Zhou), a Chu vassal in the time of King Zhuang, was sent on a diplomatic mission to Qi without asking the ruler of Song for free passage through his territory and consequently was killed en route.

WU (Emperor Wu of the Han dynasty, personal name Liu Che [r. 141–87 B.C.E.]) was the son of Emperor Jing. He became emperor at the age of about fifteen and had a long and brilliant reign. He was a first cousin once removed from Liu An, king of Huainan, who presented the *Huainanzi* to him at a court audience in 139 B.C.E.

WU (King Wu of Zhou [r. ca. 1049–1043 B.C.E.]) completed the conquest of the Shang dynasty begun by his father, King Wen of Zhou, by defeating the Shang army in the battle of Muye in 1046 B.C.E.

WU (Marquis Wu of Wei [r. 396–371 B.C.E.]), the second ruler of the independent state of Wei, expanded his state's territories through a series of aggressive campaigns.

WU HUO was a legendary strongman who served King Wu of Qin (r. 310–307 B.C.E.).

WU QI (d. 381 B.C.E.) was a famous statesman and soldier of the Warring States period. He led armies for Lu and Wei and eventually was employed as prime minister by King Dao of Chu. He led Chu effectively until the king's death, when the aristocratic clans of Chu murdered him out of resentment. The *Wuzi*, a text on military strategy, is attributed to him.

WULING (King Wuling of Zhao [r. 325–295 B.C.E.]) was a dynamic ruler who initiated political and military reforms. He expanded Zhao's territory but fell victim to factional fighting among his sons and was starved to death in his own palace.

WUMA QI (also known as Wuma Shi [fl. ca. 500 B.C.E.]) was a native of Lu and a disciple of Confucius.

XI FUJI was a minister of Cao during the Spring and Autumn period. He sent a plate of food containing the precious Chuiji jade disk to the ducal scion Chong'er during the latter's wanderings in exile. Chong'er later went on to become Duke Wen of Jin and hegemon.

XI SHI and MAO QIANG were famous beauties from the state of Yue, credited with helping engineer the destruction of the state of Wu by so distracting King Fuchai (r. 495–477 B.C.E.) that he neglected his royal duties. Their names became emblematic of perfect feminine beauty.

XI ZHONG was a cartwright of legendary skill.

XIAN (Duke Xian of Jin [r. 676–651 B.C.E.]) gave the Prince of Yu a rare jade disk called the Chuiji Jade in exchange for granting a Jin army the right of passage through Yu territory. The Jin army then treacherously conquered Yu. Later, Duke Xian had his own heir killed in order to replace him with the son he had fathered with the "barbarian" Lady Li Ji, and the struggle for title to the throne lasted for four generations.

XIANG (Viscount Xiang of Zhao [d. 425 B.C.E.]) was the leader of the Zhao clan who orchestrated the alliance that brought down Earl Zhi and led ultimately to the partition of the state of Jin into the three independent kingdoms of Hann, Wei, and Zhao.

XIANG TUO was a precocious youngster who at the age of seven supposedly instructed Confucius.

XIAO JI (Ji the Filial [ca. 1200 B.C.E.]), the son of King Wuding of the Shang dynasty, was renowned for his filial piety. He fell victim to his stepmother's slander and died in exile.

XIEZI (also known as Qi Shezi [fourth century B.C.E.]) was a "persuader."

XING CAN was a mythical rebel in the predynastic era of sage-rulers. When his head was cut off, he continued to fight, using his nipples as eyes and his navel as a mouth, singing and dancing while brandishing a shield and an ax.

XU YOU was a legendary hermit in the time of the mythical sage-rulers of prehistory.

XUAN MING was a mythical being or deity associated with the north and with the planet Mercury.

XUE (Duke of Xue, also known as Tian Ying and Lord Jingguo) was a scion of the Qi royal house during the Warring States period and the father of Lord Mengchang. He served as prime minister under King Xuan (r. 319–301 B.C.E.).

XUNZI (Master Xun, personal name Xun Kuang [ca. 310–271 B.C.E.]) was his generation's leading disciple of Confucius. The text that bears his name was an important source for the *Huainanzi*.

YAN DI, the Flame Emperor, was a mythical figure associated with the south and the planet Mars and supposed to have been a ruler during the predynastic period of ancient China. He fought, and was defeated by, Huang Di, the Yellow Emperor.

YAN HUI (fl. ca. 500 B.C.E.) was Confucius's favorite disciple. His early death greatly saddened the Master.

YAN YING (also known as Yanzi [d. 500 B.C.E.]) was a celebrated minister who served three successive dukes of Qi with great loyalty and dedication.

YANGSHE XI. *See* Shuxiang.

YAO (also known as Tang [written with a character different from that for the name of Tang the Victorious]) was a mythical sage-king in the predynastic era. Rather than pass down the throne to his unworthy son, he abdicated in favor of the supremely virtuous Shun.

YELLOW EMPEROR. *See* Huang Di.

YI YIN, a legendary minister of King Tang, the founder of the Shang dynasty, was famous for his cooking.

YIN YI (also known as Shi Yi [Scribe Yi]), the grand historian of the Zhou court in the time of King Cheng (r. 1043–1021 B.C.E.), was an astronomer and a diviner of renowned skill.

YOUYU. *See* Shun.

YU (Yu the Great) was the mythical tamer of the Great Flood and legendary founder of the Xia dynasty.

YU FU was a mythical physician, supposed to have lived at the time of the Yellow Emperor.

ZAOFU appears frequently in the *Huainanzi* as the paragon of chariot drivers. He was said to have been the charioteer of King Mu of Zhou (tenth century B.C.E.) on his legendary journey to the West.

ZENG CAN. *See* Zengzi.

ZENGZI (Zeng Can [505–435 B.C.E.]) was a prominent disciple of Confucius, mentioned in many early texts.

ZHAI JIAN (fourth century B.C.E.) was a hereditary minister at the court of Wei during the Warring States period.

ZHANG YI (d. ca. 310 B.C.E.) was a statesman, strategist, and diplomat of the Warring States period. A native of Wei, he traveled as a "roaming persuader" seeking employment at various courts until King Hui made him the prime minister of Qin. Zhang's policies greatly expanded the power of Qin. Contrary to the claim made in *Huainanzi* 9.29, his life did not end in execution.

ZHAO XUANMENG (also known as Zhao Dun and Viscount Xuan of Zhao [fl. late seventh century B.C.E.]) was a minister of Jin. He consolidated control over the Jin court and presided over a period of peace and stability. In 607 B.C.E., he fell out of favor with Duke Ling (r. 620–607) and was forced into exile. The duke had planned an ambush to kill Zhao, but he was saved by a knight named Ling Zhe, to whom Zhao had earlier provided food when he was starving.

ZHI (Earl Zhi, also known as Earl Yao of Zhi [d. 453 B.C.E.]) was a colorful figure who was a master of strategy and deceit. For example, he once gave an enormous bronze bell to the ruler of the northern Qiu You people. In order to transport the bell to their homeland, the Qiu You had to build a road, which Earl Zhi then used to invade and annex their territory. Earl Zhi is also portrayed as an example of overreaching ambition. As leader of the Zhi clan, he seemed poised to bring all the vassal clans of Jin under his sway, until his arrogant belligerence drove the Hann, Wei, and Zhao clans to unite to destroy him.

ZHI (Robber Zhi) was a legendary bandit of the Warring States period known for his daring, cunning, and ferocity. His name is preserved in the title of chapter 29 of the *Zhuangzi* and is invoked in many early texts as an exemplar of rapine.

ZHONGZI QI was a close friend of the master musician Bo Ya. When he died, Bo Ya broke his *qin* (stringed instrument) because no one else could sufficiently appreciate his playing.

ZHOU GONG (Duke of Zhou, also known as Duke Dan of Zhou [eleventh century B.C.E.]) was a younger brother of King Wu of Zhou. He served as the regent for King Cheng until the latter became old enough to assume the throne. The Duke of Zhou was regarded by Confucius as a paragon of royal virtue.

ZHU MING (also known as Zhu Rong) was a mythical being associated with the south and with the planet Mars.

ZHU RONG. *See* Zhu Ming.

ZHUAN XU was a mythical sage-ruler who supposedly lived during the predynastic era. In some traditions, he is associated with the north and with the planet Mercury, but in other traditions he is associated with the south. He fought a titanic battle with Gong Gong, during which one of the pillars of Heaven was so damaged that the land tilted upward in the northwest.

ZHUANG (King Zhuang of Chu [r. 613–591 B.C.E.]) initially had little interest in government, but through the remonstrance of loyal ministers, he became a competent and forceful leader and rose to be hegemon of the Zhou realm.

ZHUANG QIAO was a man of Chu who led a revolt during the reign of King Huai (r. 328–299 B.C.E.).

ZHUANGZI (Master Zhuang, personal name Zhuang Zhou [fourth century B.C.E.]) was a celebrated Daoist philosopher. The book that bears his name, the *Zhuangzi*, has been shown to be a work of multiple authorship, although some portions might be from the hand of Zhuang Zhou.

ZIFA (late fourth century B.C.E.) served as both a general and a civil official in the state of Chu.

ZIHAN (Sicheng Zihan [sixth century B.C.E.]) was a minister of the state of Song. Although he was renowned for his incorruptibility, his historical reputation is mixed: ultimately, he murdered the lord of Song and usurped his throne.

ZIJIAO and ZIQI (fifth century B.C.E.) were paternal uncles of Duke Sheng of Bo.

ZILU (also known as Ji Lu and Zhong You [fifth century B.C.E.]) was a disciple of Confucius. Militarily inclined, he served as a steward to the powerful Ji clan of Lu.

ZIQI and ZIJIAO (fifth century B.C.E.) were paternal uncles of Duke Sheng of Bo.

ZISI (fifth century B.C.E.) was a grandson of Confucius and an important thinker in his own right. The text that bears his name, now preserved only as fragments, was a source for the *Huainanzi*.

ZOU YAN (ca. 300 B.C.E.) was a philosopher credited with systematizing the basic properties of yin and yang and the Five Phases of *qi*, and with envisioning the world as a set of nine continents.

BRIEF BIBLIOGRAPHY

## Chinese Texts

Lau, D. C. *Huainanzi zhuzi suoyin* (淮南子逐字索引) (*A Concordance to the Huainanzi*). Chinese University of Hong Kong, Institute of Chinese Studies Ancient Chinese Text Concordance Series. Hong Kong: Commercial Press, 1992.

Zhang Shuangdi (張雙棣). *Huainanzi jiaoshi* (淮南子校釋). 2 vols. Beijing: Beijing University Press, 1997.

## Western-Language Translations and Studies

Ames, Roger T. *The Art of Rulership: A Study of Ancient Chinese Political Thought*. Honolulu: University of Hawai'i Press, 1983. Reprint, Albany: State University of New York Press, 1994. [A translation of chapter 9]

Ames, Roger T., and D. C. Lau. *Yuan Dao: Tracing Dao to Its Source*. Classics of Ancient China. New York: Ballantine Books, 1998. [A translation of chapter 1]

Kraft, Eva. "Zum *Huai-nan-Tzu*. Enfurung, Ubersetzung (Kapitel I und II) und Interpretation." *Monumenta Serica*, no. 16 (1957): 191–286; no. 17 (1958): 128–207.

Larre, Claude, Isabelle Robinet, and Elisabeth Rochat de la Vallée. *Les grands traités du Huainanzi*. Variétés sinologiques, vol. 75. Paris: Institut Ricci, 1993. [Translations of chapters 1, 7, 11, 13, and 18]

Le Blanc, Charles. *Huai-nan Tzu: Philosophical Synthesis in Early Han Thought: The Idea of Resonance (Kan-ying) with a Translation and Analysis of Chapter Six*. Hong Kong: Hong Kong University Press, 1985.

Le Blanc, Charles, and Remi Mathieu. *Mythe et philosophie à l'aube de la Chine impériale: Études sur le Huainanzi*. Montreal: Presses de l'Université de Montreal, 1992; Paris: De Boccard, 1992.

Le Blanc, Charles, and Remi Mathieu, eds. *Philosophes taoïstes*. Vol. 2, *Huainan zi: Texte traduit, présenté et annoté*. Bibliothèque de la Pléiade. Paris: Éditions Gallimard, 2003. Complete translation.

Major, John S. *Heaven and Earth in Early Han Thought: Chapters Three, Four and Five of the Huainanzi*. SUNY Series in Chinese Philosophy and Culture. Albany: State University of New York Press, 1993.

Roth, Harold D. *The Textual History of the Huai-nan Tzu*. Monographs of the Association for Asian Studies, vol. 46. Ann Arbor, Mich.: Association for Asian Studies, 1992.

Ryden, Edmund. *Philosophy of Peace in Han China: A Study of the Huainanzi Ch. 15 on Military Strategy*. Taibei: Ricci Institute, 1998.

Vankeerberghen, Griet. *The Huainanzi and Liu An's Claim to Moral Authority*. SUNY Series in Chinese Philosophy and Culture. Albany: State University of New York Press, 2001.

Wallacker, Benjamin. *The Huai-nan-tzu, Book Eleven: Behavior, Culture and the Cosmos*. American Oriental Series, vol. 48. New Haven, Conn.: American Oriental Society, 1962.

INDEX

*Admonitions of Yao*, 192
affairs, human (*shi*), 18, 31, 111, 123
    in *chap.* 14, 153, 154, 156
    in *chap.* 18, 189–96
    in *chap.* 20, 216, 219
    in *chap.* 21, 227, 229, 230, 232
    See also military affairs
alteration (*bian*), 163, 173
    in *chap.* 18, 192–93
    in *chap.* 21, 227–28, 232
    See also change; transformation
*Analects* (*Lunyu*), 112. See also Confucius
anecdotes, 135–36
animals
    in *chap.* 4, 54, 55
    in *chap.* 5, 57, 59, 60, 61, 65
    in *chap.* 8, 90
    in *chap.* 9, 102–3
    in *chap.* 11, 126, 127
    in *chap.* 13, 147, 148
    in *chap.* 14, 155
    in *chap.* 15, 167, 170, 173
    in *chap.* 16, 181, 182
    in *chap.* 17, 185–86
    in *chap.* 18, 195, 196
    in *chap.* 20, 217

    See also dragons; horses; *qilin*; tigers
archery, 60–61, 180, 186, 218
astrology/astronomy, 5, 39–40, 57, 70, 71. See also cosmology; Dipper; Jupiter cycle

Baili Xi, 203
"barbarians," 99, 123, 127, 130, 139, 150, 168, 201
Beigongzi (Beigong You), 102
bells, 25, 91, 104, 171, 207, 217, 223
    Yellow, 46, 185
*benmo*. See root and branch
Bi Gan, 103, 107, 224
Bian He, 205
    jade disk of, 162
Bian Que, 192
Bo, Duke of, 139
Bo Ya, 205, 206
Bo Yu, 148
Bocheng Zigao, 149
*Book of Documents*. See Documents

calenders, 5, 39
Chang Hong, 108
change (*yi*), 145–46, 148, 150. See also alteration; transformation

Changes (Classic of Changes; Yijing; Zhouyi),
    5, 9, 114, 116, 127, 219, 230
Chaoxian, state of (Korea), 61
charioteering, 6, 46, 71–72, 109, 126, 149, 152,
    172. See also horses
cheng. See sincerity
Cheng, King of Zhou, 108, 143
Chong'er, Prince. See Wen, Duke of Jin
Chuci (Elegies of Chu), 10, 40, 50
Chunqiu. See Spring and Autumn Annals
Confucianism, 7
    classics of, 9, 112, 124
Confucians (ru), 14, 74, 102, 111, 112, 131, 133
Confucius (Kong Qiu), 8, 28, 34
    in chap. 9, 101, 102, 108, 109
    in chap. 11, 128–29
    in chap. 12, 140, 144
    in chap. 19, 203, 205, 207
cosmology, 74
    correlative, 58, 70, 73
culture (wen), 118
customs (su), 106, 123–33, 149, 150, 203, 220,
    229

Da Bing (sage-king), 71–72
Dan, Duke of Zhou, 127
Daodejing. See Laozi
Daoism, 14, 78n.1, 136. See also Laozi
de. See Moral Potency; Potency
Dee tribes, 127, 139
Dii tribes, 127
Dipper (Big Dipper, Northern Dipper), 47,
    59n.1, 128
Divine Farmer (Shennong), 143, 149, 200, 204
Djou, King of Shang (tyrant; Djou Xin), 103,
    108, 120, 127n.2, 143, 223–24
Doctrine of the Mean. See Zhongyong
Documents (Classic of Documents; Shang shu;
    Shujing), 9, 206, 219
dragons, 43, 44, 47, 53, 55
drums, 25, 44, 99, 104, 170, 171, 174, 217, 224

Earth (earthly; di), 5
    in chap. 1, 16, 22
    in chap. 2, 30, 31, 35
    in chap. 3, 41, 42, 44, 45, 46, 47
    in chap. 4, 51, 54–55

    in chap. 5, 57, 63, 65
    in chap. 6, 68
    in chap. 7, 74, 75, 76, 78, 80
    in chap. 8, 85, 86, 87
    in chap. 9, 105
    in chap. 12, 137, 138
    in chap. 14, 155
    in chap. 15, 169, 170, 172, 173, 174
    in chap. 17, 184
    in chap. 20, 212, 216, 219, 221
    in chap. 21, 227, 228, 229, 231
    in Heaven-Earth-Man triad, 5, 74
    See also Five Phases; Heaven
education, 4, 6, 9, 149, 198, 199
emptiness (xu), 24, 34, 73, 130, 152, 165
    in chap. 14, 154, 156, 158
    See also Nothingness

fate/destiny (ming), 80, 164, 223
filial piety (xiao), 108, 117, 201, 217
Five Human Relationships, 125
Five Orbs (wu zang), 24, 36, 76, 77, 78
Five Phases (wuxing), 7, 58, 219, 228
    in chap. 4, 50, 54–55
    in chap. 8, 89–92
Five Thearchs, 83, 168, 211, 228, 229
form/formlessness (xing/wu xing), 67, 80, 138,
    179
    in chap. 1, 16, 23
    in chap. 14, 154, 156
    in chap. 15, 169, 173
fu (poetic exposition), 226
Fu Yue, 71
Fuchai, King of Wu, 141, 196
Fuxi, 149, 230

Gan Jiang (swordsmith), 99n.2
ganying. See resonance
Gao, Emperor of Han. See Gaozu, Emperor
Gao Xin. See Zhuan Xu
Gaoyang Tui, 194
Gaozu, Emperor (Liu Bang), 2–3
Genuine Person (zhenren), 8, 28, 31, 35, 74,
    154, 155
geography, 5, 49–55, 61–63
gnomons (biao), 98, 191
Gong Gong, 42, 168, 201

Gongniu Ai, 30
Gongshu (Gongsun Ban, Lu Ban), 140, 204
Gongzi Xiao Bo. *See* Huan, Duke of Qi
Goodness, 102, 107, 108, 218, 219, 220–21
    in *chap.* 10, 112, 117, 119, 120
Gou Mang, 44, 61
Goujian, King of Yue, 196
government (*zhi*), 6, 112, 139, 158, 170
    in *chap.* 5, 58, 65–66
    in *chap.* 6, 68, 70
    in *chap.* 8, 83, 84, 86, 88, 89, 92–93
    in *chap.* 11, 124, 126, 130
    in *chap.* 13, 149–50
    in *chap.* 16, 179, 181
    in *chap.* 19, 198–99, 204
    in *chap.* 20, 211–24
    centralization of, 2–3
    by sage-rulers, 4, 20
    techniques of, 8–9, 95–109
    *See also* officials/ministers; rulership; sage-rulers
Grand One (Taiyi), 87, 88, 98, 154, 155, 160, 169. *See also* Way
Grand Purity (*tai qing*), 79, 136, 137–38, 198
Great Clod, 29
Guan Zhong (Guanzi, Guan Yiwu, Zhongfu), 101, 203
*Guanzi* (*Book of Master Guan*), 9, 68, 74, 96
Gun, 201

Han dynasty, 1, 2–3, 9, 49, 213. *See also* Gaozu, Emperor; Wu, Emperor
*Hanfeizi*, 9, 96, 146, 178, 190
harmony (*he*), 44, 71, 81, 86, 105, 123, 156, 171
    in *chap.* 1, 14, 15
    in *chap.* 2, 28, 31, 32, 36
    in *chap.* 20, 212, 213, 223
    in *chap.* 21, 228
He. *See* Bian He
Heaven (*tian*)
    in *chap.* 1, 16, 19, 20, 22
    in *chap.* 2, 30, 31, 32, 33, 35
    in *chap.* 3, 39, 41, 42, 43, 44, 45, 46, 47
    in *chap.* 4, 51, 52
    in *chap.* 5, 57, 63, 64, 65
    in *chap.* 6, 68, 69, 70
    in *chap.* 7, 73, 74, 75, 76, 78, 80
    in *chap.* 9, 96, 98, 105
    in *chap.* 11, 125
    in *chap.* 12, 137, 138, 141
    in *chap.* 14, 155, 157, 160, 164
    in *chap.* 15, 167, 169, 170, 172, 173, 174
    in *chap.* 17, 184
    in *chap.* 20, 211, 212, 213, 214, 215, 216, 219, 221
    in *chap.* 21, 227, 228, 229, 231
    in Heaven-Earth-Man triad, 5, 74
Heavenly Heart (*tianxin*), 211, 215
hegemons (*ba*), 2, 87, 89, 127, 168, 207, 222
horses, 8, 19, 55, 71–72, 206
Hou Ji. *See* Millet, Lord
Hou Tu, 44
Hu tribes, 99, 127
*Huainanzi* (*Master of Huainan*)
    authorship of, 3–4
    sources of, 4–5, 9–10, 14, 40, 50, 112, 124
    structure of, 5–6
Hualiu (horse), 206
Huan, Duke of Qi (Gongzi Xiao Bo), 101, 103, 129, 141, 203
Huan Dou, 201
Huang-Lao tradition, 5
Huangdi. *See* Yellow Emperor
Hui, King of Qin, 205
Hui, King of Wei, 138–39
Hui Shi (Huizi), 138, 205
human beings (humankind, others; *ren*), 19, 74, 189–96. *See also* affairs, human; sages
human nature. *See* nature
Humaneness (*ren*), 6, 7, 8, 9
    in *chap.* 2, 27, 31, 32, 34–35
    in *chap.* 8, 84, 85, 86, 87
    in *chap.* 10, 111, 112, 114, 116, 117, 120
    in *chap.* 11, 130, 131
    in *chap.* 14, 157, 160
    in *chap.* 15, 171, 173
    in *chap.* 19, 201
    in *chap.* 20, 218, 221, 222
*hun* and *po* souls, 179

inner cultivation. *See* self-cultivation

Ji Lu. *See* Zilu
Jian, Viscount of Zhao (Zhao Yang), 142

Jie, King of Xia (tyrant), 108, 116, 120, 143, 202, 224
Jie Fan, 102
Jing, Duke of Qi, 69, 101
Jing, Emperor (Liu Qi; Han), 3
Jingguo, Lord. *See* Xue, Duke of
*jingshen*. *See* spirit, quintessential
Jizi, 107, 224
*junzi*. *See* Superior Man
Jupiter cycle, 40, 44

Kang, King of Zhou, 108
Kuang, Music Master, 69, 207
Kunlun, Mount, 50, 52, 62, 90

*Laozi* (*Daodejing*), 5, 6, 7, 9, 84, 96
　and *chap. 1*, 14, 27–28
　and *chap. 12*, 135–36, 138, 139, 140, 141, 142, 143–44
Laozi (Lao Dan), 5, 23, 135
Lau, D. C., 11
laws, 2, 6, 111, 171
　in *chap. 5*, 61, 62, 63
　in *chap. 9*, 96, 99–101, 102
　in *chap. 12*, 138–39
　in *chap. 13*, 149, 150
　in *chap. 20*, 212, 217, 218, 219, 220, 221
Li, King of Chu, 162n.1
Li Ke (Li Kui), 140–41
Li Qi, 205
*Liji*. See *Rites*
Liu An (king of Huainan), 1, 3–4, 10, 14, 166, 213, 225, 226
Liu Bang. *See* Gaozu, Emperor
Liu Chang (king of Huainan), 3
Liu Che. *See* Wu, Emperor
Liu Qi. *See* Jing, Emperor
Liu Xiang, 178
*liuhe*. *See* six coordinates
Lu Ban. *See* Gongshu
Lü Shang. *See* Wang, Grand Duke
Lü Wang (butcher), 203
Lü'er (horse), 206
lunar lodges (*xiu*), 71
*Lunyu*. See *Analects*
*Lüshi chunqiu* (*Mr. Lü's Spring and Autumn*), 5, 9, 10, 58, 68, 96, 190

Mao Qiang, 79, 86, 207–8
*Master Sun's Arts of War* (*Sunzi bingfa*), 10, 166, 170n.2
Mawangdui texts, 10, 40, 112
Mencius (Meng Ke, Mengzi), 111
*Mencius* (*Mengzi*), 112
Meng Ben (Meng Yue), 108
Mercury, 44
Miao tribes, 150, 168, 201
military affairs (*wu*), 6, 165–75, 229
Millet, Lord (Hou Ji), 50, 216
mind-heart (*xin*), 191, 192
　techniques of, 8, 25, 28, 74, 81, 157, 211
Mingtang (Hall of Light), 60, 65, 92, 108
Mizi (Mi Zijian, Mi Buqi), 144
Mo Di. *See* Mozi
Mohists, 102, 131, 133. *See also* Mozi
Moral Potency (*de*), 7, 96, 120, 133, 144, 149
　in *chap. 8*, 88, 89
　in *chap. 14*, 159, 164
　in *chap. 15*, 165, 171
　in *chap. 20*, 212, 213, 221
mourning, 46, 61, 93, 104, 131, 215, 217
Moye (sword), 99, 206
Mozi (Mo Di), 28, 34, 102, 109, 140, 146, 203, 207
Mu, Duke of Qin, 203
Murray, Judson, 12
*Music* (*Classic of Music*), 219
Music (*yue*), 8, 9, 32, 40, 59, 139, 185
　in *chap. 8*, 84, 86, 87, 88, 89, 93
　in *chap. 9*, 100, 104, 105, 106, 107, 108
　in *chap. 10*, 115, 117
　in *chap. 11*, 125, 132
　in *chap. 19*, 205
　in *chap. 20*, 217
　in *chap. 21*, 230
　*See also* bells; drums; pitch pipes; *qin*; *se*

Nameless (*wuming*), 154. *See also* Way
nature (*xing*), 8, 18, 167
　in *chap. 2*, 28, 33, 34, 36
　in *chap. 11*, 125, 127, 128, 129
　in *chap. 14*, 156, 157, 158, 161
　in *chap. 20*, 216, 217–18, 220, 223
Ning Qi, 129
non-action (*wuwei*), 8, 9, 71, 84, 120

in *chap.* 1, 20, 23
in *chap.* 9, 96, 97, 99, 100, 102
in *chap.* 12, 136, 137–38
in *chap.* 14, 154, 156, 159, 160, 162
in *chap.* 19, 197–98, 200, 202
norms (*shu*), 137–38, 163
Nothingness (non-being; *wu*), 7, 13, 73, 155, 156. *See also* non-action

Odes (*Classic of Odes*; *Shijing*), 9, 106, 107, 162, 206, 209, 215, 216, 219
officials/ministers, 62, 70, 142, 150, 171, 181, 203
in *chap.* 9, 95, 96, 97, 100, 102, 104, 106
in *chap.* 10, 116, 117
in *chap.* 11, 125, 126
in *chap.* 20, 220, 221
*See also* government; rulership
oral literature, 178, 190, 198, 225, 226

parallelism, 190
Perfected Person (*zhiren*), 8, 28, 31, 32, 74, 77–80. *See also* sages
persuasions (*shuo*, *shui*), 111, 177–87, 205, 229
phoenix (*feng*, *fenghuang*), 17, 55, 118, 212
Ping, Duke of Jin, 69, 207
pitch pipes, 46, 59, 100, 104, 132, 185, 217
six, 87, 88, 89
*See also* bells
*po* soul. *See hun* and *po* souls
poetry (*shi*), 4, 226. *See also* Chuci; Odes
positional advantage (force; *shi*), 96, 101–2, 103, 152, 166
Potency (*de*), 6–7, 8, 46, 81, 147, 157, 170, 185, 197
in *chap.* 1, 14, 17, 22, 23
in *chap.* 2, 27, 28, 30–31, 32, 36
in *chap.* 5, 64, 65
in *chap.* 8, 83, 84, 86, 87, 88
in *chap.* 9, 96, 99
in *chap.* 10, 111, 113, 114, 118
in *chap.* 11, 125, 129
in *chap.* 21, 227, 228, 229, 232
*See also* Moral Potency
primitivism, agrarian, 83–84, 146, 147–49, 200, 221–22
Puett, Michael, 12

*qi* (vital energy), 7, 53, 161, 228
in *chap.* 1, 14, 23, 24
in *chap.* 2, 30, 36
in *chap.* 3, 39, 41–42, 43, 44, 45, 46
in *chap.* 5, 60, 61, 62, 64
in *chap.* 6, 67, 68, 70, 71
in *chap.* 7, 73, 74, 75, 76, 77, 79
in *chap.* 8, 85, 86, 87
in *chap.* 9, 96, 98
in *chap.* 11, 123, 130
in *chap.* 15, 167, 175
in *chap.* 20, 211, 215, 219
*daoyin* (guiding and pulling of), 74
noxious, 161
and resonance, 5, 8
Qi (son of Yu), 131n.8
Qi, state of, 144
Qian Qie, 71–72
*qilin* (mythical beast), 17, 43, 55, 212
*qin* (musical instrument), 59, 104, 108, 118, 205, 206, 230
Qin, state of, 2
Qin Shihuangdi (Zhao Zheng), 2
Qing Nü (Gray Woman), 44
Qingxiang, King of Chu, 205
Qu Jian, 195
Queen Mother of the West (Xiwangmu), 50, 52n.1

resonance (stimulus and response; *ganying*), 5–6, 8, 84, 96, 112, 130, 185
in *chap.* 6, 68, 69–72
in *chap.* 7, 74, 78, 81
Rightness (*yi*), 6, 7, 8, 9, 150, 171
in *chap.* 2, 27, 31, 32, 34–35
in *chap.* 8, 84, 85, 86, 87, 93
in *chap.* 9, 100, 102, 103, 108, 109
in *chap.* 10, 111, 112, 114, 116, 117, 119
in *chap.* 11, 123, 125, 126, 130, 131, 133
in *chap.* 16, 180, 183
in *chap.* 20, 218, 221, 222
Rites (*Liji*; *Record of Rites*), 58, 112, 124, 219
ritual (*li*), 5, 6, 8, 32, 80, 111, 139, 150
in *chap.* 5, 58, 59
in *chap.* 8, 85, 86, 87, 93
in *chap.* 11, 123–33

250 INDEX

ritual (*continued*)
   in *chap.* 15, 166, 174–75
   in *chap.* 20, 216, 218
root and branch (*benmo*), 6, 8, 9, 34, 76, 100, 172, 191
   in *chap.* 1, 20, 28
   in *chap.* 20, 215, 220, 222, 223
   in *chap.* 21, 227, 230
Ru Shou, 44, 62
rulership, 2, 4, 6, 10, 28, 140
   in *chap.* 1, 14–15
   in *chap.* 9, 95–109
   in *chap.* 13, 146, 150–51
   in *chap.* 14, 154, 160
   in *chap.* 15, 168, 173–75
   in *chaps.* 16 and 17, 179, 181
   in *chap.* 19, 198–99
   in *chap.* 20, 211–24
   in *chap.* 21, 228–29
   techniques for, 8, 95–109
   *See also* government; officials/ministers; sage-rulers

sage-rulers, 4, 7, 8, 10, 20, 28, 146, 154
   in *chap.* 1, 14–15
   in *chap.* 6, 68, 70
   in *chap.* 8, 83–84
   in *chap.* 10, 111–12, 116
   in *chap.* 11, 124, 129, 130
   in *chap.* 12, 135–36
   in *chap.* 19, 198–99
   in *chap.* 20, 211–24
sages (*shengren*), 8, 19–20, 55
   in *chap.* 2, 28, 31–32, 34
   in *chap.* 6, 68, 70
   in *chap.* 7, 74, 76
   in *chap.* 8, 83, 93
   in *chap.* 9, 102, 107, 109
   in *chap.* 10, 115, 116, 117, 119, 121
   in *chap.* 11, 123, 124, 126, 127, 128
   in *chap.* 13, 146, 147–48, 150, 151
   in *chap.* 14, 153–54, 156, 159, 161, 163
   in *chap.* 15, 168, 173
   in *chap.* 16, 179, 182
   in *chap.* 18, 192, 193
   in *chap.* 19, 197, 198, 200–204, 206–7

   in *chap.* 20, 214, 216, 218, 219
   in *chap.* 21, 228, 230
San Miao (Three Miao tribes). *See* Miao tribes
*se* (zitherlike instrument), 59, 104, 132
seasons, 51, 76, 170, 203, 228
   in *chap.* 3, 39, 41, 43
   in *chap.* 5, 57–66
   in *chap.* 8, 87, 88, 89
   in *chap.* 20, 212, 214, 216, 218, 221
self-cultivation, 7, 8, 14, 74, 96, 136, 166, 190, 199
   in *chap.* 2, 27, 28
   in *chap.* 14, 154, 164
   in *chap.* 20, 222–24
   and rulership, 4, 6
Shang (Yin) dynasty, 107, 132, 143, 149, 150, 216
*Shang shu*. *See* Documents
Shangdi (Supreme Thearch), 52, 64
*Shanhaijing* (*Classic of Mountains and Seas*), 10, 50
Shao Hao, 44, 62
She, Duke of (Shen Zhuliang), 139
Sheng, Duke of Bo, 195
Shennong. *See* Divine Farmer
*shi*. *See* affairs, human; positional advantage
Shi Qi, 139, 195
*Shijing*. *See* Odes
*Shizi* (*Master Shi*), 9
Shu Hai, 51
*Shujing*. *See* Documents
Shun (sage-ruler), 129, 168
   in *chap.* 9, 106, 107
   in *chap.* 10, 115, 116, 119
   in *chap.* 13, 149, 150
   in *chap.* 19, 200, 201, 204
*Shuo yuan* (Liu Xiang), 178
Sicheng Zihan, 142
Sima Kuaikui, 102
sincerity (*cheng*), 112, 115, 116, 118, 131, 144, 215
six coordinates (*liuhe*), 16, 51, 87, 170
so-of-itself (spontaneously, naturally; *ziran*), 8
space-time (*yuzhou*), 41
spirit, quintessential (*jingshen*), 8, 20, 34, 72, 73–81
spirit illumination (*shenming*), 8, 24, 33, 64, 74, 111, 169

in *chap.* 8, 84, 86, 87
in *chap.* 20, 211, 214, 216
spirit transformation (*shenhua*), 170
*Spring and Autumn Annals* (*Chunqiu*), 5, 109, 219
Spring and Autumn period, 2, 87n.1, 108, 150
statecraft, 96, 99, 124
*Sunzi bingfa* (*Art of War*), 10, 166, 170n.2
Superior Man (*junzi*), 8, 108, 142, 180, 209
    in *chap.* 10, 114, 117, 118, 119, 120
    in *chap.* 14, 154, 162, 163–64

Tai Hao, 44, 61
Tai Zhang, 51
Taiyi. *See* Grand One
Tang, King of Shang (sage-ruler), 107, 143, 149
    in *chap.* 19, 200, 201–2, 203
    in *chap.* 20, 216, 224
Tang, Music Master, 206
Tang Guliang, 205
taxes, 2, 96, 103–5, 202
techniques (*shu*), 161, 162, 191, 198, 230
    of government, 8–9, 95–109
    of the mind (*xin shu*), 8, 25, 28, 74, 81, 157, 211
    of the Way (*dao shu*), 28, 31, 152
    See also *Guanzi*
Three Dynasties, 120, 150. *See also* Shang dynasty; Xia dynasty; Zhou dynasty
Three Kings, 83, 211, 229, 232
Three Miao tribes (San Miao). *See* Miao tribes
*tian*. *See* Heaven
"Tian wen" (Questions About Heaven; *Chuci*), 10, 40, 50
Tian Ying. *See* Xue, Duke of
*tianxin*. *See* Heavenly Heart
tigers, 30, 43, 44
tool metaphors (carpenter's square, level, compass), 99, 113, 191, 204
    in *chap.* 5, 58, 63–66
    in *chap.* 8, 88, 89
transformation (metamorphosis; *hua*), 8, 21, 50, 68, 80, 163, 173, 219
    in *chap.* 2, 27, 29, 30, 32, 35
    in *chap.* 3, 40, 42
in *chap.* 11, 127, 128
in *chap.* 18, 192–93
in *chap.* 21, 227–28
*See also* alteration; change
Trustworthiness (*xin*), 173, 187, 221, 222

Unhewn (uncarved block; *pu*), 78, 79, 145, 155, 227

vacuity (*xu*), 36. *See also* emptiness
Venus, 44

Wang, Grand Duke (Lü Wang, Taigong Wang), 127
Wang Liang, 71
Warring States period, 2, 166
Way (*dao*), 5–6, 8, 9, 185, 191
    in *chap.* 1, 14, 16–21, 23, 25
    in *chap.* 2, 28, 31, 32, 33, 34, 36
    in *chap.* 6, 68, 70, 71
    in *chap.* 7, 74, 76, 77, 79, 81
    in *chap.* 8, 83, 84, 86, 87, 88, 89, 93
    in *chap.* 9, 96, 97, 98, 99, 100, 108
    in *chap.* 10, 111, 113, 114
    in *chap.* 11, 124, 125, 129, 131
    in *chap.* 12, 135, 136, 137–38, 140, 141
    in *chap.* 13, 146, 152
    in *chap.* 14, 154, 156, 157, 158, 159, 160, 162, 163, 164
    in *chap.* 15, 165, 168–69, 170, 172, 173, 175
    in *chap.* 16, 179, 180, 182
    in *chap.* 19, 197, 198, 200, 202, 204, 205, 206
    in *chap.* 20, 211, 218, 221
    in *chap.* 21, 227–32
    techniques of (*dao shu*), 28, 31, 152
weights and measures, 40, 100. *See also* tool metaphors
Wen, Duke of Jin (Prince Chong'er), 143
Wen, King of Chu, 102
Wen, King of Zhou, 107, 108
Wen Wuwei (Shen Zhou), 102
Wisdom (*zhi*), 19, 20, 119
*wu*. *See* military affairs; Nothingness
Wu, Emperor (Liu Che; Han), 3, 4, 14, 225
Wu, King of Chu, 162n.1

Wu, King of Zhou, 107, 108, 143, 216, 224
Wu, Marquis of Wei, 140
Wu Huo, 102
Wu Qi, 109
Wuling, King of Zhao, 102
Wuma Qi (Wuma Shi), 144
*wuwei*. See non-action
*wuxing*. See Five Phases
*Wuxingpian* (Mawangdui text), 112
*Wuxingzhan* (*Prognostications of the Five Planets*; Mawangdui text), 10

Xi Fuji, 130
Xi Shi, 79, 86, 207–8
Xi Zhong, 204
Xia dynasty, 143, 149, 150, 216
Xian, Duke of Jin, 130
Xiang, Viscount of Zhao, 139–40, 142
Xiang Tuo, 205
Xiao Ji, 126
Xiezi (Qi Shezi), 205
*xing*. See nature
Xing Can, 54
Xu You, 25, 34
Xuan Ming, 44, 63
Xue, Duke of (Tian Ying, Lord Jingguo), 144, 194
Xunzi, 9, 96

Yan Di, 44, 168
Yan Hui (Yan Yuan), 128
Yan Ying. *See* Yanzi
Yanzi (Yan Ying), 101
Yao (sage-ruler), 25, 106, 107, 119, 129, 149, 168
    in *chap*. 19, 200, 201, 204
Yellow Emperor (Huangdi), 5, 44, 52, 62, 168, 204
Yi tribes, 123
Yi Yin (cook), 203
Yin Yi (Scribe Yi), 143
yin-yang, 6–7, 99
    in *chap*. 1, 17, 18, 23
    in *chap*. 3, 39, 40, 41–42, 43, 45, 46, 47
    in *chap*. 4, 50, 54, 55
    in *chap*. 5, 58, 60, 63
    in *chap*. 6, 67, 71
    in *chap*. 7, 74, 75, 76, 80

in *chap*. 8, 86, 87, 88, 89
in *chap*. 12, 137, 138
in *chap*. 13, 147, 151
in *chap*. 15, 169, 172n.3
in *chap*. 20, 212, 214, 216, 218
*you*. See Nothingness
Youhu clan, 131, 168
Youmiao tribes, 168
Yu (sage-ruler), 50, 51, 62, 107, 131n.8, 149, 216
    in *chap*. 19, 200, 201, 202, 204
Yu Fu, 192
Yue tribes, 99, 127
*Yueling* (*Monthly Ordinances*), 58

Zaofu, 71
Zengzi (Zeng Can), 126
Zhai Jian, 138–39
Zhang Yi, 109
*Zhanguoce* (*Intrigues of the Warring States*), 190
Zhao Xuanmeng (Zhao Dun, Viscount Xuan of Zhao), 130
Zhao Zheng. *See* Qin Shihuangdi
Zhaoyao (star), 59
Zhi, Earl (Earl Yao, Zhi Bo), 130
Zhi, Robber, 126
Zhong You. *See* Zilu
*Zhongyong* (*Doctrine of the Mean*), 112, 124
Zhongzi Qi, 205
Zhou, Duke of, 117, 127
Zhou dynasty, 1–2, 132, 149, 150
*Zhouyi*. *See* Changes
Zhu Ming, 44
Zhuan Xu (Gao Xin; sage-ruler), 42, 44, 62, 63, 168
Zhuang, King of Chu, 102, 206
Zhuang Qiao, 126
Zhuang Zhou, 28n.1
Zhuangzi, 135, 205
*Zhuangzi*, 7, 9, 28, 68, 74, 123, 129n.5, 190
Zifa (magistrate), 195
Zijiao, 195
Zilu (Ji Lu, Zhong You), 101
Ziqi, Minister of War, 195
*ziran* (so-of-itself; spontaneously, naturally), 8
Zisizi, 112
Zou Yan, 50

TRANSLATIONS FROM THE ASIAN CLASSICS

Major Plays of Chikamatsu, tr. Donald Keene 1961
Four Major Plays of Chikamatsu, tr. Donald Keene. Paperback ed. only. 1961; rev. ed. 1997
Records of the Grand Historian of China, translated from the Shih chi of Ssu-ma Ch'ien, tr. Burton Watson, 2 vols. 1961
Instructions for Practical Living and Other Neo-Confucian Writings by Wang Yang-ming, tr. Wing-tsit Chan 1963
Hsün Tzu: Basic Writings, tr. Burton Watson, paperback ed. only. 1963; rev. ed. 1996
Chuang Tzu: Basic Writings, tr. Burton Watson, paperback ed. only. 1964; rev. ed. 1996
The Mahābhārata, tr. Chakravarthi V. Narasimhan. Also in paperback ed. 1965; rev. ed. 1997
The Manyōshū, Nippon Gakujutsu Shinkōkai edition 1965
Su Tung-p'o: Selections from a Sung Dynasty Poet, tr. Burton Watson. Also in paperback ed. 1965
Bhartrihari: Poems, tr. Barbara Stoler Miller. Also in paperback ed. 1967
Basic Writings of Mo Tzu, Hsün Tzu, and Han Fei Tzu, tr. Burton Watson. Also in separate paperback eds. 1967
The Awakening of Faith, Attributed to Aśvaghosha, tr. Yoshito S. Hakeda. Also in paperback ed. 1967
Reflections on Things at Hand: The Neo-Confucian Anthology, comp. Chu Hsi and Lü Tsu-ch'ien, tr. Wing-tsit Chan 1967
The Platform Sutra of the Sixth Patriarch, tr. Philip B. Yampolsky. Also in paperback ed. 1967
Essays in Idleness: The Tsurezuregusa of Kenkō, tr. Donald Keene. Also in paperback ed. 1967
The Pillow Book of Sei Shōnagon, tr. Ivan Morris, 2 vols. 1967
Two Plays of Ancient India: The Little Clay Cart and the Minister's Seal, tr. J. A. B. van Buitenen 1968
The Complete Works of Chuang Tzu, tr. Burton Watson 1968
The Romance of the Western Chamber (Hsi Hsiang chi), tr. S. I. Hsiung. Also in paperback ed. 1968
The Manyōshū, Nippon Gakujutsu Shinkōkai edition. Paperback ed. only. 1969
Records of the Historian: Chapters from the Shih chi of Ssu-ma Ch'ien, tr. Burton Watson. Paperback ed. only. 1969
Cold Mountain: 100 Poems by the T'ang Poet Han-shan, tr. Burton Watson. Also in paperback ed. 1970
Twenty Plays of the Nō Theatre, ed. Donald Keene. Also in paperback ed. 1970
Chūshingura: The Treasury of Loyal Retainers, tr. Donald Keene. Also in paperback ed. 1971; rev. ed. 1997
The Zen Master Hakuin: Selected Writings, tr. Philip B. Yampolsky 1971
Chinese Rhyme-Prose: Poems in the Fu Form from the Han and Six Dynasties Periods, tr. Burton Watson. Also in paperback ed. 1971
Kūkai: Major Works, tr. Yoshito S. Hakeda. Also in paperback ed. 1972
The Old Man Who Does as He Pleases: Selections from the Poetry and Prose of Lu Yu, tr. Burton Watson 1973
The Lion's Roar of Queen Śrīmālā, tr. Alex and Hideko Wayman 1974
Courtier and Commoner in Ancient China: Selections from the History of the Former Han by Pan Ku, tr. Burton Watson. Also in paperback ed. 1974
Japanese Literature in Chinese, vol. 1: Poetry and Prose in Chinese by Japanese Writers of the Early Period, tr. Burton Watson 1975
Japanese Literature in Chinese, vol. 2: Poetry and Prose in Chinese by Japanese Writers of the Later Period, tr. Burton Watson 1976
Love Song of the Dark Lord: Jayadeva's Gītagovinda, tr. Barbara Stoler Miller. Also in paperback ed. Cloth ed. includes critical text of the Sanskrit. 1977; rev. ed. 1997
Ryōkan: Zen Monk-Poet of Japan, tr. Burton Watson 1977
Calming the Mind and Discerning the Real: From the Lam rim chen mo of Tsoṇ-kha-pa, tr. Alex Wayman 1978
The Hermit and the Love-Thief: Sanskrit Poems of Bhartrihari and Bilhaṇa, tr. Barbara Stoler Miller 1978
The Lute: Kao Ming's P'i-p'a chi, tr. Jean Mulligan. Also in paperback ed. 1980
A Chronicle of Gods and Sovereigns: Jinnō Shōtōki of Kitabatake Chikafusa, tr. H. Paul Varley 1980
Among the Flowers: The Hua-chien chi, tr. Lois Fusek 1982
Grass Hill: Poems and Prose by the Japanese Monk Gensei, tr. Burton Watson 1983
Doctors, Diviners, and Magicians of Ancient China: Biographies of Fang-shih, tr. Kenneth J. DeWoskin. Also in paperback ed. 1983
Theater of Memory: The Plays of Kālidāsa, ed. Barbara Stoler Miller. Also in paperback ed. 1984
The Columbia Book of Chinese Poetry: From Early Times to the Thirteenth Century, ed. and tr. Burton Watson. Also in paperback ed. 1984
Poems of Love and War: From the Eight Anthologies and the Ten Long Poems of Classical Tamil, tr. A. K. Ramanujan. Also in paperback ed. 1985
The Bhagavad Gita: Krishna's Counsel in Time of War, tr. Barbara Stoler Miller 1986
The Columbia Book of Later Chinese Poetry, ed. and tr. Jonathan Chaves. Also in paperback ed. 1986
The Tso Chuan: Selections from China's Oldest Narrative History, tr. Burton Watson 1989
Waiting for the Wind: Thirty-six Poets of Japan's Late Medieval Age, tr. Steven Carter 1989
Selected Writings of Nichiren, ed. Philip B. Yampolsky 1990
Saigyō, Poems of a Mountain Home, tr. Burton Watson 1990

*The Book of Lieh Tzu: A Classic of the Tao*, tr. A. C. Graham. Morningside ed. 1990
*The Tale of an Anklet: An Epic of South India—The Cilappatikāram of Iḷaṅkō Aṭikaḷ*, tr. R. Parthasarathy 1993
*Waiting for the Dawn: A Plan for the Prince*, tr. with introduction by Wm. Theodore de Bary 1993
*Yoshitsune and the Thousand Cherry Trees: A Masterpiece of the Eighteenth-Century Japanese Puppet Theater*, tr., annotated, and with introduction by Stanleigh H. Jones, Jr. 1993
*The Lotus Sutra*, tr. Burton Watson. Also in paperback ed. 1993
*The Classic of Changes: A New Translation of the* I Ching *as Interpreted by Wang Bi*, tr. Richard John Lynn 1994
*Beyond Spring: Tz'u Poems of the Sung Dynasty*, tr. Julie Landau 1994
*The Columbia Anthology of Traditional Chinese Literature*, ed. Victor H. Mair 1994
*Scenes for Mandarins: The Elite Theater of the Ming*, tr. Cyril Birch 1995
*Letters of Nichiren*, ed. Philip B. Yampolsky; tr. Burton Watson et al. 1996
*Unforgotten Dreams: Poems by the Zen Monk Shōtetsu*, tr. Steven D. Carter 1997
*The Vimalakirti Sutra*, tr. Burton Watson 1997
*Japanese and Chinese Poems to Sing: The* Wakan rōei shū, tr. J. Thomas Rimer and Jonathan Chaves 1997
*Breeze Through Bamboo: Kanshi of Ema Saikō*, tr. Hiroaki Sato 1998
*A Tower for the Summer Heat*, by Li Yu, tr. Patrick Hanan 1998
*Traditional Japanese Theater: An Anthology of Plays*, by Karen Brazell 1998
*The Original Analects: Sayings of Confucius and His Successors (0479–0249)*, by E. Bruce Brooks and A. Taeko Brooks 1998
*The Classic of the Way and Virtue: A New Translation of the* Tao-te ching *of Laozi as Interpreted by Wang Bi*, tr. Richard John Lynn 1999
*The Four Hundred Songs of War and Wisdom: An Anthology of Poems from Classical Tamil, The* Puṟanāṉūṟu, ed. and tr. George L. Hart and Hank Heifetz 1999
*Original Tao: Inward Training* (Nei-yeh) *and the Foundations of Taoist Mysticism*, by Harold D. Roth 1999
*Po Chü-i: Selected Poems*, tr. Burton Watson 2000
*Lao Tzu's Tao Te Ching: A Translation of the Startling New Documents Found at Guodian*, by Robert G. Henricks 2000
*The Shorter Columbia Anthology of Traditional Chinese Literature*, ed. Victor H. Mair 2000
*Mistress and Maid (Jiaohongji)*, by Meng Chengshun, tr. Cyril Birch 2001
*Chikamatsu: Five Late Plays*, tr. and ed. C. Andrew Gerstle 2001
*The Essential Lotus: Selections from the* Lotus Sutra, tr. Burton Watson 2002

*Early Modern Japanese Literature: An Anthology, 1600–1900*, ed. Haruo Shirane 2002; abridged 2008
*The Columbia Anthology of Traditional Korean Poetry*, ed. Peter H. Lee 2002
*The Sound of the Kiss, or The Story That Must Never Be Told: Pingali Suranna's Kalapurnodayamu*, tr. Vecheru Narayana Rao and David Shulman 2003
*The Selected Poems of Du Fu*, tr. Burton Watson 2003
*Far Beyond the Field: Haiku by Japanese Women*, tr. Makoto Ueda 2003
*Just Living: Poems and Prose by the Japanese Monk Tonna*, ed. and tr. Steven D. Carter 2003
*Han Feizi: Basic Writings*, tr. Burton Watson 2003
*Mozi: Basic Writings*, tr. Burton Watson 2003
*Xunzi: Basic Writings*, tr. Burton Watson 2003
*Zhuangzi: Basic Writings*, tr. Burton Watson 2003
*The Awakening of Faith, Attributed to Aśvaghosha*, tr. Yoshito S. Hakeda, introduction by Ryuichi Abe 2005
*The Tales of the Heike*, tr. Burton Watson, ed. Haruo Shirane 2006
*Tales of Moonlight and Rain*, by Ueda Akinari, tr. with introduction by Anthony H. Chambers 2007
*Traditional Japanese Literature: An Anthology, Beginnings to 1600*, ed. Haruo Shirane 2007
*The Philosophy of Qi*, by Kaibara Ekken, tr. Mary Evelyn Tucker 2007
*The Analects of Confucius*, tr. Burton Watson 2007
*The Art of War: Sun Zi's Military Methods*, tr. Victor Mair 2007
*One Hundred Poets, One Poem Each: A Translation of the* Ogura Hyakunin Isshu, tr. Peter McMillan 2008
*Zeami: Performance Notes*, tr. Tom Hare 2008
*Zongmi on Chan*, tr. Jeffrey Lyle Broughton 2009
*Scripture of the Lotus Blossom of the Fine Dharma*, rev. ed., tr. Leon Hurvitz, preface and introduction by Stephen R. Teiser 2009
*Mencius*, tr. Irene Bloom, ed. with an introduction by Philip J. Ivanhoe 2009
*Clouds Thick, Whereabouts Unknown: Poems by Zen Monks of China*, Charles Egan 2010
*The Mozi: A Complete Translation*, tr. Ian Johnston 2010
*The Huainanzi: A Guide to the Theory and Practice of Government in Early Han China*, by Liu An, tr. John S. Major, Sarah A. Queen, Andrew Seth Meyer, and Harold D. Roth, with Michael Puett and Judson Murray 2010
*The Demon at Agi Bridge and Other Japanese Tales*, tr. Burton Watson, ed. with introduction by Haruo Shirane 2011
*Haiku Before Haiku: From the Renga Masters to Bashō*, tr. with introduction by Steven D. Carter 2011
*The Columbia Anthology of Chinese Folk and Popular Literature*, ed. Victor H. Mair and Mark Bender 2011
*Tamil Love Poetry: The Five Hundred Short Poems of the* Aiṅkuṟunūṟu, tr. and ed. Martha Ann Selby 2011
*The Teachings of Master Wuzhu: Zen and Religion of No-Religion*, by Wendi L. Adamek 2011